Aristocrats Facing Change

VICTOR AZARYA is lecturer, Department of Sociology and Social Anthropology, Hebrew University, Jerusalem.

AZARYA, Victor. Aristocrats facing change: the Fulbe in Guinea, Nigeria, and Cameroon. Chicago, 1978. 293p map bibl index 77-15025. 19.00 ISBN 0-226-03356-2. C.I.P.

What is the relative importance of internal versus external factors in accounting for types of social and cultural changes under conditions of rapid change? To answer this question, Azarya compares three similar aristocratic groups of Fulbe (Fulani) at three historical stages, precolonial, during decolonization, and after independence. He determines how the three groups responded to differing situations of change in their control over the resources that provide power, wealth, and prestige (Azarya modification on the Weberian definition of dominance) in the context of their involvement with politically important centers (as defined by Shils). Azarya develops a set of six factors (testable hypotheses) that are important in accounting for the differing forms of change in these cases. He concludes that external factors are more important than internal social system factors and should be emphasized in studies of rapid social change. Secondary source materials are supplemented by materials from five months' research in Cameroon and Senegal. The presentation is sometimes repetitive; the writing is readable but undistinguished. Good notes, bibliography, and index. Recommended for upper-division and graduate libraries.

CHOICE *NOV.*
Anthropology

Aristocrats Facing Change

The Fulbe in Guinea, Nigeria, and Cameroon

Victor Azarya

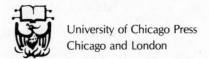

University of Chicago Press
Chicago and London

Victor Azarya teaches in the Department
of Sociology and Social Anthropology at the
Hebrew University of Jerusalem, Israel.

The University of Chicago Press, Chicago 60637
The University of Chicago Press, Ltd., London

Library of Congress Cataloging in Publication Data

Azarya, Victor.
  Aristocrats facing change.

  Bibliography: p.
  Includes index.
  1. Fulahs. 2. Africa, West—Social conditions.
I. Title
DT474.5.A94   301.45'963   77-15025
ISBN 0-226-03356-2

To My Parents

Contents

      Futa Jallon, Northern Nigeria, and
      North Cameroon   167
9   Further Developments in the Status
      of the Fulbe in Postcolonial Futa Jallon,
      Northern Nigeria, and North
      Cameroon   189

      Conclusion   207
      Notes   235
      Selected Bibliography   273
      Index   283

Tables

Preface

This book is the result of a long-standing interest in the use of sociological tools of analysis to elucidate transformations that have occurred in the last centuries in "developing" countries, particularly in Africa, hoping to arrive at something more than a chronicle of political-military fortunes or a more "technical" survey of economic growth possibilities. Beyond the obvious aim of shedding light on the contemporary history of West Africa, I wished to illustrate the operational use of some general theoretical concepts and approaches which have not been tested enough in a systematic way in the study of concrete cases. Focusing on social inequality, I attempted to operationalize the Weberian multidimensional approach. Shils's center-periphery scheme was used to present what seemed to me a better general explanation of colonialism and decolonization. By choosing to study three different geographical areas, I raised the problem of comparative study of social change in which the inherent tensions between historical particularism and regularities sought by sociological analysis were most apparent.

The collection of data for this work occupied a large part of my scholarly career. It started when I was a graduate student of sociology and African Studies at the Hebrew University of Jerusalem, expanded with my doctoral thesis at the University of Chicago, and has been continuing ever since. The fieldwork proper was carried out in 1972 when I spent half a year in West Africa, most of it in Cameroon. Some of the ideas in this book were included in a paper on North Cameroon published in 1976 by Sage Publications, Inc. in their Studies in Comparative Modernization series. The data that appear in this book have been updated several times (for the last time they were updated to Fall 1976) to keep up with the rapidly changing contemporary African scene, though significant changes will undoubtedly have occurred before the book appears in print.

I am well aware that some imbalance exists in the way data were collected for the three areas discussed in the book. Data on North Cameroon were based mainly on extensive interviews conducted with informants during a five-month stay in that country. Unfortunately I did not know the Fulbe language (Fulfulde) and had to use interpreters in most interviews. I apologize for the possible mistakes that I might have made in the few words in Fulfulde that were used in the book. I also consulted some unpublished material at the Cameroon Service of Archives, at the Institut de Recherches Camerounaises, and at the University of Yaoundé. All this information was added to the standard published material to which I already had access.

Compared to the relatively abundant and partly firsthand Cameroonian data, my information on Nigeria and Guinea was mostly based on published material since I could not visit either country. Data on Nigeria were almost completely based on published material (except for occasional talks with Nigerian students in the United States), but this was not a serious handicap because the published material on Nigeria is one of the richest compared to other African countries. In the case of Guinea, standard published material was supplemented by visits to research and documentation centers in Paris and to the Institut Fondamental d'Afrique Noire in Dakar, Senegal, where rare or unpublished material was consulted. I also conducted some interviews with Guinean refugees in Senegal and with Frenchmen who had lived in Guinea. Obviously those informants were a very biased source of information; they were almost all strongly opposed to the present Guinean regime. For this reason I treated the interview data on Guinea with utmost skepticism and tended to disregard it when it seemed to deviate from documentary sources.

The names of all the people who have helped me in this study are too many to mention separately; their contribution was nonetheless crucial to this enterprise. Some of them, including most of my informants in the field, cannot be named here also because their anonymity was a condition of their cooperation. Unfortunately very few of them will ever read this book or even be aware of its existence. I would like to thank them all wholeheartedly. I also hope that the few who will read the book will receive kindly those parts where I chose not to agree with them.

I owe the greatest intellectual debt to two of my teachers and colleagues at the Hebrew University, Professor Shmuel N. Eisenstadt, who most profoundly influenced my sociological thinking, and Professor Nehemia Levtzion, who kindled in me a passionate interest in West Africa. I would like to thank also the participants of the various African Studies seminars at the Hebrew University in 1968–70. Amid their friendly atmosphere and high intellectual standards many of the ideas formulated here originated.

At Chicago the two people who were of greatest assistance to me were Professor Morris Janowitz and the late Professor Lloyd A. Fallers. Professor Fallers, whose premature death was a great shock to all his students and colleagues, showed a keen interest in my work, despite his deteriorating health, and helped me beyond measure with detailed comments and thoughtful suggestions. To Professor Janowitz I am especially indebted for the part he played in seeing the book through to its completion. He was my constant guide and mentor at the University of Chicago in 1970–73 and introduced me to the exceptional qualities of scholarly life there. The Center for Social Organization Studies that he conducted was the same invaluable sounding board for half-baked ideas that the African Studies seminars had been at the Hebrew University.

In Cameroon and Senegal, I was privileged to have access to the library and facilities of the Institut de Recherches Camerounaises (also called the ORSTOM center), the University of Yaoundé, the Institut Fondamental d'Afrique Noire in Dakar. I also benefited from exchanges with many itinerant or resident scholars including Thierno Diallo, Oumar Ba, Jean Yves Martin, Guy Pontié, Vouter Van Beek, Hans Wilhelm, and particularly Eldridge Mohamadou at the Centre Linguistique et Culturel in Yaoundé. My good friend and travel companion Dr. Ulrich Braukämper of the Frobenius Institute in Frankfurt certainly remembers the long days spent together in the Cameroonian Savannah. Thanks are due also to Mme Rohrich of Bonakou Accueil in Douala, to Mme Bue of the Foyer International in Yaoundé, and to Dr. Norman Haupt, the director of the Baptist Mission in Victoria, for their hospitality during my stay in Cameroon. Above all, I would like to express my gratitude to the government of Cameroon for its invaluable assistance during my field trip. The interviewing tours would not have been possible without the support of Cameroonian government officials at all levels, who not only solved many of the crucial logistics problems encountered in my constant traveling, but also demonstrated a generally open-minded and helpful attitude that could serve as model to many other countries.

Many eminent scholars, besides those mentioned above, provided constructive criticism of my work and read parts of the manuscript. I would like to thank particularly here Professors Philip Foster, Ralph Austen, Donald Levine, Edward Shils, Joseph Ben David, Aristide Zolberg, and Pierre F. Lacroix. A special note of gratitude is due to Professors Remi Clignet and Philip Foster and to the African Studies Committee of the University of Chicago for providing the financial assistance that made possible my trip to France and Africa. In Jerusalem, Doctors Naomi Chazan and Michel Abitbol of the Truman Institute at the Hebrew University were especially helpful in the hectic days of rewriting the conclusion. I would like also to thank Lucille McGill, Regina Alkalay, Hilda Sofer, and Ruth Horowitz for their impressive typing under pressure of repeated "final" drafts of the manuscript.

Finally, it is a pleasure for me to thank my family, especially my wife, Mireille, who in the long years in which this work was in process not only typed several versions of it but became its most solid support. This book would certainly not have been completed without the serenity of family life which she provided and which I apologize for having taken too much for granted sometimes. To my parents, to whom this book is dedicated, go my deepest thanks and appreciation for their trust in me, for having always backed me in all the arduous and unpathed ways that I took, even when they did not quite see where they would lead.

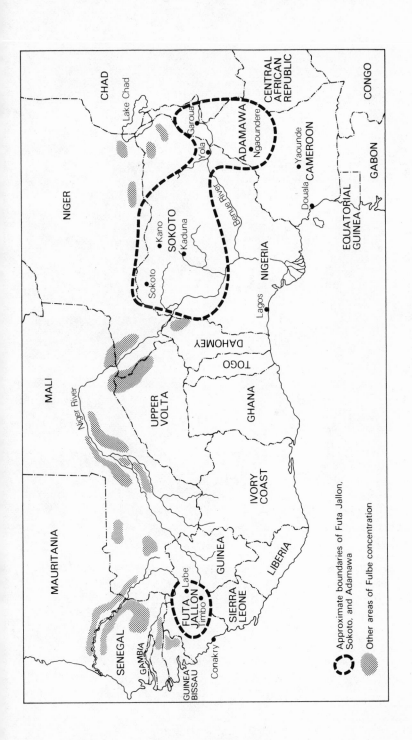

Introduction

The general purpose of this work is to study in a comparative framework the position of aristocratic groups in three precolonial West African societies and to examine the transformation that they underwent in the colonial period and after independence. The three precolonial societies—Futa Jallon in today's Guinea, the Sokoto Caliphate in today's Nigeria, and Adamawa in today's Cameroon[1]—were chosen because they were all societies dominated by the Fulbe people and had striking similarities with regard to the formation of the respective states; their economic, political, and religious systems; and the privileged position that the Fulbe occupied in each of them.[2] The three societies were certainly not identical; many important differences existed between them, as we shall see in detail later. But their general similarity and the connection of all three societies to the same Fulbe element provided a common framework into which all three societies could be placed and their subsequent variation from it and from each other could be more easily traced. The explanation of this variation is the basic issue to which this research addresses itself.

How can we characterize this variation that needs to be explained, or, in other words, of what is our "dependent variable" broadly conceived? In answer, we start from the premise that every aristocratic group's adjustment to change is limited by its wish to maintain some kind of overall superiority over other groups, nonaristocratic elements in society. If a social change results in the elimination of that superiority, this is considered not a successful adjustment on the part of the aristocratic group but, on the contrary, the destruction of its aristocratic status. The crucial issue determining the aristocracies' adjustment to change is not their relative success in adjusting to innovations, but rather the effect of such adjustment on their overall superiority or dominance vis-à-vis other populations in society. Stressing this aspect of adjustment, this book proposes to explore the extent to which Fulbe aristocracies could maintain their dominant position compared with other populations, in three different areas, in a time of rapid change.

To operationalize the concept of "dominance" (or "superiority"), which is central to this study, we consider a dominant group to be one which controls, more than any other group in that society, the resources which maximize power, wealth, and prestige[3] (resources such as land, professional skills, military force, religious piety, or other commodities, attributes, or activities). This classification of basic social goals and desires is obviously influenced by the now classic tridimensional approach to social stratification which developed with some modifications out of Max Weber's original differentiation between "class," "status," and "party,"[4] "power" having replaced "party" in subsequent studies using the same approach. A classification of major social rewards presented by Eisenstadt comes closest to defining our triad of prestige, power, and wealth. Rewards that are based on differential allocation of esteem and deference without the use of coercion correspond to what we call prestige. Rewards that are based on differential amounts of obedience that can be exacted from others by force correspond to power. Rewards that are based on obtaining differential amounts of valuable possessions, commodities, and services are a rough approximation of wealth.[5] Resources that provide wealth, power, and prestige either can be earned as rewards for the roles performed in society (doing something or being something) or they can be purchased by, or exchanged for, other resources. In order to purchase more resources through exchange or to accede to roles and positions providing such resources as reward, one can use the wealth, power, or prestige resources already acquired. Wealth, power, and prestige can then be "means" as well as "ends." They can be used to purchase resources that would bring the owner more of the same resource, or they can be converted to other types of resources. Wealth resources can be used to increase one's wealth or to convert it to power or prestige; power resources can be used to purchase more power or can be converted into wealth or prestige; likewise, prestige can be used for self-aggrandizement or for conversion to wealth and power.[6]

However, this exchange or conversion is certainly very different from the simple exchange mechanism that we learn from basic economic models and analyses. The main difference is very aptly described by Eisenstadt in the following terms:

> When a simple case of exchange is effected by an exchange medium, the person who, as we say, "purchases" a commodity usually ends up with more of the commodity and less of the medium of exchange than he possessed before the transaction. The "cost" of the commodity is measured in terms of the number of exchange medium units that have to be given in return for a particular number of commodity units. . . . But when an officer orders the soldiers under his command to do various things, and obtains their compliance, he does not thereby diminish his stock of power. When a religious elite exacts certain observances from its followers, it does not surrender a portion of its influence in a quid pro-quo exchange. When an aristocracy habitually obtains deference from commoners, it gains in prestige, even though prestige is the expended medium of exchange.
>
> In short, the very possession of medium of exchange, such as prestige or power, is tantamount to a title to certain rewards. This anomaly, of course, greatly impairs the "purity" of a social exchange system.[7]

The competition and exchange directed toward maximizing wealth, power, and prestige are, of course, regulated by certain norms and values that remain outside the competition and exchange process proper. Values and norms play an important role in determining how social roles and functions are evaluated and what rewards are accorded to them; they also set the rates of exchange between different resources and between wealth, power, and prestige. The value of each resource—that is, the extent to which it acquires wealth, power, or prestige—derives from some general understanding among the participants in the distributive process. However, there may occur important changes in those values in time, as we shall see later. Also, at the same point in time different groups may attribute different values to resources, and that may affect their effort to acquire those resources. Those who value a certain resource more than another may try to enter into exchange with other people whose priorities regarding the two resources are reversed.

Social inequality is then the picture that emerges from the distribution of resources among different groups or categories of people. Because it is based on three separate dimensions,

those of wealth, power, and prestige, it can account for incongruences between one's positions in different dimensions—
for instance, occupying a high position on the prestige scale
while having a low position on the wealth scale, or being strong
in power but weak in prestige. The extent of interconvertibility
between the three sets of resources is inversely related to the
existence of such incongruences. The more freely wealth,
power, and prestige resources are converted into one another,
the easier it is to acquire the missing resources by the conversion of others (for instance, acquiring wealth by the use of
power or acquiring power by the use of prestige) and so to
balance one's position in the overall social inequality scale.

Because the distribution of resources is a continuous, ongo-
ing process, minor changes in the distribution of resources
occur constantly, but these changes do not affect the general
structure of inequality.[8] Changes reach a significant proportion
only if they modify a certain group's general opportunity to
accede to resources of wealth, power, and prestige or if they
modify the value attached to those resources and modify their
rates of exchange. One way in which such significant change
occurs is when some new resources competing with old resources or new uses that modify the value of old resources are
introduced into the society by inventions, innovations, im-
ports, and impositions from outside. As we shall see later, the
ability of dominant groups to acquire new resources or to put
old resources to new uses that increased their overall power,
wealth, or prestige value constitutes the ultimate test of their
successful adjustment to change, that is, of their adoption of
innovations while preserving the dominant positions that they
held before the change.

In addition to studying social inequality resulting from the
distribution of wealth, power, and prestige resources, this book
tries to examine the position of the Fulbe in terms of the closely
related question of their participation in the "center" or the
"periphery" of the respective societies. The changes with
which the Fulbe are confronted, and in the face of which they
have to maintain their dominance, are studied here in the context of new center formation by alien (colonial) elements and
indigenous participation in that center. In defining the center
we closely follow Shils:

> Society has a center. There is a central zone in the structure of
> society. This central zone impinges in various ways on those

who live within the ecological domain in which the society
exists. Membership in the society, in more than the ecological
sense of being located in a bounded territory and of adapting
to an environment affected or made up by other persons located in the same territory, is constituted by relationship to
this central zone. . . . The center, or the central zone, is a
phenomenon of the realm of values and beliefs. It is the center of the order of symbols, of values and beliefs, which gov-
ern the society. . . . The center is also a phenomenon of the
realm of action. It is a structure of activities, of roles and
persons, within the network of institutions. It is in these roles
that the values and beliefs which are central are embodied
and propounded.[9]

"Periphery" is that part of society which stays outside the center. It is less affected by norms, values, activities of the center,
and it takes a minor role in the creation, modification, preservation of those values, norms, activities. Center and periphery are
defined in a very abstract way which does not readily expose
the institutions which emanate from, or shape, the center in
concrete cases. To pinpoint those roles, structures, social
groups that are located at the center or in the periphery is the
crucial and at the same time most difficult task in applying the
center-periphery conceptual framework to specific case studies
as this book tries to do. Geographical center, urban center,
communication and trade center, central government, ruling
elite, dominant religion or ideology are not equivalent to "center" in the sense Shils used it, but all or some in different
occasions form together those activities, institutions, values,
groups from which a center is composed. In the periphery are
included at various times nonrulers, nonelites, ethnic and religious minorities, rural areas, uneducated people, etc., none
of whom is equivalent to periphery but each of whom forms
an important component of the amorphous body called periphery. There are, of course, great margins of overlapping
between center and periphery. These depend on such factors
as the center's penetrations into the periphery, peripheral participation in the center, and communication between center and
periphery.

The properties of the occupants of the center and the periphery are very closely related to the form of inequality existing in
society, since they determine to a large extent the distribution
of wealth, power, and prestige in that society. The occupants of
the center, as custodians of the basic norms of the society, have

a determining influence on the values (or rates of exchange) of different resources, and they can regulate the access of other groups to resources. In other words, they are in control of the rules of the distributive process and can determine them in a way that would bring them greatest advantage. However, beyond that, their closeness to the basic goals and values of society, their influence on setting the "right" order, are also, almost by definition, sources of power and prestige. Wealth, on the other hand, is not directly related to centrality. It is often seen as too profane to be closely related to central positions, to basic norms and values, it is purposely kept at some distance from the center. This does not mean, of course, that occupants of the center do not find ways to accumulate wealth. They usually do so by converting to wealth the prestige and power obtained by their centrality. As a result, they usually do become wealthier than all other peripheral groups. Nevertheless, the lack of essential, direct relationship between centrality and wealth, unlike power and prestige, creates the opportunity for certain peripheral groups to amass considerable wealth of their own, at the margin, though under the control, of people occupying central positions.

The close connection between occupying a central position in society and controlling power, prestige, and to some extent wealth not only helps us identify the dominant group in question but also enlightens important aspects of its adjustment to change. In studying the extent to which an aristocratic group maintains its dominance in changing conditions we shall examine mainly the following points:[10]

A. Inner structural transformations within the group; in what way and to what extent new roles are adopted, old roles are modified, new activities are undertaken by the group.

B. The group's participation in other groups, frameworks which are larger than or cut across its own unit, especially, in our case, the group's participation in the new colonial and post-colonial center.

C. The extent to which the group in question, while undergoing change, maintains or increases its control over the resources that enable it to maximize wealth, power, and prestige, and the extent to which it translates them to new resources corresponding to overall changes introduced in the society, modifies them while keeping them under its control.

D. The extent to which, despite its participation in new groups and frameworks, the basic collective identity of the group in question is kept among its members, and how this is reflected in the cultural status symbols and the style of life of the group members.

It should be pointed out here that in this work we deal simply with social change and not with modernization in order not to get involved in the complex problem of trying to define modernization and deciding whether the social change observed in West Africa is a modernizing change or not. The social change that we study is divided into two stages, the establishment of the colonial system and the achievement of independence. The first stage of change, the establishment of the colonial system, must be distinguished from earlier contacts of Europeans with African societies many centuries prior to the colonial period, in that it involved, unlike earlier contacts, the establishment of European political rule and administration over large African territories and precolonial social and political systems. We can see in the establishment of the colonial system the formation of a new center by alien European elements in colonial territories. This center was distinct from, and rival to, the precolonial traditional centers and introduced (in fact imposed) far-reaching innovations to the colonial territories. The second stage of change, "decolonization," was the process in which indigenous elements entered the colonial center, gradually gained control of it, and created on its bases a new postcolonial center politically independent from the colonial power. The two stages occurred at almost the same time in the three societies. The precolonial period in which we are interested extends from state formation by Muslim Fulbe in the mid-eighteenth century (in Futa Jallon) and at the beginning of the nineteenth century (in Sokoto and Adamawa) to the end of the nineteenth or beginning of the twentieth century. The establishment and consolidation of the colonial system extended roughly from the end of the nineteenth century to the end of World War II. The process of decolonization started at the end of World War II, reached an important turning point with the achievement of independence in 1958 in Guinea, in 1960 in Nigeria and Cameroon, and continued until the present with the consolidation of the three societies' postcolonial structures.

Finally, this work raises the central question of whether the differential adjustment to change found among the dominant aristocratic groups in the three societies is related to the respective societies' or social groups' internal adjustment capabilities or to external factors that functioned independently of the societies or social groups in question and imposed upon them a certain pattern of adjustment. In the social science literature dealing with problems of social change there has been a tendency to concentrate on societies' internal abilities to adjust to change and to detect structural or cultural attributes within societies that could explain differential patterns of adjustment. An underlying hope in this effort is that by explaining differential adjustment to social change on the basis of internal attributes of societies, we can overcome the arbitrariness and unpredictability of explanations that rely on coincidental, external, historical factors. However, the emphasis on internal attributes—adjustment capabilities—as explanatory variables of social change also derives from a conceptualization of societies as rather tightly knit social organisms manipulating and controlling forces of change within themselves and in their environment. The societies are pictured, so to speak, as deciding what to take and what not to take from changes that develop within themselves and outside, and their adjustment is made dependent mostly on their own decisions or predispositions in their encounter with forces of change. It is therefore their own attributes and capabilities that determine whether they would adjust to forces of change (probably by some self-transformation to ease the pressure) or would be overwhelmed by them. This conceptualization of interplay between society as an organism and the force of change was reinforced when some social scientists defined modernization (or modernity) in terms of an ability of social systems to initiate, absorb, and sustain changes. By looking at societies' capability to adjust to changes, these social scientists hoped to learn about their modernizing potentialities, but obviously this could only be done by assuming that adjustment to change depended primarily on some internal attributes and capabilities and that external intervening factors were negligible.[11]

This approach was also, in part, the result of the reaction of the systemic-functionalist approach to the criticism that its analytical framework neglected to, or even was unable to, explain phenomena of social change, that it treated change as an exter-

nal and to some extent accidental factor that could not be accounted for in the system itself. To disprove this criticism and
show that the systemic-functional approach did account for
change, a great effort was made to show how internal properties
of social systems were influential in determining what changes
would be adopted, or initiated, within the system and how
those internal properties, as if giving a manipulative capacity to
the system to cope with forces of change, affected the outcome
of change that the social system underwent. However, in their
effort to head off criticism and show their analytical
framework's ability to explain change, the proponents of this
approach tended to forget that some changes were indeed due
to external, "historical" factors, unaccountable by the social system itself, but deriving from situational factors, from the historical context in which the system was found. In other words,
they failed to see that their approach's original inability to explain changes was due not only to deficiencies of their analytical
scheme or neglect on their part but also to the very properties of
the social system since the social system had very little control
over them.

As comparative history amply illustrates, there are many cases
in which a society's—or, as in our case, a social group's—
differential adjustment to change depends more on external factors on which the society or group in question has very little
influence and which are generally unrelated to any internal adjustment capability that the society or social group might have.
In many cases societies or groups are unable to cope with
changes that are forced upon them; they simply accept the
changes because they have no other choice. This is especially
true in colonial societies where, more than in any other
societies, changes were externally induced by the colonial
power, leaving practically no say to the societies or populations
on which they were imposed. In dealing with such conquest
situations it becomes dangerous to focus primarily on internal
adjustment capabilities. External, historical factors—such as
how changes were introduced, by whom, with what new
societies or social groups the society or group in question was
forced to unite and compete for resources, etc.—have to be
given serious consideration before any internal adjustment
capability is put forward as an explanatory variable.

The comparative framework of this study will, I hope, help us determine what role internal and external factors played in the Fulbe's differential adjustment to change in three different areas and to what extent each group controlled those factors and manipulated them to its advantage. Certainly both internal properties of the groups and external, situational factors played an important role in their adjustment to change, and the task of this study is to detect each of them. However, the existence of great similarities between the three aristocracies in the pre-colonial period (as we shall see in the first part of the book) helps us narrow the focus of the study, since it limits (though by no mean eliminates) the possibility that their differential adjustment to change derives from preliminary differences that existed between them before colonial change. Factors of their differential adjustment to change are then searched mainly in the forces of change themselves, and the main question is to what extent the three aristocratic groups controlled and manipulated to their advantage those forces of change and whether this con-trol could explain the differences that are found between their respective adjustment to change. The assumption of pre-liminary similarity between the three groups leads us to focus more strongly on external, historical factors, in counterbalance to earlier studies of adjustment to change which have stressed internal "systemic property" factors. If we indeed have three aristocratic groups who presented important similarities in the precolonial period, they could be expected to have more or less the same internal adjustment capabilities. If, in spite of that, they adjusted differently to a far-reaching social change, then apparently their internal attributes were not the determining factors of their differential adjustment to change, or at least their internal attributes were significantly modified by the forces of change at the early stage of transformation and that affected their ability to adjust to later stages of transformation. But, beyond these general hypotheses, any further discussion of the subject should await the close examination of the case of the Fulbe of Guinea, Nigeria, and Cameroon in the following chapters of the book.

Finally, it should be stated that, beyond anything else, this work is a result of the author's fascination with the pos-sibilities, but also difficulties, offered by the application of sociological tools and concepts to the understanding of history.

In this sense, perhaps the ultimate test that should be applied to this work is the degree to which it contributes to the illumination of some important aspects of the history of West Africa.

Part One The Fulbe in the Precolonial Period

1

The Formation of Fulbe States in Futa Jallon, Sokoto, and Adamawa

The Fulbe in West Africa

Fulbe Identity, Culture, and Early History

The Fulbe are a West African people, more than 6 million strong, who are scattered throughout West Africa from Senegal and Gambia in the west to Chad and Central African Republic in the east. Their greatest concentration is in Northern Nigeria where there live 3 or 4 million Fulbe. Other important concentrations are found in Senegambia (300,000), in the Futa Jallon area in Guinea (800,000), the Massina area in Mali (500,000), and northern Cameroon (400,000).[1]

There are some important differences between the Fulbe and most other West African populations among whom they live. First of all, the Fulbe have basically nonnegroid physical traits, though they vary widely in the purity of those traits. Second, the Fulbe are originally a pastoral people, unlike most other West African populations who occupy themselves with agriculture. It is assumed that in the past all the Fulbe were nomadic cattle herdsmen who, in their search for water and grazing land for their cattle, scattered all over West Africa. A large part of them have since become sedentary, but they still try to refrain from agriculture and keep special ties to cattle. Wherever they went, the Fulbe stressed their common culture and tradition to offset dangers of assimilation into the great majorities of non-Fulbe people among whom they lived. Out of their culture and traditions developed a special code of behavior and morality, called *Pulaaku*, which came to symbolize and set the boundaries of Fulbe identity.[2]

The fundamental virtues of Pulaaku are stoic sobriety, reserve, and strong emotional attachment to cattle. A true *Pullo* (singular of Fulbe) is supposed to be gentle, proud, introverted, but helpful to fellow Fulbe when they need help. He attains respectability by keeping himself physically and psychologically at a distance from other people (especially non-Fulbe) and by refraining from displaying his feelings, whether joy, pain, anger, or curiosity. A true Pullo should be taciturn, should conceal his real thoughts, should despise the common vivacity of non-Fulbe living around him. He also should despise conspicuous richness and consumption, should live poorly, pay no attention to external signs of material comfort, and be content with the little that he has. This detachment from material commodities and human beings is offset by great attachment to cattle. Occupying oneself with cattle gives great personal satisfaction, and the number of cattle owned is an important sign of social standing. Agriculture, on the other hand, is despised as an unworthy occupation undertaken out of sheer necessity. While cattle no doubt provided the pastoral herdsmen's basic means of subsistence and had a thesaurized capital value for sedentary Fulbe, their importance far exceeded their economic value. They were hardly ever consumed for their meat and reluctantly sold in exchange for other products. The pastoralist Fulbe developed strong symbolic connections between their life and that of their cattle. Most legends relate to cattle the origins and existence of the Fulbe as a separate people.[3]

The Fulbe consider themselves as belonging to one of four general lineages corresponding to the four descendants of their common ancestor. The four branches (*Yettoré*), namely, *Ba*, *Bari*, *Diallo*, and *Sow*, are recognized by all Fulbe communities but not much importance is attributed to that affiliation.[4] Greater importance is attributed to different groups which cut across Yettoré lines and were formed in the various stages of Fulbe history, especially in times of migration and political confrontation. At the highest level these groups developed into major branches, four of which—the *Vollarbé* (or *Dayébé*), the *Ouroubé*, the *Yirlabé* (or *Yillaga*), and the *Férobé*—are found all over West Africa, and affiliation to them constitutes the second highest basis of identity below overall Fulbe identity. Below that level, lineage affiliation assumes primary importance again, the Fulbe being divided into various patrilineages which are subdivided at various levels but are also intersected by territorial groupings and by groups migrating together under the leadership of an *Ardo* (literally meaning the one who walks in front, i.e., the guide).[5]

The origin and early history of the Fulbe people has always intrigued historians and has been subject to various speculative theories, none of them very reliable.[6] Most historians seem to agree, however, that sometime in their history, probably around the tenth century, the Fulbe were concentrated in today's northern and eastern Senegal where they led a predominantly pastoral life. Later historical studies generally tend to see in this place also the place of origin of the Fulbe, thus discounting the legends of their coming from the east and hypothesizing that they were formed by a mixture of local negroid people and white people coming from the north.[7] This accounts also for their less negroid physical traits, which have intrigued historians and ethnographers for many years. Whether this hypothesis is true or not, it seems more certain that at some time after the tenth century a large number of Fulbe started to move eastward in search of better pastures, less crowded places, or an escape from hostile neighbors. This migration developed gradually over many centuries as a result of which the Fulbe spread all over West Africa.

Parallel to their migration the Fulbe also gradually adopted Islam. A small section of them, called *Torodbé*, foresook their pastoral life, settled in towns, mixed with other Muslims, and, together with Berber and Arab clerics, formed the most learned and respected layer of Muslim religious leaders in West Africa. However, other Fulbe, and especially those who continued their nomadic pastoralism far from centers of communication and commerce, adopted Islam later and more superficially.

In most of the places to which they spread, the Fulbe were subjected to populations whom they despised. Their frustration at such subjection increased after they became Muslim. Most of their rulers were either outright pagans or, as in Hausaland, were nominally Muslim but were tolerant of pagan practices and poor observers of the Islamic law (*Sharia*).[8] Islam increased the feeling of cultural and religious superiority of its believers toward pagans or superficially Muslimized people, and hence it increased the frustration of its believers at being ruled by nonbelievers. Moreover, Islam made it a religious duty for its believers to liberate themselves from nonbelievers' rule through flight (*Hijra*) and holy war (*Jihad*). It is not surprising, therefore, to find the Muslim Fulbe, especially their Torodbé branch, at the forefront of the Islamic ferment which, in the eighteenth and nineteenth centuries, erupted in a series of Muslim holy wars (Jihads) against pagan or superficially Muslimized regimes.[9] Where those wars, under Fulbe leadership, succeeded, as in Futa Jallon, Massina and Sokoto, the Fulbe formed new states and came to ruling positions over other populations.

Fulbe Holy Wars in Futa Jallon, Adamawa, and Sokoto

The Fulbe migrating into Futa Jallon, Adamawa, and Sokoto were at first nomadic cattle herdsmen. Most of them were still pagans, but the proportion of Muslims among them increased as migration progressed. Their migration was slow and peaceful. They came in small groups with the permission of local rulers; they accepted the territories allotted to them and paid grazing dues. As long as their penetration was peaceful, the Fulbe were generally welcomed by the non-Fulbe populations, who looked forward to selling to the Fulbe their various agricultural products in exchange for milk, dairy products, and occasionally meat. The cattle of the Fulbe also provided them with valuable manure to fertilize their land. The local rulers were pleased with the presence in their territory of Fulbe herdsmen, who represented a further source of tribute. Muslim Fulbe were also highly valued for their services as officials, teachers, and advisors in the courts.[10]

Before the Fulbe penetration, Futa Jallon, Sokoto, and Adamawa were ruled by a great number of small kingdoms or chiefdoms. In Futa Jallon and Adamawa those consisted mainly of pagan chiefdoms and segmentary groups, while in Sokoto they were nominally Muslim Hausa city-states, more developed politically and economically and united by a common language and culture. Unlike Futa Jallon and Adamawa, which were located at the peripheries of main economic, political, and cultural centers, Hausaland was an important center of trade, communications, and learning. So, in Hausaland the migrating Fulbe encountered incomparably more developed and culturally united societies than in Adamawa and Futa Jallon and, as we shall see later, this had very important consequences for subsequent Fulbe history in Hausaland as compared to Futa Jallon and Adamawa.

Historical data on the Fulbe penetration to Futa Jallon are obscure and very confusing.[11] Apparently the Fulbe entered Futa Jallon in two distinct phases. Until the seventeenth century the Fulbe came in small groups, were mostly pagan, and were integrated among the various local groups dominated by the *Jallonké* people. After the seventeenth century there began a more intensive second wave of Fulbe immigration composed of larger groups, among whom an increasing majority were Muslims. Unlike their predecessors, the latecomers, especially the Muslims among them, were not smoothly integrated into the different populations of Futa Jallon, and they were less willing to accept Jallonké domination. At the beginning of the eighteenth century their discontent erupted in a revolt proclaimed to be a Jihad as a result of which the Muslim Fulbe became the ruling element in Futa Jallon. The Jihad was launched in 1725 by clerics representing nine leading Muslim families. One of the clerics known for his great Islamic knowledge, Ibrahima Sambego (called Karamoko Alfa), was chosen as leader of the Jihad and head of the new state. At first the Jihad seemed to be basically a religious war fought between Muslims and pagans, whether Fulbe or not. Many pagan Fulbe who had emigrated earlier opposed the Jihad and allied themselves with the Jallonké against their Muslim kinsmen. The war lasted for a very long time, and the Muslim Fulbe had many serious reverses including a temporary capture of their capital Timbo, but finally under their second leader Ibrahima Sory, chosen for his military capabilities, the Jihad was won. By the 1770s Muslim Fulbe control was established all over Futa Jallon. The country was divided into nine very autonomous provinces, each under the rule of one of the nine Fulbe families who led the Jihad. In 1776 Ibrahima Sory was given the religious title of *Almamy* (corresponding to Imam, i.e., the leader of the Muslim community). After the Jihad was won, the original religious basis of the war started to be discarded in favor of the idea of Fulbe ethnic supremacy. The few non-Fulbe people who had participated in the Jihad out of religious faith were gradually eliminated. Among the pagan populations who fell under Fulbe rule, the non-Fulbe were made captives while the Fulbe who had opposed the Jihad were permitted to become free commoners upon acceptance of Islam.[12]

The Fulbe penetration into what was later to become Adamawa occurred mainly in eighteenth century. At the time of their penetration, the strongest political system that the Fulbe encountered was the kingdom of Mandara, located on the

slopes of the Mandara hills and in the plain of Diamaré. It had
recently freed itself from Bornu tutelage and had also superficially adopted Islam. All the other populations were organized
in small chiefdoms or village communities. Almost all were pagan. Until the end of the eighteenth century the Fulbe penetration into Adamawa was slow and peaceful, in small groups,
mostly pagan. Islam made slow progress, though Muslim clerics
were present among the migrants and were generally respected.
Here too the Muslim Fulbe were more frustrated than the pagan
ones at their state of subservience to local non-Fulbe populations, and later in the eighteenth century they started sporadic
revolts against non-Fulbe rulers. These revolts gained religious
legitimacy when a Muslim scholar named Modibo Adama
brought the news of the Jihad launched by another Pullo,
Usman dan Fodio, in Hausaland, urged the local Fulbe to join
it, and was later chosen by Usman dan Fodio to head the Jihad
in Adamawa. The Jihad gave new momentum to the Fulbe
struggle. A great number of Muslim Fulbe heads of families
rallied to Adama and either spread the Jihad into their own
region (the Benue valley and the plain of Diamaré) or started to
conquer new territories to which they brought Islam (Adamawa
highlands).[13] In this way between 1808 and the 1930s the Jihad
spread all over what later became Adamawa. The defeated
non-Fulbe groups were subjected, enslaved, or driven to the
tops of hills inaccessible to Fulbe cavalry, while still-pagan
Fulbe were pressed to accept Islam and were then accorded
their freedom. Modibo Adama settled at the town of Yola in the
Benue valley and made it his capital. The Fulbe heads of
families who spread the Jihad to different regions established
autonomous chiefdoms (lamidates) subjected to Yola, which itself was part of the empire of Sokoto. The state thus formed was
named by its founder Adamawa, and it established the Fulbe as
the ruling element in the area.[14]

The earliest Fulbe penetration to Hausaland probably occurred in the fifteenth century during their eastward migration
toward Bornu. According to the Kano Chronicle, the first Fulbe
who settled in Hausaland were literate Muslims.[15] They were
probably clerics and teachers who preferred to settle in the
Hausa towns which had already accepted Islam (Kano and Katsina) or were about to accept it (Zaria). They were certainly
more attracted to Hausa towns than to grazing land, water,

or any other need of pastoral life. Following those few pioneers, other Fulbe continued to come to Hausaland between the sixteenth and nineteenth centuries. They came in small groups and accepted the rule of the local people. Hausaland at that time was governed by different Hausa states (Katsina, Kano, Gobir, etc.) which for most of their history had been vassals of Bornu or Songhay but had started to gain their independence in the seventeenth century. By the eighteenth century, one of them, Gobir, reached a predominant position in the area. In Hausaland the Fulbe encountered developed political, economic, and cultural centers situated in large towns with a cosmopolitan population, big and active marketplaces, stations of the trans-Saharan trade, schools, courts, and administrative organizations. Consequently, the Fulbe who spread all over Hausaland by the end of the sixteenth century consisted not only of cattle herdsmen but also of a sizeable number of people (whether Muslimized before or after arrival to Hausaland) who were attracted to urban centers where they were employed as clerics, teachers, judges, and councilors at the courts of Hausa rulers. These Muslim Fulbe, instead of despising the local culture, as in Futa Jallon and Adamawa, were attracted to it and were ready to absorb it. As a result of that, not only did a much greater extent of permanent settlement take place among the migrating Fulbe, but those who became sedentary also adopted the Hausa language and customs. However, they still kept close ties with their kinsmen continuing the pastoral life and paid frequent visits to each other. Many of them continued to own large herds of cattle herded by their clients, kinsmen, or hired workers. As M. G. Smith reports:

Numbers of Fulani settled themselves in separate wards within the walls of the main Habe towns, adopted Hausa language and culture and increasingly adhered to the religion of Islam. Their nomadic brothers, meanwhile, continued to pasture their cattle and migrate unmolested within the confines of Habe territory, using the settled Fulani as liaison with the local Habe rulers to ensure free passage and grazing rights. The nomads retained their culture, language and racial exclusiveness, while the bilingual settled Fulani, through intermarriage, came more and more to adopt Habe customs and language, losing their racial purity while still remaining dependent on their relations with the Habe rulers.[16]

The urbanized Fulbe distinguished themselves from the Hausa by surpassing them in Islamic learning and piety. They excelled in teaching and in administrative and judiciary positions. They constituted the most orthodox Muslim faction and resented the superficiality of Islam as practiced among the Hausa; they were at the forefront of movements for religious reform. They also shared the mounting discontent of their Fulbe kinsmen who, as in other places, resented the excessive cattle taxes that were imposed on them, the various kinds of oppression to which they were subjected, and in general their subservience to what, in their eyes, were unworthy, inferior non-Fulbe people. This feeling, as in other places, led to the launching of a Fulbe revolt in the form of the Jihad at the beginning of the nineteenth century. However, in Hausaland, in contrast to every other place, the Fulbe Jihad was started by urbanized Fulbe who had already absorbed much of the local non-Fulbe culture. The Fulbe Jihad in Hausaland was launched in 1804 by Usman dan Fodio, one of the most highly acclaimed clerics of his time. He launched the Jihad after his previous public criticism of the state of religion and administration in the state of Gobir led to more oppression of Muslims in that state. As the news of the Jihad reached the different parts of Hausaland, the Fulbe located in those areas rallied to the Jihad and assured its ultimate success.[17]

By 1810 almost all the Hausa states were defeated. Usman dan Fodio distributed flags to his major disciples and supporters, advising them to carry the Jihad to their own territories. These people conquered almost all of Hausaland and beyond, forming in each place a Muslim state subordinate to Usman dan Fodio. In this way a large Fulbe-ruled empire was formed and called the Sokoto empire after the name of the town that was built as its capital.

At the beginning of the Jihad the followers of Usman dan Fodio did not consist only of Fulbe. Many Hausa people sided with him for religious reasons and because they saw in him a defender of poor people's interests. They even took an active part in the war. One of his major flagbearers, Yakubu, who founded the emirate of Bauchi, was not Pullo. Many Hausa people continued to play important roles in the various emirates that were formed. However, the crucial factor contributing to the victory was the help received from the pastoral Fulbe groups scattered throughout Hausaland. It was mainly through their solidarity with Usman dan Fodio that the Jihad could spread so rapidly across Hausaland. For those people the idea of establishing Fulbe supremacy counted much more than the religious ideas of Usman dan Fodio. Later the idea of Fulbe supremacy asserted itself even more at the expense of the religious Islamic mandate[18] and received its clearest illustration when the Fulbe attacked Bornu, which was among the oldest Muslim states in the area and was ruled at the time by a Muslim no less scholarly than Usman dan Fodio himself. Although the Fulbe tried to justify their attack (which failed) on the basis of alleged religious laxity and impropriety in Bornu, there seems to be no doubt that what was really at stake was political supremacy in the central-Sudan area.[19]

Relations between Fulbe and Non-Fulbe Populations Following the Holy Wars

The above description of the formation of Fulbe states in Futa Jallon, Adamawa, and Sokoto has shown how closely the Islamization of the Fulbe was related to Fulbe state formation and to the establishment of Fulbe domination in those areas; it illustrated how Islam was used to further the Fulbe's sense of superiority over non-Fulbe populations. In Futa Jallon and Adamawa the aim of establishing the rule of Islam obviously meant the rule of Fulbe, since they were the only "genuine" Muslim people of the region. In Hausaland, on the other hand, things were not quite as simple. There were many very respectable Muslims among the Hausa. Moreover, the Fulbe themselves had absorbed Hausa culture to such an extent that they could hardly repudiate it as being a pagan culture. Therefore, the Fulbe had to accept the general Muslim identity of the Hausa, though stressing its superficial and incomplete nature. Unlike the local populations in Futa Jallon and Adamawa, the Hausa were considered to be part of the Islamic community (and generally not enslaved unless caught in enemy armies) and even had access to some high positions in the emirates. A clear distinction was made between the Hausa and the pagan hill tribes or the populations of the Middle Belt which became the main targets of slave raids. Therefore, the relationship between Fulbe and Hausa remained quite close, and assimilation between the two groups continued after the Jihad.[20] In Hausaland the Fulbe were simply the aristocratic ruling elements of a Muslim community which comprised also the Hausa, while in Futa Jallon and Adamawa the Fulbe alone formed the Muslim community, almost all the non-Fulbe being outside the community and so prey to war and slavery. For this reason, very little conscious effort was made in Adamawa and Futa Jallon to spread Islam among non-Fulbe populations.[21]

Among the Muslim non-Fulbe populations who were politically predominant in their region before the Jihad there was almost universal resistance to the Fulbe Jihads. Some of them were successful in their resistance and never fell under Fulbe political rule. Such was the case of the Kanuri in Bornu, a few Hausa kingdoms in Hausaland, and to some extent the Mandara in Adamawa.[22] Others, such as most of the Hausa in Sokoto, were defeated by the Fulbe and had to accept their rule. However, being considered Muslim by the Fulbe, they were accepted as part of the Islamic community. They were granted freedom and enjoyed some minimal rights of citizenship together with Fulbe commoners. They tended to accept the basic legitimacy of the new social order and of the new rulers.

Besides the Muslim non-Fulbe groups who were politically predominant in the region before the Jihad, there were also some Muslims who belonged to ethnic groups living outside the boundaries of the Fulbe states in question. These Muslims formed small minorities mostly occupied either with trade or with koranic teaching. The Moors, the Dyakhanke, the Toucouleurs in Futa Jallon, the Shuwa Arabs, the Kanuri, the Kotoko in Sokoto and Adamawa belonged to that category. They too enjoyed the rights of Muslim commoners, and their position on the scale of prestige corresponded to that of their ethnic group's perceived Islamic identity.

Among the pagan non-Fulbe populations, those who tried to resist the Fulbe were mostly either utterly destroyed or driven off to areas inaccessible to the Fulbe. Those who were more or less successful in their resistance[23] lived in the constant fear of Fulbe attacks, either at the margin of the territories controlled by the Fulbe or on hilltops within those territories. Because of their constant confrontation with the Fulbe, these groups remained least influenced by Islam, by the Fulbe language and customs; they preserved their own traditions more or less intact. The groups whose resistance collapsed[24] suffered extreme destitution and social disorganization as a result of Fulbe domination. They were reduced to remnants by slave raids; thousands of people disappeared each year, either being taken as slaves or dying in the massacres accompanying the raids or from the famine that followed because all crops were taken or burnt by the raiders.

Some pagan populations did not resist the Fulbe but tried to come to some kind of coexistence with them.[25] They accepted Fulbe sovereignty and provided the Fulbe an annual tribute, including a quota of slaves, in return for which the Fulbe recognized their autonomy in local affairs and undertook not to attack them, though even that did not protect them totally from occasional Fulbe slave raids. Those people generally showed greater readiness to adopt Islam and aspects of Fulbe culture and social organization. However, they were not encouraged in that attempt by the Fulbe, and even when their Islamization was acknowledged they were left outside the community of free Muslims because they were pagan at the time of the Jihad and so their servile status preceded their adoption of Islam.

We can see from this brief discussion that, with the exception of those populations fully acknowledged by Fulbe to be Muslim, the formation of Fulbe hegemony caused a great breakdown in non-Fulbe populations. Social structures were dislocated, economic activities were disrupted, social groups were dispersed and some so seriously dismembered that they stopped being viable social units. Furthermore, those who tried to escape from Fulbe slave raids by retreating to inaccessible swamps or tops of hills thereby retreated to places inaccessible to any civilizing influence. At their place of refuge they cut themselves off from contact with important centers and routes through which trade and communications passed and changes and innovations were diffused to the region. Their "uncivilized" nature was thus reinforced. As we shall see later, this factor was of crucial importance at the time of colonial penetration. These people were the last to come into contact with Europeans and with the innovations that followed the establishment of the colonial system.

Structure of Government and Distribution of Power

We have stated in the preceding sections that the holy war and state formation in Futa Jallon, Sokoto, and Adamawa resulted in the Fulbe's coming to ruling position. We should now examine this assertion more closely by investigating the extent of Fulbe control over power resources in society, in terms of positions which offered to their occupants greatest decision-making authority and control over forces of coercion such as the military. In doing that we shall have to describe briefly the main features of the government structure in each state.

The position of head of state in each country combined in itself the supreme political and religious leadership. In Futa Jallon, the head of state, or *Almamy*, was chosen from the lineages of the first head of state, Karamoko Alfa, and his successor and cousin Ibrahima Sory. The death of Ibrahima Sory had created a big succession crisis between his and Karamoko Alfa's lineages. To solve the crisis, a rare system of joint rule was instituted according to which two almamys, one from each lineage, were chosen and the two candidates held office in rotation for two years each. This pattern of biannual rotation intensified the rivalry between the *Alfaya* and *Soriya* branches instead of reducing it. The clashes and struggles accompanying succession were now repeated almost every two years. Even when the rules of rotation worked properly, each almamy provided a built-in opposition to the actions of his counterpart, the result being great immobility and virtual paralysis of the exercise of government at the top level. This, in turn, increased the political intervention of the council of clerics and enhanced the autonomy of provincial chiefs.[26]

The head of state in Sokoto was the sultan of Sokoto who also held the title of *Sarkin Musulmin* (chief of the Muslims). The first head of state, Usman dan Fodio, was, like his Futa Jallon counterpart, above all an important Islamic scholar who preferred to leave military and political matters to his kin and lieutenants and occupy himself more with religious and scholarly matters. He was succeeded by his son Mohamadu Bello, who, besides being recognized supreme political and religious head of the empire, was also the ruler of all the eastern provinces. Bello's uncle Abdullahi, who was his main opponent for succession, was made Emir of Gwandu and given the rule of all the western provinces of the empire. Mohamadu Bello was succeeded as head of Sokoto by his brother Attiku, and thereafter all but one of the sultans of Sokoto came from the descendants of either Bello or Attiku.[27]

The head of state of Adamawa (called *Lamido*[28]) was an autonomous ruler subordinate to the sultan of Sokoto. The first head of state, Adama, was, like his counterparts in Sokoto and Futa Jallon, above all a pious Muslim cleric and a scholar of great fame; he was called simply *Modibo,* meaning "the learned man." He was succeeded by his son, Lawal, and thereafter the rule remained always in Adama's lineage. While no succession crises occurred in Adamawa, Adama's successors faced recurrent endeavors by subordinate provincial chiefs to break away from Adamawa and declare their independence or their direct allegiance to Sokoto. In some cases they could not prevent the separation of some provinces from Adamawa.[29]

In all the states, the head of state was assisted in government functions by advisory councils, and executive officials. In Futa Jallon the central advisory councils, composed mainly of clerics, were quite powerful autonomous bodies with well-articulated separate functions, and they restrained the almamy's power. Through those councils the power of the religious elite was asserted. In contrast, the executive officialdom was much less developed. Their functions and attributes were generally not well defined, and most of them were called simply "followers" of the rulers.[30] In Sokoto and Adamawa, on the other hand, while the advisory council, called *Fada,* had much less precise functions and was much more dependent on the head of state who appointed most of its members, the state officialdom was much more developed. The head of state was assisted by officials generally appointed by him and performing precisely defined and differentiated bureaucratic functions. The position of the officials was formalized by attaching to each office a title which defined the specific function of the officeholder and gave him specific rights and privileges, such as exploitation of land and slaves and control over some subordinate emirates and chiefdoms. Most of the offices, their titles, and the functions of their holders were adopted from the Hausa system.[31]

Provincial government in each state was held by powerful chiefs (called emir in Sokoto, lamido in Futa Jallon and Adamawa). Emirs and lamibé had their own army and their own autonomous government. They were assisted by their own councils and executives whose functions were similar to the central ones. They sent yearly tributes to the head of state and put their army at the head of state's disposal in times of war.

They were forbidden to launch wars independently, though minor slave raids were permitted. The head of state also had veto power over the election of new provincial chiefs. Provinces varied widely in size and power. The bigger and more powerful a province, the more autonomous it was toward central authority. In Futa Jallon, for example, the province (called *Diwal*) of Labé comprised about 50 percent of the population of the whole country, and its chief's power did not fall from that of the almamy.

Below the province, the basic administrative unit in Futa Jallon was the *Missidé,* generally translated into "village" but which should rather be called parish since it meant "place of prayers" and determined also the local religious community. Missidés were, in turn, subdivided into hamlets which if inhabited by Fulbe were called *Fulasso* and if inhabited by people of servile status were called *Runde.* For these hamlets the missidé was the administrative and religious center where the mosque, the school, and the local chief's residence were located. Gradually other people having relations with the local authorities set up their residences around this center. Each missidé was headed by a chief of missidé (village head) generally chosen from the family who built the mosque at that location and so made it develop into a missidé. The chief of the missidé was chosen by the local council of elders who assisted him in his functions which included collection of taxes, arbitration in local litigation and feuds, recruiting soldiers for the province chief, setting up grazing areas for cattle herds, and hospitality to strangers.[32]

In Sokoto, emirates were in turn divided into provinces ruled by autonomous provincial chiefs and into districts ruled by district heads (*Hakimai*) appointed by emirs or by provincial chiefs. District heads were usually fief holders, appointed by the emirs or the provincial chiefs, controlling land which was related to their official title. The extent to which official titles and the fiefs related to them were inheritable varied by emirates. Usually the district heads were stationed in the capital of the emirates; they were represented in their district by subordinate retainers, called *Jakadu,* who collected the taxes, recruited military contingents, administered the fief holder's estate, and kept law and order in the area in liaison with village heads. Beneath the districts were the villages, headed by village chiefs usually selected by the village population and confirmed in office by the district head. The village heads were assisted by an advisory council of elders of the village.[33]

Among the subordinate emirates of Sokoto, Adamawa was the largest and the most distant from Sokoto and perhaps because of that also one of the most autonomous states of all. It was divided in its turn into many lamidates among which were Maroua, Rey Bouba, Ngaoundéré, Tibati, Banyo. Below them, villages, headed by village chiefs (*Jauro'en*), were the basic units of local territorial administration. However, in the lamidates founded on the Adamawa plateau (Banyo, Tibati, Tignère, Ngaoundéré) the Fulbe population was so mobile and the density of the population so small that although villages did exist they did not become the basic units of local administration until the colonial period. The unit of local administration was the *Tokkal* (plural, tokké) which had no territorial basis and which indicated a group of families traveling together.[34]

In all three societies positions of power were dominated overwhelmingly by the Fulbe. The heads of state, the emirs, the lamibé were, almost without exception, Fulbe[35] belonging to families who had taken a leading role in the Jihad. In Futa Jallon those were the nine leading families of the Jihad; in Adamawa and Sokoto they were the families of those delegated by Usman dan Fodio and Adama to spread the Jihad. Since the emirs and provincial chiefs were also the commanders of their own army, the bulk of the armed forces was controlled by the royal Fulbe families. In Futa Jallon, but not in Sokoto and Adamawa, the armies were made up principally of Fulbe soldiers. The Fulbe of Futa Jallon were quite exceptional in precolonial West Africa in being very reluctant to use slaves or other non-Fulbe subjects in their armies.[36] The almamys had small private armies consisting of slaves, but their force was secondary compared to the larger and stronger provincial armies consisting of Fulbe soldiers. In Sokoto and Adamawa, slaves were used as soldiers, but the command of the armies generally remained in Fulbe hands.[37]

The Fulbe were also predominant among councilors and titled officials. In Futa Jallon virtually all the clerics and officials down to the heads of Missidé were Fulbe belonging to families who had taken a leading role in the Jihad, and this excluded all the Fulbe commoners who were pagan before the Jihad. Not only all the non-Fulbe, but even the Fulbe commoners, who generally did not hold political positions higher than that of hamlet head, were completely barred from those positions. However, regarding *informal* power positions the situation was somewhat different. The almamys and provincial rulers were surrounded by some non-Fulbe people, especially trusted domestic slaves to whom they delegated much power. These people were despised for their status and origin but feared for their power.[38] However, there were only a handful of these people around each ruler, and since they were mostly slaves who were completely dependent on the person of the ruler, they could not challenge the general overwhelming control of the Fulbe aristocracy over power resources.

In Sokoto, Fulbe political dominance was somewhat more limited than in Futa Jallon. In the Hausa-inhabited areas of the empire, the Hausa generally participated in government in subordinate administrative tasks. There were some top official positions open to Hausa and also some official titles held exclusively by slave officials. This practice was inherited from the pre-Jihad Hausa government structure, in which many top government offices were held by slaves. The changes brought after the Fulbe came to power varied from emirate to emirate. In Zaria the power of slave officials declined rapidly, and they became simply administrative subordinates. In the emirates of Kano, Katsina and Daura, on the other hand, slave officials had a prominent place.[39] The subordinate retainers of the fief holders, the jakadu, were almost always chosen from among domestic slaves, and they had complete power in the fief, delegated to them by their masters.[40]

In Adamawa, non-Fulbe people participated less in the government apparatus as officials and local chiefs than in Sokoto but more than in Futa Jallon. In all the lamidates of Adamawa, people of slave status held some official positions and in some places even participated in the advisory councils of the lamibé. In certain lamidates, such as Rey Bouba and Tibati, there was a greater reliance of Fulbe chiefs on some non-Fulbe people (the Mboum in Tibati and the Dama in Rey Bouba) against their fellow Fulbe kinsmen. These two lamidates were also among those which tried most to detach themselves from Adamawa's suzerainty, and one can assume that by allying themselves with some local groups against the Fulbe, the lamibé in those places were trying to establish the basis for independence from Adamawa.[41]

Regarding the differentiation among Fulbe themselves, in both Sokoto and Adamawa most Fulbe councilors and officials belonged to aristocratic families who had played a leading role in the Jihad and who were thus differentiated from Fulbe commoners who played a marginal role in the Jihad and did not control political positions. However, this division was not as stressed as that which existed between aristocratic and commoner Fulbe in Futa Jallon. In Sokoto, following the great degree of assimilation of sedentary Fulbe into Hausa culture, the sedentary Fulbe commoners as a group were not very visible and were easily assimilated along with the Hausa into the general group of sedentary Muslim commoners (*Talakawa*) as differentiated from the ruling class (*Sarauta*) where the Fulbe clearly predominated. For this reason in Sokoto, sedentary Fulbe commoners were ignored as Fulbe (they spoke Hausa, engaged in occupations characteristic of the Hausa, intermarried with Hausa, and were in fact very difficult to differentiate). The only visible differentiation among the Fulbe was that between the Fulbe associated with the ruling class and the pastoral Fulbe herdsmen who continued their traditional occupation at the periphery of the society. In Adamawa, sedentary Fulbe not belonging to the ruling aristocracy still kept their distance from the non-Fulbe populations and were clearly visible in the Benue valley and on the plain of Diamaré. On the Adamawa plateau, on the other hand, there were few sedentary Fulbe commoners. Almost all the Fulbe not holding political and religious positions were pastoral cattle herdsmen.

As a whole, we can conclude that power obviously rested with the Fulbe in all three states, and the extent of power controlled was closely related to the role that one's family had played in the Jihad which led to state formation. One's family's role in the Jihad also differentiated between the ruling Fulbe—who had taken a leading role in the Jihad and were permanently settled, taking up religious and political administrative occupations—and the Fulbe commoners who had taken a marginal role in the Jihad, did not occupy political-administrative positions, and most of whom continued their nomadic pastoral life.

2

The Precolonial Economic, Cultural, and Social Stratification Structures

Distribution of Wealth in Precolonial Futa Jallon, Sokoto, and Adamawa

At the time of their migration to Futa Jallon, Adamawa, and Sokoto, the Fulbe were essentially nomadic, pastoral cattle herdsmen. Their economic system was almost entirely based on cattle. They lived on milk and butter which were either directly consumed or exchanged for agricultural products supplied by the local non-Fulbe populations. The Fulbe deeply disliked agriculture and considered it to be the most humiliating of all manual work, but it was undertaken by their wives as a part-time occupation, and when reliance on cattle could not ensure their subsistence (mainly due to the small size of their herd) the men joined their wives in agriculture, hopefully for a short time only. Many Fulbe families also kept permanent houses on the transhumance cycle of cattle where part of the family, usually the older people, were left, where the family gathered for social occasions and festivities, usually, in the rainy season, and around which some agriculture was undertaken.[42]

An exception to this predominance of pastoralism or semisedentarism among the Fulbe before the Jihad was the permanent settlement of Fulbe in Hausa towns. As seen earlier, those Hausa towns were the seats and centers of pre-Jihad states and were important trade and communications stations as well as regional Islamic centers attracting some Fulbe to administrative and religious positions and opportunities, cultural activities, and trade possibilities. Those Fulbe settled permanently in those towns and thus became fully sedentary prior to the Jihad. In Futa Jallon and Adamawa the Fulbe did not encounter such developed urban centers and no similar urbanization or any kind of full sedentarism took place before the Jihad. However, even in Hausaland, the Fulbe who became fully sedentary before the Jihad constituted only a small minority of the whole Fulbe population.

Slaves

With the Jihad and Fulbe state formation, the Fulbe economy underwent great changes. Most important, the place of cattle as the primary economic resource was taken by slaves. The families who had participated in the Jihad, and especially those who had led it, acquired a great number of slaves from the pagan non-Fulbe populations and from captured enemy forces. The greater one's family's role in the Jihad and the higher his position in the political hierarchy, the more slaves he accumulated (i.e., conversion of power resources into slaves). Slaves were either used as personal servants assisting in the household work or were put to work in agriculture, on land belonging to their masters. They were usually settled in separate slave villages called *Runde* and were also given small parcels of land for their own use where they worked a few days a week and from which they supplied part of the products to their master. They were also used to clear the bush, thereby enlarging the cultivatable land on which their masters could claim legitimate right of control. Following the great increase in the number of slaves owned by the Fulbe and the realization of the profitable way in which they could be made to work in agriculture, the economy of the ruling, slave-owning Fulbe became increasingly oriented toward the exploitation of agricultural slave labor.[43] The value that slaves gained with this reorientation of economic activities is most eloquently described by M. G. Smith: "The most significant form of capital in Zaria consisted in slaves. Such slave capital was legitimate and its accumulation was sanctioned by religion; it was self-reproducing, self-supporting, and provided regular annual returns on investment; it was liquid, and could easily be sold; on the whole it appreciated rather than otherwise, despite the rule against the sale of local-born slaves (dimajai); it was eminently inheritable, and it possessed political and military significance under the prevalent pattern of state organizaton."[44] Consequently the exploitation of slaves and hence their number grew very rapidly in all three societies. By the end of the nineteenth century the slave population in Futa Jallon amounted to about one-third of the total population, and in some parts the proportion rose to one-half. Smith's study of the emirate of Zaria in Sokoto indicates that at the same period close to half the population of Zaria was made up of slaves.[45] As for Adamawa, it was the greatest supplier of slaves for the whole empire of Sokoto. Visiting Adamawa in 1851, the European traveler Barth wrote: "Slavery exists on an immense scale in this country and there are many private individuals who have more than a thousand slaves.... Muhammed Lowel had all his slaves settled in Rumde or slave villages where they cultivate grain for his use or profit.... I have been assured that Mohammed Lowel (the Emir) receives every year in tribute, besides horses and cattle, about 5,000 slaves."[46]

Besides agriculture, the slaves could be used in many other tasks. Some were used in construction works. Many were trained as soldiers, others as craftsmen. Most tribute from vassals and local rulers to emirs and lamibé included a quota of slaves. The domestic slaves were generally the luckiest of all as they could develop personal ties with their masters. The position and privileges of household slaves were closely related to the position of their masters. Household slaves of rulers and state officials were generally their most trusted councilors and, as such, held considerable power. Some of them, especially in Sokoto and in a few lamidates of Adamawa, were even appointed to top executive positions. Such slave officials clearly occupied a more privileged position than many free persons.

Finally, many slave girls were taken as concubines by their masters. Their sons were considered free Fulbe and were entitled to succeed their father like any other children.[47] Since the taking of wives from the slaves was very widespread, the settled Fulbe and especially the ruling groups rapidly lost their nonnegroid traits and were physically differentiated from the pastoral Fulbe who remained endogamous and preserved their original physical characteristics. This deepened the division between sedentary and pastoral Fulbe.[48]

The slaves who were privately owned were differentiated from the slaves who belonged to the state and who were under the custody of the head of state or his agents. The slaves belonging to the state were part of the *Beital,* or the public treasury of the country, administered by the ruler or his agents. In this category of slaves of the state were included all the pagan populations directly ruled by the state, whether they were actually used as slaves working in state farms, in public works, being enrolled in the army, etc. or were simply tax-paying subjects having a servile status but not being actually enslaved. The term *Matchoudo* (plural, *matchoubé*) literally meaning slave, was used to designate all the populations collectively considered pagan at the time of the Jihad. The privately owned actual slaves constituted only a small part of this population.[49]

While first-generation slaves were considered basically as a commodity, second-generation slaves could not be sold, and close ties existed generally between them and their masters. Fulbe slave owners were urged to offer to worthy Muslimized second-generation slaves the opportunity to buy their freedom. Their adoption of Islam did not earn the slaves the automatic right to become free, but proof of sincere and thorough Islamization was a moral incentive for their masters to grant them freedom. Slaves who earned their freedom continued to maintain close relations with their ex-masters. They continued to serve them and show them deference. In fact, there existed so little visible difference between an enfranchised and a second-generation slave that the word *Dimadio* (plural, *rimaibé* or *dimajai*) was intermittently used for enfranchised slave and inalienable second-generation slave.[50]

The increasing importance of slave labor agriculture accelerated the trend toward sedentarization among the Fulbe, and it also changed its basic reasons. It was no longer poverty measured in lack of cattle that induced Fulbe families to permanent settlement but, on the contrary, wealth measured in agricultural products supplied by their slaves. At the same time, although cattle lost their value as an economic resource they continued to be valued as a prestige resource, and this accounted for the fact that, even after taking up a sedentary life and orienting their economy toward the exploitation of slaves in agriculture, the leading Fulbe families continued to own large herds of cattle whose care was left to hired, poorer Fulbe herdsmen. Ownership of cattle showed that, although permanently settled, the rich sedentary Fulbe had not forsaken completely their traditional Fulbe life. It is interesting to note that the wealthy Fulbe who became sedentary by making others work for them in agriculture and who owned cattle herded by others did not lose their Fulbe identity, while those Fulbe who became sedentary because of poverty and had to take up agriculture usually did.[51] In other words, it was not sedentarism per se that was anathema to Fulbe identity but agricultural occupation and loss of cattle. With agricultural products being supplied by servile labor, cattle being herded by hired herdsmen, household work being done by women helped by domestic slaves, the remaining specialized goods and services supplied by craftsmen or traders consisting mostly of non-Fulbe groups, the slave-owning Fulbe, especially those belonging to the leading families of the Jihad, could establish themselves in permanent settlements where they could dedicate themselves to learning, religion, and political and military activities. This is the functional setting which explains the close relationship between the high economic and political position achieved by the Fulbe after the Jihads and their taking up a sedentary life in a permanent settlement.[52]

Land

With the formation of the Fulbe-ruled states and the process of sedentarization that followed, one other item that gained great economic value was land. As long as the Fulbe were pastoral herdsmen, land served them only for grazing. Where land was abundant, as on the Adamawa plateau, there was no reason for delimiting property rights on it. Where land was scarce, as on the plain of Diamaré and the Kano-Katsina area, then it clearly belonged to non-Fulbe populations who before the war were in a politically superior position to the Fulbe. The Fulbe had to pay dues to the owners of the land in order to graze their cattle or simply pass through. With the Jihad, the Fulbe who came to a ruling position took away all the land that they wanted from the local populations. This was in keeping with the Maliki Law of Islam which permitted the Faithful to arrogate to themselves the land that they conquered in the process of Jihad.[53] "Living" lands in conquered territories, that is, lands which were cleared from the bush, were then distributed in different ways. Some of it was treated as *Kharajj* land, land that was left to the conquered population, who could work on it and pass it to their descendants but had to pay a land tax (Kharajj) as tribute to the rulers for permitting them to cultivate the land. Other lands were allocated to the family of the ruler, to his aides, his companions-in-arms, and in general to all Muslim conquerors (most of whom were Fulbe) for their private use; they could install on them their slaves to work in agriculture. The ruling groups also received as fiefs control over some Kharajj land inhabited by conquered populations. In this case ruling groups not only paid no tax for controlling that land, but on the contrary received a share of the Kharajj collected from the conquered population who worked on the land. Part of the fiefs were noninheritable and were attached to certain political offices, in which case control over land was temporary and was clearly related to the title of the officeholders. Finally, some land was kept vacant by the ruler, either for possible allocation in the future or for public utilities such as mosques, wells, marketplaces. Land reserved for public religious purposes was called "dedicated" *Wakf* land. However, this term was also applied to many newly conquered areas which were put under the direct control of the Fulbe conquerors.[54]

Regarding the inheritable land, there has been much confusion among scholars as to whether land was privately owned or was legally the property of the state or local communities. We shall not enter here into this discussion, which is well covered in the literature but still remains inconclusive.[55] In theory, it seems that some limitations did exist on private ownership of land. However, in practice, the possessors of land acted very much as if they owned it and, especially in Futa Jallon, there were no inhibitions on selling, renting, loaning, or entering into any other transactions. Whether this was simply tolerated by the local authorities or was part of peoples' ownership rights is not clear. It is agreed, however, that in each case heads of local communities had some control over local land, at least in allocating empty lots to strangers or to new households and in reallocating land whose possessor died without inheritor or left the village with little prospect of return.[56]

The legal complexities of land tenure should not divert us from our principal issue, which is the extent of Fulbe control (whether legally owning or not) over land, and in this point we find significant differences between the three societies. In the areas of Sokoto inhabited by the Hausa, Fulbe control over land was less extensive and less direct because the Hausa, like other Muslim subjects, were allowed to keep their land on the condition that they pay tributes to the local rulers or fief holders. By contrast, in areas inhabited mostly by pagans (such as

Adamawa) more land was taken from the conquered populations and put under the direct control of the Fulbe conquerors.
In Futa Jallon, on the other hand, since a great proportion of the
subjected populations were themselves Fulbe and were left to
control their own land, we find that although the Fulbe clearly
controlled most of the land compared to non-Fulbe populations,
the ruling group's control over land was not much greater than
that of the Fulbe commoners.

Nevertheless, beyond those differences between the three
societies, it is clear that in each society the Fulbe exerted greater
control over land than non-Fulbe populations.[57] This control,
and indeed the general land-tenure system established after
state formation, was a clear illustration of the conversion of
power resources into land which could be used both as a wealth
resource, in the form of agricultural products, and as a further
power resource, in the form of political control exerted on the
population inhabiting that land. As a wealth resource, possession of land was complementary to possession of free labor
force (whether servile or not) in the sense that possession of
both was essential in order to make economic profit from each.
Like slaves, land was purchased by power resources and, while
partly reconverting into power, it also brought considerable
wealth to its new holders. This in turn contributed greatly to
ensure the economic as well as political dominance of the Fulbe
compared to other populations in the three societies.

Trade and Craftsmanship

Until now we have discussed three major economic
resources—cattle, slaves, and land—whose control by the Fulbe
determined the latter's overall economic dominance in precolonial times. One of those resources, cattle, had always been
controlled by Fulbe. The two other resources, land and slaves,
which surpassed cattle in economic value, came under Fulbe
control only after the Jihads as a result of their coming to a
politically dominant position. Now we should turn our attention to two sets of economic activities which remained outside
the direct control of the Fulbe even after they came to a ruling
position, namely, trade and craftsmanship.

With regard to trade, important differences are detected between the three areas. Trade flourished in Hausaland before the

Jihad. The Hausa towns were important centers on West African trade routes. A well-developed system of markets existed in Hausaland with use of standard currencies and a wide range of goods brought from very distant areas. The Hausa excelled in trade, while the Fulbe shunned and despised it. Even those Fulbe who were attracted by the administrative and educational opportunities of Hausa towns were not attracted by their commercial opportunities. This situation did not change after the Jihad. The Hausa continued to control trade activities, and the Fulbe were satisfied with taxing them.[58] In contrast with Hausaland, Adamawa was located outside the main trade circuits of West Africa. No important markets were held, nor did any important caravans traverse it. Local populations were hostile to traders, in whom they saw precursors of foreign invaders. The formation of the Fulbe state and its attachment to Sokoto caused a slight development of commercial activities by opening up the area to a few Hausa traders, but by no means could the area be compared with the lively commerce of Hausaland. Here too the Fulbe kept their distance from trade but taxed it heavily. A somewhat different pattern was observed in Rey Bouba where trade was monopolized by the lamido; no private traders were allowed into the territory and all markets were banned, the lamido having complete control over the distribution of goods in his territory.[59]

In Futa Jallon too commercial activities were marginal prior to the Jihad. With the establishment of the Fulbe state, however, a significant development occurred in commerce. The area was integrated in the Dyula trade network of Western Sudan, both as a transit area and as principal exporter of cattle and importer of slaves. Commerce developed even more after the opening of European trade posts in the Guinean coast in the mid-nineteenth century. Futa Jallon provided the main link between those stations and the Dyula trade of the interior. Still, the structure of commerce in Futa Jallon was quite different from that of Hausaland. The rising importance of trade routes in Futa Jallon did not lead to the propagation of private commercial enterprise and opening of a multitude of markets throughout the country. Commerce in Futa Jallon was much more a "state affair." It was either directed by the state itself, as in much of the slave and cattle trade, or else it was allowed only to a few

Dyula merchants who received special permission from the highest ruling authorities and were forced to organize in big caravans closely controlled and often given military escort by the ruling authorities. The whole trade was monopolized by a few Dyula who either worked as the state's agents or were allowed private commerce because they enjoyed privileged relations with the political authorities without which no trade was possible.[60] In any case, here too the Fulbe kept away from trade and contented themselves with taxing it heavily.

Craftsmanship was another activity from which Fulbe kept their distance. Craftsmen were usually organized in specialized groups with hereditary transmission of the crafts and restricted interaction with other groups, though important differences existed between the three societies with respect to the degree of closure of craftsmen's groups. It seems that the Fulbe adopted the existing patterns that they encountered in each location as they arrived there in the course of migration. In Hausaland, where caste-like organizations were rare, no such organizations for craftsmen were established after the Jihad. Craftsmen were organized in specialized occupational groups with special training and patterns of preferential marriage among themselves, but there was no strict endogamy, no restrictions on interaction with people outside the group, and apprentices for the profession could be taken from outside. The craftsmen called themselves Hausa, like the majority of the population. In Adamawa and Futa Jallon, on the other hand, many of the local groups encountered by the Fulbe did have in their society caste-like organizations of craftsmen, and therefore the Fulbe also adopted this pattern. In Adamawa, generally speaking, the only craftsmen organized in castes were the blacksmiths, while in Futa Jallon, under the influence of the predominance of castes in Western Sudanese societies, most of the craftsmen were organized in caste-like organizations.[61] However, after the Jihad, when the Fulbe came to ruling positions and acquired many slaves, they tried to reduce their dependence on closed groups of artisans by forcing the latter to teach their craft to slaves. By controlling their slaves, who became craftsmen, the Fulbe gained better control of the specialized products of craftsmen and did not have to pay for them.[62] This was true also of Hausaland, where no caste organization of craftsmen had existed in the first place and so the training of slaves as craftsmen was all the easier. The craftsmen were generally free to sell their products and services to anyone in society, but they were heavily taxed by local rulers.

Taxes and Other Economic Returns of Political Officeholding

We have seen so far various ways in which the power position achieved by the Fulbe was used to acquire wealth resources. Besides being used in purchasing commodities that served as wealth resources, the ruling positions were themselves sources of considerable income collected in the form of war booty, taxes, tribute, and presents. War booty was a principal source of revenue as far as slaves were concerned. Except for natural reproduction, the greatest number of slaves were acquired as prisoners taken in wars and periodic raids carried by Fulbe rulers against pagan populations living at the periphery of their lands. In those wars and slave raids, one-fifth of all the goods captured, including slaves, horses, cattle, and weapons, belonged to the emir or lamido who had ordered the expedition; the rest of the goods were distributed among the participants, and the higher one's position was in the chain of command, the bigger was his share.

The main taxes collected in Futa Jallon, Sokoto, and Adamawa included the tithe (*Zakaat*); the land tax (Kharajj); the cattle tax (called *Jangali* in Hausaland); the inheritance tax; dues and fees received in markets and from craftsmen; tribute paid by someone who assumed office (*Kurdin Sarauta* in Hausa); tribute sent by subordinate chiefs to their suzerain; and a special tribute (*Jizye*) paid by non-Muslim subjects as a sign of subjection to Muslim rule.[63] The main tax, the zakaat, was regarded in theory as alms paid by Muslims to a public fund (Beital, deriving from the Arabic word *Beit el Mal*) from which the head of state or his agents were supposed to cover the needs of the poor. However, since the rulers had exclusive control over that fund and nobody could question the way it was used, the zakaat soon lost its almsgiving aspect and became simply the main tax paid to the ruler by the Muslim community. Taxes were paid by subjects to their immediate rulers, who sent part of them to higher authorities while keeping a part for themselves. It was common practice for officials and local chiefs to extort from subject people more taxes than were determined at higher echelons in order to keep a greater share for themselves.

Beyond these official sources of revenue, officeholders were the recipients of considerable unofficial income in the form of gifts and commissions for services rendered, including appointment to office. Candidates for office, if they were to have any chance at all, had to invest a great amount in gifts to people who could affect their appointment. The economic payoffs that the office would bring was expected to cover the preliminary investment. The higher a person's position in the political hierarchy, the more people in inferior positions needed his services and favors, the more gifts (called *Gaisuwa* in Hausa, meaning "greeting gifts") he received and hence the higher his informal income was in addition to the official revenues attached to his office.[64]

Thus, in various formal and informal ways, the political position that one occupied could be translated into income, the power resource being used to acquire more wealth. This was done directly and officially in the form of tax shares, fees, dues, tribute, etc., less officially in the form of "greeting gifts," and indirectly through the general political and social changes which gave the politically dominant group control over land and slaves. While power resources could thus easily be converted into wealth, the same cannot be said of the conversion of wealth into power. Although appropriate gifts could play an important role in political appointment, most top-ranking political positions were limited to a small group, generally closed on the basis of ascriptive criteria. For the ones outside that group, the economic resources were not of great help in opening the gates of high political office. For example, no matter how wealthy they were, merchants were definitely outside the political elite and could not expect to use their wealth to enter it. The few people who did manage to enter the political elite from outside the closed aristocratic group did not owe this to their wealth but rather to the prestige deriving mostly from their Islamic fame and knowledge. Noneconomic considerations, such as family ties, personal trust, political alliances, or religious prestige, played a more important role than any economic considerations in the access to positions of greatest power.

Distribution of Prestige in Precolonial Futa Jallon, Sokoto, and Adamawa

Islam

Following the holy wars and Fulbe state formation, Islam formed the basis of legitimacy of the new social and political order in Futa Jallon, Sokoto, and Adamawa. Collective values and goals from which derived most prestige were based on Islam. People known for greatest piety or knowledge of Islam, or those who belonged to the oldest Muslim families, enjoyed greatest prestige. This prestige was also an important prerequisite for selection to high political office, thereby illustrating the conversion of prestige into power. The founders of the states, Karamoko Alfa in Futa Jallon, Usman dan Fodio in Sokoto, and Modibo Adama in Adamawa, were all Islamic scholars first and political or military leaders second; it was their religious leadership that earned them the position of head of state. The same was true also of many of their subordinate emirs and provincial rulers.[65] Most political offices were defined in religious, Islamic terms; the official activities and decisions were explained and legitimized on a religious basis. Furthermore, fields such as the educational and the judicial were left completely to the control of Muslim clerics.

The judicial system in all three societies was based on Islamic law, which could be supplemented, but not modified, by executive orders of rulers or their agents. In theory, the heads of state (and the autonomous emirs or provincial rulers) were also the supreme judges in their role of religious heads of their country or province, but they always delegated their judicial powers to the *Chief Alkali*, who held the supreme Islamic court, the highest judicial body in the country. Under the supreme Islamic court was organized a network of lower Islamic courts held by Alkali (Islamic judges), the lowest level being the arbitration courts at villages headed by the village head and local elders and clerics.[66]

Muslim clerics also completely controlled the educational system of Futa Jallon, Sokoto, and Adamawa. In all three states basic education was given in koranic schools scattered all over the country where pupils learned to recite prayers and the rudiments of literacy.[67] Students who wanted to pursue their studies beyond the level of the koranic school went to study with higher teachers. At the successful completion of studies which enabled them to read and write Arabic and explain the basic tenets of Islam, they became *Mallams* (meaning teachers in Arabic) as they were called in Sokoto and Adamawa or *Karamoko* as they were called in Futa Jallon. Those who continued even higher studies could reach the status of *Modibo*, meaning scholar or erudite (in Futa Jallon, however, Modibo was used for relatively lower-level clerics, while higher scholars were *Thierno* or *Alfa*[68]). The fame of some of these scholars was so widespread that they had students and followers from all over West Africa.

When they were not themselves part of the political structure, the Muslim clerics and scholars held a relatively autonomous position vis-à-vis political authorities. Their religious prestige, deriving from their position as custodians or interpreters of the basic norms and values of society, protected them to a certain extent from abuse and persecution by political authorities. They were the group of people who, when located outside the political apparatus, were best protected against that apparatus due to their role as legitimizers of the apparatus. The political authorities tried to control them by coopting them into the political structure, by appointing them to official positions, advisory councils, etc., and in fact the great majority of clerics were incorporated in this way in the political structure of the society.

The position of clerics was in principle open to anybody who could excel in Islamic knowledge and prove himself by his sound judgment and advice. There existed some non-Fulbe among top clerics in all three societies. In general, Islamic scholars were geographically very mobile people, traveling from place to place for purposes of study, preaching, or on their way to or from Mecca. Many clerics were thus foreigners in the country, and their consequent detachment from competing factions of rulers and rivals was an asset in their employment by local political authorities. Nevertheless, the great majority of clerics in all three societies were Fulbe, and so the Fulbe controlled the positions conferring highest religious prestige. Beyond that, the Fulbe as a whole were considered to be the most orthodox Muslim people, the model of Islam for others in all three societies, and hence they enjoyed greater prestige than other local populations in terms of general proximity to Islam.

Fulbe Identity and Way of Life

A second set of traits conferring prestige, which supplemented that of Islam, derived from the virtues of the Fulbe ethos and way of life. These traits by definition were controlled by the Fulbe since they formed part of Fulbe identity. The prestige related to being or acting like Fulbe derived from the fact that the Fulbe were already the dominant group in society and could impose their own cultural standards on the rest of the population. However, it derived also from the fact that the Fulbe way of life was perceived as being basically a Muslim way of life, thereby bringing one closer to prestige derived from Islam. Certain aspects of the Fulbe way of life were blended together with Islam and presented as parts of true Islamic behavior. Interestingly, this occurred just as the Fulbe themselves were undergoing a deep transformation in their way of life through sedentarization and in Hausaland also considerable acculturation to Hausa culture. In other words, those Fulbe who were in the process of losing some of their traditional ethnic characteristics came to a dominant position and put to the forefront the virtues of a Fulbe way of life according to a revised Islamic version. On the other hand, the pastoral Fulbe, who showed greatest attachment to the traditional Fulbe way of life but were not counted among the most orthodox Islamic populations, held relatively lower prestige. By stressing less the pastoral aspects of Pulaaku and bringing it closer to the Islamic mode of behavior, the sedentary Fulbe were able to position themselves as the cultural model for the whole population, and that entitled them to greatest prestige.

In Adamawa and Futa Jallon, since the great majority of the non-Fulbe people were pagan at the time of the Jihad, the Fulbe were considered the only true Muslim group in the area and Fulbe identity was practically indistinguishable from Muslim identity in the eyes of most non-Fulbe populations. Consequently the Fulbe language, the importance attributed to cattle, the Fulbe patterns of dress, and other Fulbe customs started to spread to non-Fulbe people in the process of their Islamization. In the areas of Sokoto inhabited by the Hausa, on the other hand, because the bulk of the non-Fulbe population, the Hausa, were considered at least nominally Muslim[69] even before the Jihad, Islamic identity was not confused with Fulbe identity. Therefore, Islamization did not lead to Fulbeization as it did in Adamawa and Futa Jallon. On the contrary, in Hausaland many aspects of Hausa culture and social organization (for instance, their language, their distinctive architecture, their patterns of government) were adopted by the Fulbe themselves, and therefore not only Fulbe traits but also many Hausa traits were used as models of the right way of Islamic life The adoption of Islam by pagan non-Fulbe populations brought them closer to Hausa identity and not to the Fulbe identity which was restricted either to the ruling group or to pastoral herdsmen.

In our discussion of the distribution of prestige so far we have seen the close relationship and easy interconvertibility that existed between power and prestige resources. The relationship between prestige and wealth resources, on the other hand, was less close and more indirect. Generally speaking, prestige was not readily convertible into wealth unless it passed through the intermediary of power. Those who held most prestige in society were not necessarily among the wealthiest, and to the extent that they were, their wealth derived mostly from the economic payoffs of their political position and not directly from their prestige. The clerics and scholars, though enjoying relatively great religious prestige, were not wealthy unless they held also some political position. They were conventionally required to shun wealth and live mainly on charity, though they received small fees and presents from their pupils, from their followers, and from people who came to seek their help and advice. The conversion of wealth into prestige was somewhat easier. The wealthier could afford more thorough Islamic education for themselves or their sons, as they had more leisure and could pay the teachers. Wealth could purchase prestige also through lavish almsgiving. Buying cattle and building a large herd was another very typical Fulbe way of converting wealth into prestige. However, highest prestige was still inaccessible on the sole basis of wealth, and prestige acquired through wealth was considered of less value than prestige with which one was born or which was acquired through noneconomic means.[70]

The Jihads and state formation in Futa Jallon, Sokoto, and Adamawa could be represented as the building of new "centers" in those areas. The overall dominance of the Fulbe, especially in terms of power and prestige resources, could then be explained by the fact that they founded those new centers and occupied dominant positions in them. Islam and Fulbe identity were the two essential traits that helped to characterize those centers, to distinguish them from the periphery, and to delimit participation in them. For this reason they were also the bases of hierarchical differentiation between the various populations living in the three societies. In the first place, Muslims were differentiated from pagans; only the former were considered to be part of the community (the *Umma*) represented by the state, and they became the free subjects (*Rimbé*) of the Fulbe rulers. Those who were pagan at the time of their subjection were classified as nonfree (Matchoubé) even if subsequently they adopted Islam. Second, the Fulbe were differentiated from the non-Fulbe. Although in principle no difference was supposed to exist between different members of the Islamic community, the Fulbe generally held a superior position in terms of proximity to the center and in terms of control over power, prestige, and wealth resources. Third, state formation caused an important differentiation among the Fulbe themselves on the basis of the extent of participation in it. The families which led the Jihads constituted a ruling aristocracy who enjoyed greatest prestige by virtue of belonging to the lineage of the founding fathers. They also had the virtual monopoly of ruling positions and concentrated in their hands the largest amount of wealth, counted mainly by the number of slaves and the amount of land that they controlled. Access to their positions was closed to all other people, even to Fulbe who did not belong to their lineage. Their superior status was expressed in a special style of life characterized by refraining from all manual labor and dedicating oneself to religious, political, administrative, and military functions.[71]

Part Two Colonial Changes

3

Principal Characteristics of Colonial Systems

The Establishment of Colonial Rule

Futa Jallon, Adamawa, and Sokoto fell under colonial rule at the turn of the twentieth century. The Fulbe rulers' reaction to it was quite similar in the three areas. At first they tried to resist the increasing European presence and pressure, the resistance culminating in a military confrontation in which the Fulbe armies were easily defeated by the European forces and colonial rule was established in Fulbe-held territory. However, the military clashes were short-lived; feeling the futility of resisting the European militarily, the Fulbe rulers cut short their resistance and shifted to collaboration with the European forces in the hope of remaining intermediaries between the colonial power and the native population of the region and so maintaining their ruling position and their general domination over other groups.

French penetration to Futa Jallon took place between the 1830s and the 1890s. It started with the establishment of trade ports on the Guinean coast. Entering into trade relations with coastal people who were vassals of the Fulbe brought the French into direct contact with Futa Jallon. Between the 1840s and 1890s many French missions visited Futa Jallon, at first mostly for trade purposes, but since the 1880s with more political aims—to sign a treaty of protection which would bring Futa Jallon into the French orbit (and remove from there any British presence). For a long time the Fulbe put up a subtle but firm resistance to French pressures. In 1888 the reigning Almamy Soriya refused to sign a treaty on the pretext that his Alfaya counterpart would not sign it. A treaty signed in 1891 was repudiated two years later on some technicality. The French put an end to those delaying tactics in 1896 by a military action which profited from the struggle between the two ruling families. When the reign-

ing Almamy Bubakar Biro, of Soriya family, refused to hand
over the rule to his Alfaya counterpart, the French troops moved
against him and were assisted by the Alfaya family, part of
Bubakar Biro's own Soriya family, and many provincial chiefs.
Having killed Bubakar Biro in battle, they established a French
protectorate in Futa Jallon and incorporated it in the colony of
Guinea.[1]

With the establishment of French colonial rule in Futa Jallon,
the Fulbe chiefs kept their ruling position but could not prevent
the fragmentation of their provinces and the loss of autonomy.
At first the French removed from the control of the almamys the
province of Labé, which was the largest in the country and in
which lived close to half of the population. In 1905, under the
pretext of putting an end to the continuous conflicts between
the two royal families, the French abolished the system of rotation and divided the territories still under almamys' rule into
two regions, each ruled by one family. Between 1905 and 1919
the provinces were even further fragmented into smaller units
called "cantons." The provincial rulers, including the two
almamys, were reduced to the status of canton chiefs.[2]

There were hardly any movements of opposition or rebellion
against the French among the Fulbe chiefs of Futa Jallon. One
notable exception was the discontent expressed by Alfa Yaya,
chief of Labé, when his territory was broken up into several
smaller districts and parts of them remained in Senegal and
Portuguese Guinea. The French, fearing that Alfa Yaya might
prepare an uprising against them, deposed him and exiled him
first to Dahomey (1905) and then to Mauritania (1911).[3]

In Adamawa the establishment of colonial rule followed an
intense competition between the British and the Germans, resulting in the partition of Adamawa between the two colonial
powers. After the Germans beat the British in installing a protectorate on the Cameroon coast a great race started between the
British, the Germans, and the French, in the typical fashion of
"scramble for Africa," for the acquisition of as much territory as
possible between the coast and Lake Chad, through explora-
tion, signing of protection treaties with local chiefs, or military
conquest if necessary. This scramble brought the colonial powers to Adamawa and ended in a series of agreements between
1885 and 1894 in which the boundaries between the three colonial powers' spheres of influence were delimited. According to

those agreements the largest part of Adamawa, including the important provinces of Maroua, Rey Bouba, Ngaoundéré, Banyo, and Tibati, was left to the Germans and became part of Cameroon, while the capital Yola and a small part of Adamawa territory were left to the British and later became part of Northern Nigeria. The French had the smallest part, composed only of the province of Binder incorporated to Chad.[4] The Adamawa head of state, the lamido of Yola, who remained on the British side, was thus separated from most of his provinces. After 1894, each colonial power started to establish its authority over the areas allocated to it. Meeting with Fulbe resistance, they had to turn to military measures, easily defeating each Fulbe chief and replacing him with another member of the ruling family who showed more readiness to cooperate with the colonial power. In 1899 the Germans launched the military conquest of Adamawa and completed it in about four years. In the meantime, the British captured Yola in 1901. The lamido of Adamawa, Zubeiru, who fled to Maroua, was defeated there by the Germans in 1902 and later was found dead, possibly killed by the pagans of the Mandara hills. His death cut the last tie that linked the various provincial rulers on the German side of Adamawa to Yola, which remained on the British side. Each provincial chief became an independent ruler free to deal separately with the German colonial administration.[5]

In Adamawa too the military campaigns were relatively short. The Fulbe, realizing their military vulnerability, were quick to come to terms with the colonial forces. Cooperative chiefs kept their offices, and the Fulbe as a whole continued to provide the ruling element of the area. The only significant movements of opposition to colonial rule came from people who proclaimed themselves to be *Mahdi*[6] and either proclaimed holy war against the Europeans or simply predicted their future ousting from Adamawa. These movements were easily put down by colonial forces, and their instigators were put to death. The Fulbe rulers were ready to lend their support in suppressing Mahdist movements, for those movements, preaching social and religious reforms, had always been a threat to the established Fulbe political leadership.[7]

Adamawa did not remain under German rule for long. During World War I Cameroon was conquered by British and French troops, and after the war it became a mandate of the

League of Nations, divided into French and British administrative zones.[8] France took about four-fifths of the territory, including almost all of Adamawa, while the British took two separate strips of territory bordering Nigeria and including the capital of the German colony, Buea, and the area of the richest plantations around Mount Cameroon. The change in colonial power meant a new need for adjustment for the Fulbe rulers of Adamawa. At first, as the war started between the German and Franco-British forces, the Fulbe did not know which side to take. Many who were suspected of leaning toward the French or British were deposed and even executed by the Germans (such as the lamibé of Mindif and Kalfou). The lamido of Maroua, who sided with the British, fled from Maroua and stayed with the British troops until the Germans were driven out of Maroua. Others remained loyal to the Germans but then were deposed by the French or the British (such as the lamibé of Tibati, Banyo, and Golombé). Only very few could hold a position of apparent neutrality and retain their position despite the change in the ruling colonial power. Notable among them was the lamido of Rey Bouba.[9]

The principal instrument of early British penetration into the areas ruled by the Sokoto caliphate was the Royal Niger Company, founded in 1879 and granted a royal charter in 1886. From its base at Lokoja the Royal Niger Company engaged in intensive commercial relations with the Sokoto empire. However, those relations gradually developed into increasing political interference in the outlying emirates of Sokoto. The first military confrontation occurred in 1897 when the Royal Niger Company troops attacked the emirate of Nupe, accusing it of conducting slave raids and obstructing trade with Lokoja. Then the company attacked the emirate of Ilorin, which had helped Nupe, and Ilorin accepted the company's suzerainty. Not surprisingly, these actions led to a rapid deterioration of the relations between the British and Sokoto.[10] In the meantime, agreements were reached between the British and the French determining the boundaries between their respective zones of influence according to which almost all of the Sokoto empire fell within the British sphere. In 1899, in order to formalize its colonial rule in Nigeria, the British government withdrew the royal charter from the Royal Niger Company, and in 1900 it took over all the territories administered by the company. All the northern territories, including the Sokoto empire, formed the Protectorate of Northern Nigeria. Effective control over those territories was established by military conquest between 1900 and 1903.[11] Very few emirates submitted to British rule without a fight, at least not until 1903 when the British troops easily conquered the emirate of Kano and shattered its reputation for invincibility. Finally, the Sultan of Sokoto's army was defeated, the Sultan fled, and Lugard at the head of the British troops entered Sokoto. A new sultan was elected and Lugard, in a speech approving the new sultan's election, set the basis of British colonial rule in the old empire of Sokoto.

> The old treaties are dead and you have killed them. Now these are the words which I, the High Commissioner, have to say for the future. The Fulani in old times under dan Fodio conquered this country. They took the right to rule over it, to levy taxes, to depose kings and to create kings. They in turn have by defeat lost their rule which has come into the hands of the British. All these things which I have said the Fulani by conquest took the right to do, now pass to the British. Every Sultan and Emir and the principal office of state will be appointed by the High Commissioner throughout all this country. The High Commissioner will be guided by the usual laws of succession and the wishes of the people and the chiefs but will set them aside if he desires for good cause to do so. The Emirs and Chiefs who are appointed will rule over the people as of old time and take such taxes as approved by the High Commissioner, but they will obey the laws of the Governor and will act in accordance with the advice of the Resident.[12]

British colonial rule was established along the lines which were announced in Lugard's speech. The precolonial rulers, most of whom were Fulbe, remained in ruling positions as long as they cooperated with the British colonial administration. In 1914 the Protectorate of Northern Nigeria was amalgamated with the Protectorate of Southern Nigeria to form the Protectorate of Nigeria, whose first governor general was Lord Lugard.[13]

As in Adamawa and Futa Jallon, there were hardly any serious movements of revolt and opposition to the British in Sokoto after colonial rule was established. The only serious incident occurred in 1906 in Satiru near Sokoto, where a self-styled Mahdi proclaimed holy war against the British and defeated a small British detachment. One Fulbe emir, that of Hajjeia, sided with the insurgents and another, the emir of Gwandu, showed signs of hesitation, but the Sultan of Sokoto put his own troops at the service of the British and was instrumental in crushing the rebellion.[14] Possibly the Sultan realized that the rebellion had no chance of success, but also he might have feared the success of a Mahdi who could challenge his own religious prominence and ruling position. This incident was considered a test of the relations between the Fulbe rulers and the British, and the Fulbe came out strengthened from it since Sokoto's support for the British showed the latter that they could rely on the Fulbe rulers for local administration of the territories of the old Sokoto empire. The revolt emphasized the interdependence of the Fulbe rulers and the British administration in colonial Northern Nigeria.

The general features of colonial government in the three areas were similar in that in all three territories precolonial ruling groups and patterns were maintained and precolonial chiefs occupied an intermediary role in the local administration. They were responsible for maintaining law and order, collecting taxes (including forced labor in Guinea and Cameroon), and transmitting and applying the rules and policies of the colonial government to their subject populations. Differences between the three territories occurred mainly in the extent of political autonomy left to the chiefs in carrying out their functions and in the size of territorial units and political apparatus left to their control. French colonial rule in Guinea, as in most other colonial territories, was characterized by the greater control of French officials and relatively little autonomy left to the traditional African rulers. Within Guinea, Fulbe-ruled areas fared better than other regions in the degree of autonomy left to the traditional chiefs and in the extent to which precolonial political structures were used in local government. However, compared with their counterparts in Northern Nigeria and North Cameroon,[15] the chiefs of Futa Jallon were more restricted in political power, their selection more closely controlled by the French, and their precolonial territory more fragmented; they were regarded more as local agents of an alien central government than as autonomous heads of local governments as in the British and German systems.[16]

In North Cameroon under German rule, much more autonomy was accorded to indigenous rulers in local government. Precolonial political structures were maintained and enlarged to include marginal groups and territories which did not form large enough political units of their own.[17] The German system was not altered in the first years after the establishment of French rule. Because the French received control of Cameroon in the middle of World War I, at a time of most serious shortage of manpower and other resources, they had to rely on the administrative framework left by the Germans and made extensive use of the African chiefs and traditional government structures. Later, as more resources and manpower became available, the French authority asserted itself more closely. French colonial rule in Cameroon took a middle road between that in other French colonial territories and the traditions of indirect rule left by the Germans.[18]

The British colonial administration system in Northern Nigeria bears a striking similarity to the German administration in North Cameroon. It constituted a refinement of the same system, which stressed heavy reliance on traditional rulers and traditional systems of rule and was originally devised to respond to the same need—that of ensuring effective political and military control over vast colonial territories despite very limited colonial manpower and material resources. However, while the development of the German system was cut short by the events of World War I and never had time to crystallize, the British system was gradually elaborated and developed into what came to be the classic example of indirect rule.[19] In this system the British did not simply rely on precolonial rulers and government structures for local administration. They also consolidated those native administrative systems by improving some of their methods, inducing them to adopt some modern techniques, helping them to become more efficient organizations, while at the same time respecting their autonomy and local power. A good case in point was the development of "native treasuries"[20] to which went the bulk of the taxes collected by native authorities and from which the native authority personnel, including the emirs and later the district heads and chiefs, were paid fixed salaries (instead of keeping a share of the collected tax as in North Cameroon and Futa Jallon). British officers supervised the native treasuries, but they interfered little in the way native treasury funds were spent. Since most of the taxes, which in other colonial territories would go to the European colonial government, ended up here in a fund controlled by local chiefs, the formation of native treasuries made the native authorities financially much more independent of the European administration and so enhanced their overall autonomy.

The British, in fact, interfered in the Northern Nigerian native administration more than the Germans did in North Cameroon, but their interference resulted in such things as a regularized taxation system, the reorganization of treasuries and new accounting procedures, and a better-organized system of native courts which corresponded to the real administrative needs of the native authorities and meant more rather than less power and autonomy for the local rulers. With British help and advice, native authorities modified their structures and developed their organization to meet new needs, respond to more complicated situations, and still remain basically traditional in orientation while holding broad decision-making power. British indirect rule, therefore, did not simply mean to rule through native authorities by leaving local government to them, but rather to provide them with the means of effective rule in rapidly changing conditions.

The Formation of the Colonial Center

In our introductory section we raised the possibility of conceiving the establishment of the colonial system as the formation, by alien, European elements, of a new "center," distinct from and rival to preexisting indigenous centers. Conceptualizing the establishment of the colonial system as the formation of a new colonial center may help us gain a better understanding of the general social transformations that accompanied colonialism. It also provides an opportunity to test the center-periphery scheme in a concrete example involving large-scale social change.

The colonial centers formed in Guinea, Cameroon, and Nigeria were in many ways very different from precolonial centers. They were formed by different people, were usually geographically situated in a different place, had very different bases of legitimacy and support, and were formed in rivalry and struggle with precolonial centers. Colonial centers were above all characterized by their "alien" nature. Their formation was completely externally induced, and they were controlled by elements foreign to the region. In the three colonial territories examined here (but not in other territories where large-scale white settlement occurred), before indigenous participation in the colonial center started, the colonial center was held exclusively by officials who did not consider themselves to be part of the social system whose center they occupied. After a certain number of years of duty they left the territory and returned to their own society. Also, the structures, the organization patterns, and the underlying normative framework of the colonial centers were imported from outside and served above all the aliens who built and occupied the new center. The colonial centers were not independent centers; they were rather administrative agencies or outposts of metropolitan centers located far away. The new centers were imposed on the population by a foreign power, an invading external element. At first the colonial centers had no legitimacy in the eyes of the indigenous populations, but since power relations were clearly unfavorable to the indigenous people, they tried to adjust to the new order as best they could with occasional outbursts of revolt when adaptation seemed impossible to certain groups or when they thought that power relations had improved in their favor. These revolts were usally put down without difficulty and colonial law and order were restored. With the consolidation of colonial rule, the colonial center started to gain some legitimacy. For most indigenous populations the formation of new centers as a result of conquest was not uncommon and quite acceptable. It had always occurred in the precolonial period. Its legitimacy was accepted especially by the Fulbe, since they had formed their own center by the same method of military power and conquest, as Lugard wisely reminded them in his first speech in Sokoto in 1903. Later, the colonial center gained legitimacy also through the services that it provided for the indigenous populations and the various innovations that it introduced to the colonial territories.

Besides their alien nature and their close association with external forces and foreign elements, the colonial centers were characterized by the great extent of the transformations they caused in colonial territories. Colonial centers were the seats and channels through which far-reaching innovations were introduced. The existence of colonial centers was justified by their builders, not only on the basis of effective administration of colonial territories, but also on the basis of the development of commercial activities, the exploitation of the natural resources of the territories, the provision of goods produced in Europe, the introduction of the rudiments of western technology, knowledge, and patterns of organization. These innovations were partly introduced to meet the needs of European personnel stationed in the colonial territories, but they were also directed toward the indigenous population, to enlighten them, to broaden their horizons, to put them on the path of development—in short, to provide them with a share (albeit a very small one) of the progress and development that a "modernizing" West was experiencing at home. Despite important differences in their policies and in their general outlook on their role in colonial territories, it seems that all three colonial powers, France, Britain and Germany, had some commitment to such a "civilizing" mission.

We can state, therefore, that all colonial centers combined in themselves two main functions. They were the centers of the administration and political regulation of the colonial territory, and at the same time they were the locus of the introduction of large-scale changes and innovations into the colonial territories, such as the development of new towns, the development of cash economy, the growth of trade and its redirection toward new stations, the greater mobility caused by improved transportation and communications, and the introduction of western technology, of new skills and professions, of western education, religion, art, consumption, and style of life. In other words, the colonial centers were set to preside over the "orderly" introduction of great social transformations into colonial territories, though the extent to which those transformations were introduced varied greatly from one colonial territory to another.

The two facets of the colonial centers' functions, the administrative and regulative on the one hand, the innovative on the other, were closely interrelated. Some innovations made the administrative role of the center more effective. On the other hand, the scope of innovations was sometimes limited by the necessities of the center's regulative, administrative role. This was the case in the colonial center's tolerance of the continued

existence of precolonial centers. The necessity of keeping a regular administrative framework in the colonies for which they
did not have sufficient manpower and material resources led
the colonial powers (reluctantly in the French case, quite will-
ingly in the case of the British and the Germans) to delegate
some power to precolonial centers and keep them as loci of
local, regional administration in the periphery. Also, in order to
keep some basic order in a period of large-scale change, the
colonial powers found it convenient to keep the precolonial
centers as the main loci of symbols and ultimate values of indigenous societies. This no doubt limited the scope of colonial
transformation, but it prevented a general breakdown of the
social and cultural order and ensured an easier acceptance of
colonial presence at the periphery. With the formation of colonial centers, the precolonial centers became part of the periphery vis-à-vis the new center, but within the periphery they did
not lose completely their own centrality.

We can say, therefore, that the colonial system established
some kind of duality[21] in which the traditional sector around
the surviving precolonial centers coexisted with the western
sector formed around the new colonial center. In other words,
the precolonial centers were allowed in the colonial system to
function as subcenters within the periphery, affecting those
areas that the colonial center could not or chose not to reach.
The precolonial centers were subordinate to the colonial centers
politically, but not culturally. The two centers had very different
bases of legitimacy, upheld different normative frameworks,
and usually (though with some overlapping, especially in
Northern Nigeria) offered different kinds of services and responded to different kinds of needs and motivations of the
populations. Precolonial centers affected more the cultural,
symbolic spheres of life of the indigenous population, while the
colonial centers functioned in more instrumental spheres. The
most important point that we should stress regarding this duality is its very existence, the fact that the colonial system allowed
for (and even encouraged) the dual coexistence of colonial and
precolonial centers and of corresponding western and traditional sectors. The duality was an acknowledgment of the alien
character of the colonial center and hence of its inability or
unwillingness to respond to all the needs of the indigenous

population. Later, with increasing participation of the indigenous population in the center during decolonization and after independence, the center's tolerance of autonomous traditional centers within its periphery declined considerably. The center became more exclusive, more monopolistic, and expanded its direct control over the periphery. We shall see later the importance of this change in the center-periphery relationship on the position of the Fulbe in the late colonial and postcolonial periods in Futa Jallon, Northern Nigeria, and North Cameroon.

We have stressed so far that colonial centers were basically alien and that the indigenous population took no part in their formation. However, as a result of innovations introduced to the colonial territory through the new centers, indigenous people were increasingly attracted to them. They gradually made their ways to the colonial centers and to the western sectors built around them. For example, immigration to a city built by the colonial administration as its economic or administrative headquarters marked some access to (or participation in) the colonial center. Successful employment in that city in the colonial administration or in a colonial economic enterprise acquiring new western professional skills generally meant an even greater participation in the center. Becoming Christian, learning how to speak the European colonial language, going to western schools, enjoying western books, movies, western fads and fashions which reproduced some kind of European style of life were comparable participations in the center in the cultural, educational spheres. Having a say in the policymaking of the central political institutions, being a member of municipal councils, political associations, colonial assemblies or organizations was participation in the political sphere.

Indigenous participation in the colonial center was, in part, an almost automatic result of the colonial innovations themselves. Such was the case with indigenous immigration into new cities, being drafted into the army, employment in European-run enterprises, adoption of colonial currency as a means of exchange, etc. However, in other cases, especially in those related to the political sphere, indigenous participation in the colonial center was not automatic at all; it was earned after struggle between the indigenous people who wanted greater participation and expatriates who opposed their penetration into the colonial center for fear that they might occupy a too-influential position in it. Generally speaking, participation in the political sphere was the hardest to achieve because this, more than other kinds of participation, gave to the indigenous participants greater opportunities of dominating the center; hence, they put into greater jeopardy the superordinate-subordinate relationship which existed between the expatriate community and the indigenous population and which was basic to the colonial situation.

The participation of the indigenous population in the colonial center, then, developed more in the economic and cultural than in the political sphere, and in each case the rate of opening of colonial centers to the indigenous participation always fell short of the aspirations of that population and caused bitter frustration among its members. Moreover, this feeling was exacerbated by the many personal grievances experienced by the Africans in the western sector. Western school graduates (and drop-outs) had difficulty in finding employment which they considered equivalent to their skills and status; traders, entrepreneurs, and workers were hurt by the competition of expatriate elements (Syro-Lebanese traders, European companies). All the Africans participating in the center suffered in one way or another from different forms of discrimination and injustice in their contact with Europeans and with the colonial administration. Being in more intense contact with Europeans, they felt more strongly the basic inferiority and helplessness of indigenous populations in their encounter with Europeans in the colonial framework. They also found themselves in a very insecure position at the margin of the colonial center, which was reluctant to receive them and at the same time in growing rivalry with the traditional elite whose position they started to threaten. The emergence of this new westernized indigenous group with great aspirations and bitter frustrations was the indirect, but perhaps most important, transformation that the colonial center had created in the colonial territories. As we shall see later, in creating that new elite but not being able to respond to its aspirations and grievances, the colonial center opened the way to its own elimination as a result of decolonization. This new elite was the first group to use western methods and elements of western culture to protest against the general colonial situation. Their anticolonial protest started in ostensibly nonpolitical spheres, but as soon as the ban on indigenous political activities was lifted, they became involved in the political arena. Out of this emerged the anticolonial political movements which, in turn, opened the way to decolonization.

4

The Impact of Colonial Changes on the Status of the Fulbe in Futa Jallon, Northern Nigeria, and North Cameroon

Having discussed in general terms the establishment of the colonial system in Guinea, Nigeria, and Cameroon, we should now assess its impact on the Fulbe's position in Futa Jallon, Northern Nigeria, and North Cameroon. For this purpose we shall turn again to the principal resources for wealth, power, and prestige which determined the overall dominance of the Fulbe in the precolonial period, and we shall examine what modifications occurred in the uses, values, and distribution of those resources. The main purpose of the analysis is to see whether or not the Fulbe could adjust themselves to colonial changes in such a way as to be able to control new resources or to put old resources to new uses in order to increase their value as factors of dominance. In addition, we shall also examine to what extent and in what fields the Fulbe participated in the colonial center in comparison both with local non-Fulbe and with other populations coming from other regions of the colonial territory.

Political, Administrative Offices

We have seen that in all three areas studied here, the traditional precolonial political structures were preserved—incorporated in some way into the colonial local government system—and the political officeholders in those structures generally kept their positions in the colonial period. The traditional ruler-subject relationship was preserved, and the Fulbe kept their ruling positions within the limits tolerated by each colonial power. Most of the changes were made at the highest level, since it was there that political officeholders could most challenge the supremacy of the colonial government and the sovereignty of the colonial power.

Comparing the three societies studied here, we have seen that the power value of indigenous ruling positions was lower in Futa Jallon than in North Cameroon and Northern Nigeria because chiefs held much less political autonomy and their territory was fragmented into smaller units. Therefore, although continuing to occupy local political offices, the Fulbe chiefs of Futa Jallon incurred greater loss of power than those of Northern Nigeria and North Cameroon. Also, the Fulbe rulers lost control of the non-Fulbe inhabited areas at the fringes of Futa Jallon (such as the *Tenda*[22] areas in the northwest and the Baga-, Nalou-, and Landouma-inhabited areas in the coastal zone). The Northern Nigerian and German-ruled North Cameroon precolonial territorial units were less fragmented, and precolonial rulers had much greater autonomy in local government. The Fulbe also continued to rule over most non-Fulbe people who were subject to them in the precolonial period. In Northern Nigeria during the first years of colonial rule even some pagan groups who had successfully resisted the Fulbe in the precolonial period, such as the hill tribes of Jos, were put under Fulbe rule by the British. This naturally created great opposition among those pagan groups, and joint British and Fulbe expeditions were sent to pacify them. However, later, especially in the 1930s under Governor Cameron, the British reversed their policy and removed many pagan groups from direct Fulbe control, including most of those who had never been conquered by the Fulbe before.[23]

In North Cameroon under German rule all pagan populations, whether they were subdued by the Fulbe in the precolonial period or not, were forcibly put under Fulbe rule. Since the pagan populations had originally retreated into the most remote and inaccessible places, when the Germans penetrated into North Cameroon their first contact was with the Fulbe, who easily convinced them that recalcitrant pagans in the mountains were simply in rebellion against their Fulbe rulers. Many joint German and Fulbe military expeditions were carried out to pacify them and put them under "colonial," that is under Fulbe, rule.[24] In this way the Fulbe, besides maintaining their ruling position within their precolonial boundaries, got the opportunity to use the colonial power's military force to extend their rule over pagan populations whom they had not been able to subdue with their own military forces in the precolonial period.

The French who replaced the Germans were also tempted at first to rely for local government on the Fulbe, who easily concealed from them the difference between the docile non-Fulbe populations, mostly former slaves, living in areas conquered by them and the hostile, resistant non-Fulbe living in areas beyond their control. Moreover, the few French officials stationed in the area depended on the Fulbe rulers as indispensable intermediaries between themselves and the local population. "We do not know a single person in town besides the lamido and his dignitaries and we could not survive more than a few days without his cooperation," wrote one French official stationed in Ngaoundéré in 1918.[25] However, the French tendency to rely on the Fulbe as intermediaries was strongly resisted by pagan *Kirdi*[26] groups who had profited from the temporary breakdown of colonial rule during World War I to detach themselves from Fulbe rule. The result was continuous clashes between the Fulbe, aided by the French, and the recalcitrant Kirdi. Every tax-collection tour turned into a full-scale military expedition. One of the most serious such clashes occurred in 1937 when the lamido of Mayo Loué, returning from a tax-collection expedition, was attacked by Guidars near Lam. The chief barely escaped, but all the tax was captured by the Guidar who immediately brought it directly to the nearest French administrative post, thus expressing their wish to be directly ruled by the French and not through the Fulbe.[27] This and other similar incidents gradually influenced the French to detach some Kirdi populations from Fulbe control.[28] The only lamidate which was untouched by this policy was that of Rey Bouba, which also remained the largest lamidate in size and the one in which the chief enjoyed the greatest political autonomy during the entire colonial period. However, in other lamidates too, sizeable Kirdi populations remained under Fulbe rule. In 1934, in the chiefdom of Ngaoundéré, only three-fifths of the population was Fulbe, one-fifth was Mboum, and one-fifth was Dourou. In Tibati only one-fifth of the population was Fulbe, the others being Mboum, Vouté, Baya, and Tikar. On the Mandara hills the Fulbe chief of Mokolo ruled in 1942 over a population of 1,357 Fulbe and 18,267 non-Fulbe.[29]

The Kirdi populations ruled by the Fulbe were usually headed by local chiefs, called *Arnabé*, who were subordinate to the Fulbe rulers. Those who were removed from Fulbe control were organized by the French in two different ways. Some of them who seemed not to have any centralized authority system of their own were directly attached (in groups of villages) to a

French administrator. Others were organized in canton chiefdoms similar in structure to the Fulbe chiefdoms. Kirdi chiefs,
sometimes lacking traditional legitimacy, were installed in the
new cantons.[30] Most Kirdi canton chiefs adopted Islam, took
the Fulbe title of lamido, and tried to copy the Fulbe chiefs as
much as possible in political government patterns (appointing
executive officials with Hausa titles, entertaining clerics and
other dignitaries, etc.) as well as in general style of life (owning
and riding horses, raising cattle, dressing like Fulbe, speaking
exclusively *Fulfuldé* [the Fulbe language], studying Islam or
sending their children to koranic schools, etc.).[31] In their eyes,
the Fulbe chiefs were the perfect model of autocratic rulers, and
they thought that imitation of the external signs of Fulbe life-
style and patterns of rule would strengthen their own political
position over their subjects. It seems that this view was shared
by French colonial officials. In 1926 the Kirdi chief of Musgoy
was rewarded with the medal of indigenous merit because he
showed "a political authority comparable to that of the best
Fulbe Lamibe" and so was "a model for all the other Kirdi
chiefs."[32]

The Military and Police

In all three Fulbe societies, with the establishment of colonial
rule, the Fulbe lost control of the military. The colonial armies
which had defeated them became the dominant military force.
The colonial system was established as a result of military conquest and, especially in the first years, relations between the
colonial administration and the indigenous people were
primarily based on military power and coercion. For this reason
the military domination of the colonial territory and the elmina-
tion of any possible military challenge by an indigenous group
was absolutely essential to the colonial government. Military
control was carried out by the same detachments which had
conquered the territories and which were stationed in various
posts scattered throughout the territory. These colonial armies
were often composed of African soldiers and even of soldiers
originating from non-Fulbe people in the Fulbe-ruled areas
(some of them later passed to the police and formed the nucleus
of the colonial police force).[33] This, of course, created a strong
antipathy among the Fulbe toward the soldiers of the colonial
armies. As Ahmadu Bello, the late prime minister of Northern

Nigeria and a member of the royal lineage of Sokoto, observed, "We did not like the soldiers; they were our own people and had conquered us for strangers and had defeated our people on the plain just before us."[34]

In Northern Nigeria and Futa Jallon, the precolonial armies were disbanded and the Fulbe rulers were prohibited from raising armed forces. All military functions became the responsibility of the colonial armed forces. In North Cameroon under German rule, on the other hand, the Fulbe lamibé were allowed to keep their own private armies, and they occasionally took advantage of this to launch slave raids against nearby pagan populations, despite the Germans' prohibition of slave trade and raids. During World War I, the Germans even distributed guns to the chiefs' private armies in order to fight the French and British, but many chiefs preferred to launch slave raids instead.[35] In the first years of French colonial rule in North Cameroon the Fulbe chiefs continued to have their own armed forces, but later the French gradually cut down that military force and transformed it into a local police force.

While the Fulbe were not allowed to have their own army, they were allowed to have their own police force to keep law and order in the territory and serve as palace guards. These guards, called *Dogari* in Northern Nigeria and North Cameroon, were non-Fulbe people, mostly of slave or enfranchised slave status. In Northern Nigeria the native administration police force was reorganized in the 1920s. In addition to the Dogari, a new local police force, the *Yan Doka* (called *Yan Gadi* in Kano) was formed in big towns. The native authority police force was forbidden to bear arms. In 1929, the Kaduna Police School, established for the colonial police force, extended its training facilities also to the native authority police.[36] In French-ruled North Cameroon, lamibé who had the means to buy arms distributed them to their guards. In most lamidates this force was composed of a few inadequately trained, scarcely armed guards, but in the lamidate of Rey Bouba they formed (and still do) a very disciplined, well-armed force stationed throughout the lamidate and exerted effective military control over the territory.[37] Generally speaking, in both North Cameroon and Northern Nigeria the native authority police force was too small in size for the population it was supposed to control. In Sokoto province, for instance, there were 600 native author-

ity policemen for a population of more than 2.5 million people
in 1958. In Zaria province, for a population of 825,000 there
were about 250 native authority policemen.[38] However, what-
ever its size and military power, this native police force controlled by the Fulbe chiefs gave them an important means of
coercion over their subject population and reinforced in the
eyes of the local population the continuing political authority of
native rulers.

One other important function of the local police was to enforce the decisions of the native courts. In Northern Nigeria and
North Cameroon the Fulbe chiefs had their own prisons in addition to the prisons maintained by the colonial government.
According to Hailey, at the end of World War II there were in all
of Nigeria forty-seven government and sixty-seven native authority prisons. The largest prison controlled by native authorities was the Central Prison of Kano, which had over 1,000
prisoners.[39] The dogari served as guards in the native authority
prisons. They were used, in cooperation with colonial police, to
catch fugitives and delinquents, bring them to court, and escort
them to prison.

Traditional Justice

Little change occurred in the judicial system with the
establishment of colonial rule in Futa Jallon, Adamawa, and
Sokoto. The indigenous population remained bound by Islamic
law and the traditional judicial system composed of a network
of Islamic courts held by Kadis (or Alkalis) appointed by the
chiefs. Most of the Islamic judges were themselves Fulbe and
were selected from among the strongest supporters of the Fulbe
chiefs. The Islamic courts were seen in each territory as the
judicial appendage of native authority rule, and they were
under firm Fulbe control, though in the colonial period this
control was limited by the extent of colonial interference in
traditional justice and by the range of activities that were taken
away from native court jurisdiciton and put under direct control
of the colonial court. In Futa Jallon these courts had jurisdiction
only in civil matters, mainly cases of divorce, inheritance, and
land ownership litigation. More serious cases, including criminal cases, were judged by mixed courts presided over by the
commanding official, assisted by two Africans. The mixed
courts applied the local religious or customary law mixed with

some French laws and colonial decrees. All litigation involving
expatriates and some of the more serious criminal cases were
judged by courts applying only French laws.[40] In North Cameroon, under German rule, Islamic courts were empowered to
judge criminal cases, but the death penalty had to be approved
by the governor. Residents served also as the supreme judicial
authorities of their areas, receiving appeals from judgments of
the customary courts. With the advent of French rule, native
courts applying religious laws continued to function, but above
them a system of mixed courts was created, presided over by
French officials assisted by local dignitaries. After 1946, all criminal cases were removed from the jurisdiction of native courts.[41]
In Northern Nigeria, besides appointing the personnel of the
native courts with the approval of the residents and/or the
lieutenant governor, the native rulers were allowed to establish
their own courts, called emir's courts or judicial councils, for
dealing with certain matters deriving from their executive orders. The emir's court also constituted the final native court of
appeal. Native courts had jurisdiction over both criminal and
civil cases, but the death sentence had to be approved by the
lieutenant governor. Also some serious offenses, such as taking
slaves, offenses against British rule, and cases involving British
citizens or other aliens (including nonnative Nigerians), were
judged by provincial courts (later modified into magistrates'
courts) which applied British laws and ordinances and not native law.[42]

Fulbe control over the traditional judicial apparatus not only
gave them political power, it also continued to enhance their
prestige. They were the main interpreters of what was right and
wrong. They provided the wisest men, those to whom people
turned to ask advice, those who could interpret the religious
laws and translate them into regulations binding the everyday
life of the population.

The maintenance of the traditional judicial apparatus also
meant continuing discrimination against pagan populations. In
predominantly Muslim areas the only recognized native court
system was the Islamic courts. The pagans in those areas were
judged by Muslim judges, who were naturally prejudiced
against them and who had little knowledge of pagan customs.
In Islamic law a non-Muslim person's testimony in court was
worth less than that of a Muslim. Islamic law also prescribed

different punishments for Muslims and non-Muslims for the same crime.[43] In cases opposing pagans to Muslims, from the outset, the letter of the law, the court procedure, and the natural prejudices of the judge were all set against the pagan.

Taxes and Other Economic Returns of Political Officeholding

The collection of taxes was one of the most important functions for which the colonial administrations needed the native authorities, and the general effectiveness of chiefs was generally measured by their ability to collect taxes regularly without needing help from colonial forces. In return, the chiefs' share from the tax provided them with the direct economic reward for their local government functions, supplemented also by unofficial fees, customary gifts presented by people who needed the native official's help or service. The Fulbe, who controlled most of the native authority offices, continued to be the principal recipients of official and unofficial revenues that derived from administrative positions, but the amount of those revenues changed from place to place.

In German North Cameroon virtually nothing was changed in the traditional taxation system. The Fulbe chiefs were the recipients of traditional taxes collected by their subordinate district and village chiefs as in the precolonial period. Part of the tax was then sent to the German colonial authorities in the form of tribute, just as it was sent to the head of state sitting in Yola in the precolonial period. Under French and British rule, on the other hand, some changes did occur. Most precolonial taxes were reorganized into two major types: (a) a capitation tax (called Kharajj in Northern Nigeria) imposed on the sedentary agricultural population, and (b) a cattle tax (Jangali in Northern Nigeria) per head of cattle imposed on pastoralist groups. However, other customary taxes (such as the inheritance tax), as well as traders' and craftsmen's dues, continued to be paid to local authorities.[44]

The big difference between the French and British taxation system was that in French-ruled North Cameroon and Futa Jallon the largest part of the tax went to the French colonial treasury. Local chiefs retained only about 10 percent of the tax collected, thus incurring a serious loss of revenue.[45] In Northern Nigeria, on the other hand, after the formation of native treasuries, the British share of taxes did not amount to more than 50 percent (later it fell even lower), the rest going to the native treasuries and so being at the disposal of native authorities. Fees, fines, death duties collected in the native courts, market fees, and the accession duty (Kurdin Sarauta) went entirely to the native treasuries and were not shared with the colonial government.[46] This system gave to the native authorities financial strength unequalled in most other African colonial territories. Although their personal income was separated from the public fund of the native authorities as organizations, the emirs and other top officeholders in native authorities had their economic position strengthened since they indirectly controlled a much larger chunk of wealth and decided how it would be spent. Some reports on North Cameroon suggest that there too the Fulbe chiefdoms had their own native treasury from which the chiefs, officials, guards, and judges were paid,[47] but we do not know how substantial those native treasuries were and how separate they were from the Fulbe chiefs' own resources. In any case, it is certain that they were far less developed than in Northern Nigeria.

The financial strength of the native authorities in Northern Nigeria enabled them to enter into the so-called western sector. They financed (in some cases supported by government grants) such innovations as western educational institutions, hospitals, factories, agricultural and veterinary stations, land surveys, mixed farming, and population resettlement schemes, in addition to their traditional responsibility for markets, waterworks, forestry, local road construction, police, prisons, judicial services, etc. In 1947 Northern Nigerian native authorities ran 397 primary schools (out of a total of 1,121) and eleven middle schools. They built and maintained eight hospitals, providing 873 beds out of a total of 1,906. They also maintained 214 health and welfare centers, and some made contributions to mission leper settlements and dispensaries.[48]

We can see, therefore, that by leaving a greater share of taxes to the native authorities, the British enabled them to undertake or at least finance many local services and development activities which in North Cameroon and Futa Jallon were undertaken directly by the French administration or were not undertaken at all. In Northern Nigeria these activities were undertaken mostly with British technical help and guidance and even at British initiative. As Lord Hailey rightly pointed out, many of these activities could be regarded as "institutions which are financed from native authority funds, but which in other respects merely represent services which the government might have provided from general revenues, had it received for itself a larger share of the resources provided by local taxation."[49] Nevertheless, it was upon this financial strength and autonomy of the native authorities, which gave the impression that the latter were in control of things even in the western sector, that the whole idea of British indirect rule in the old empire of Sokoto rested. As the range of activities financed by the native administration expanded, so did the range of activities and commodities controlled by officeholders in the native administration. This not only consolidated the political power of the officeholders but also granted them greater direct and indirect economic returns in the form of dues, fees, gifts and other means of capitalizing on one's political position. Since the Fulbe controlled most native administration offices, they were the principal beneficiaries of the added power and the consequent economic returns gained by those offices with the expansion of their activities.

Slaves

In all three territories the establishment of colonial rule was soon followed by an official declaration abolishing enslavement and slave trade. However, beyond that, realities varied in each colonial territory. Under German rule, although formally abolished, slave raids and trade continued in North Cameroon, and the Germans made little effort to stop them. It is known, for example, that the lamido of Ngaoundéré organized slave raids into the Laka country between 1904 and 1914 and that many slaves were captured under the eyes of German military forces. This expedition, which was carried out in semisecrecy, was called for this reason the "war without drums."[50] The Germans recognized the servile status of people who were already enslaved before the colonial period. The only slaves freed by the Germans were those of the chiefs who fought against the Germans, and they were then sent to the south as laborers in plantations or in road construction. With the establishment of French rule, slavery was outlawed and greater efforts were made to effectively stop it. Still some slave trade, especially of kidnapped children and women, continued well into the

1950s.[51] In Northern Nigeria, the British proclaimed in 1901 that all slaves' children born after that date were to be free, while those who had been slaves before that time were given the opportunity to buy their freedom through native courts.[52] In Futa Jallon, slavery was denied recognition of courts and its trade was abolished. In 1905 a decree was issued prohibiting "an agreement having as its object the alienation of the liberty of a third party."[53] The decree prohibited enslavement, but no measures were taken to enforce this. Nothing was done to free existing slaves except in specific political circumstances when the French wanted to punish the master. On the contrary, a colonial decision restricting the movement of people to places where they could not prove means of subsistence was used to return some runaway slaves to their masters.[54]

The abolition of slavery could have dealt a very serious blow to the Fulbe, since it could have removed their most important economic resource. However, since the legal emancipation of slaves was not accompanied by any change in land ownership, the former slaves remained economically dependent on their masters, who controlled the land. In order not to be evicted from that land, former slaves had to supply their old masters with a share of the crops. They also had to work part-time on their master's other fields and to perform various menial jobs and other services for them.[55] So, even when slavery was abolished, its value as a wealth resource was preserved in the form of free manpower, and the economic system based on the exploitation of free labor survived. Moreover, because the Fulbe held political power in the area, they also had political means of putting pressure on their former slaves. Recalcitrant former slaves could be recruited for public works, could be sent to military service, or could be refused all kinds of services by the local chief. A former slave who refused to work in his master's fields could find himself working without pay in road construction.[56]

There were also other, less coercive factors which bound former slaves to their masters. In the precolonial period close, intimate relations had developed between masters and slaves, especially second-generation ones. Slaves felt security under their master's protection, and they expected to learn about Islam from them. Some even adopted their master's name and tried to link themselves to his lineage. These relations did not

cease after the slaves were granted their freedom. Most of them
continued to show deference to their masters and to serve them
voluntarily. Many sent their children to serve their masters so
that they would grow up with the master's own children and receive the same education. Here we see how the master's prestige
resources, his name, lineage, and proximity to Islam were used
to preserve his influence over his former slaves.

One possibility for the former slaves to detach themselves
from their master was to leave their native area. They could,
and did, go to the urban centers that were being formed and to
plantations, mining areas, and construction sites where they
could escape from their inferior status in their traditional environment and also could hope to find some work that could make
them economically more independent of their old Fulbe masters. However, the former slaves lacked more than other people
the education, occupational skills, and psychologial mobility
necessary to undertake long-range migration and be successfully absorbed in the new place.

So, generally speaking, the legal emancipation of slaves did
not radically change their subordination to their Fulbe masters.
The Fulbe could still make use of their manpower, though undoubtedly within certain limits. The combination of land and
slave ownership, which had become the basis of Fulbe economic dominance in the precolonial period and was closely
related to the Fulbe's political dominance, was maintained despite the legal abolition of slavery. In a sense, with the abolition
of slavery the position of slaves was transformed into that of
lowest-status subjects and clients of the Fulbe aristocracy.[57] The
Fulbe could use them for economically profitable ends, as illustrated above, or they could use them for political purposes, as a
basis of support or as aides. People of servile status continued
to serve as bodyguards and sometimes also as executive officials
or advisors of the Fulbe chiefs. The Fulbe could ask of former
slaves and their descendants certain types of service that the
free status of other clients precluded them from asking. Also,
because the former slaves did not have any other basis of support and had no attachment to any other group, they were
among the most loyal supporters and collaborators of their
former masters.

Land and its Products

The close relationship between control of land and manpower

gained increased importance in the colonial period because of
their rapidly rising value with the development of cash crops.
Those who controlled the largest plots on which cash crops
could be grown or those who had (or could afford to buy)
enough manpower or machine power to cultivate their land
became the principal beneficiaries of the development of new
sources of wealth related to land, under colonial encouragement
and guidance. While the value of land rose, the traditional
land-tenure patterns (i.e., the distribution of the rising wealth
resource) remained basically unchanged. In all three places land
tenure was considered to be regulated by native law and cus-
tom, and the colonial governments tried to interfere as little as
possible with it. In none of the territories did the colonial authorities encourage European settlement or other colonial enterprises that would lead to large-scale expropriation of land
belonging to the local indigenous people (with the possible
exception of the tin mines on the Jos plateau in Northern
Nigeria). On the contrary, colonial authorities encouraged the
local population to raise the value of the land by taking up
cash-crop production.

The legal confusion as to whether land was owned by private
individuals or by local collectivities was not solved under the
colonial system. In Northern Nigeria the dominant approach
apparently denied private ownership of land and limited per-
missible transactions involving land. This conflicted with the
increasing pressure for unrestricted transactions following
land's increasing cash value. As a result, private land transactions developed with or without the native authorities' acqui-
escence.[58] In North Cameroon and Futa Jallon, too, while legal
property rights were not clear, free transactions of land developed with little objection from native authorities.[59]

No matter whether private ownership of land existed or not,
the Fulbe aristocratic families continued to control the largest
parcels of land and hence benefited most from its increasing
wealth value. We should bear in mind, however, that in Hausaland Fulbe control over land was much less extensive than in
other areas since the Hausa, as free subjects, had always been
entitled to control their own land. Hausaland was an area of
small-size family-run farms, and it was on those farms that
most cash crops of Northern Nigeria were cultivated.[60]
Nonetheless, in all three societies, the Fulbe were, as a whole,
the owners of larger plots of land than other groups, and they

had the manpower necessary for cultivation (mostly former slaves) without which the amount of arable land had no significance.[61] Furthermore, the native courts' authority to settle problems of land ownership was also an advantage to the Fulbe, since they were more strongly represented than any other group among the native judges and among the chiefs who appointed them.

Development of Cash Crops and Exploitation of Natural Resources

The production of agricultural surpluses, submitted as tax to rulers or sold in markets, was by no means a new phenomenon in the three territories studied here. However, in the colonial period, the growing demand for certain agricultural products in internal and overseas markets greatly increased the scope of surplus production. Also, following the growing need of producers for the colonial currency which became the generalized means of exchange (and only mode of tax payment), surplus production was directed into specific crops and specific markets (mainly the export market) which could provide the greatest amount of cash in accepted currency. Economic activities were thus more attracted to a cash and export nexus.

In Northern Nigeria, the three most important export items were peanuts, cotton, and tin. Except for tin, which was extracted by European mining enterprises and in which African participation was minimal, the producers and principal beneficiaries of the major export products were the indigenous population. Peanuts and cotton started to be exported shortly after the establishment of colonial rule, but only after 1911–12, when the railroad link between Lagos and Kano was completed, did exports take on major proportions. After World War II Nigeria became the world's largest exporter of peanuts. The main peanut cultivation area was Kano, thereby helping the area preserve its economic dominance within the old Sokoto caliphate. Cotton production, though rising sharply, lagged behind peanuts in export. The main areas of cotton cultivation were Zaria, Katsina, and Sokoto provinces.[62] Peanuts and cotton also brought some of the earliest industrial activities into Fulbe-inhabited areas, though they were controlled by expatriates. The mechanized separation of cotton lint from the seed was started in the early colonial years by the British Cotton

Growing Association, which had pioneered cotton growing in Nigeria. After World War II, an increasingly large proportion of cotton was directed toward local textile manufacture instead of export, as a result of the formation of the first local textile plants (in Kano in 1949, in Kaduna in 1959). In the 1940s, mechanized peanut-crushing mills were started in Kano, mainly by Syro-Lebanese entrepreneurs, and thereafter a growing quantity of peanut oil was produced for local use and export.[63]

Before World War II peanut and cotton were purchased for export in local markets directly by foreign (mainly British) trading companies operating through contractors and middlemen, but in 1949 the British established special marketing boards to which cotton and peanuts had to be sold. The private companies functioned as licensed buying agents for the marketing board at prices set by the board. In 1954 the separate produce marketing boards were united in regional all-purpose marketing boards; in the north the Northern Regional Marketing Board was formed.[64] The marketing boards also set quality standards which were to be met by cotton and peanuts directed to export, and native examiners were trained to examine the quality of the products at buying stations. The quality standard set by the examiner obviously had a crucial effect on the earnings of the farmers. Consequently, the post of product examiner became one of the most powerful, most highly prized, and most hotly contested positions among the local population. The native administrations (and hence the Fulbe) succeeded in most cases in controlling the recruitment of product examiners and thus could exert a very strong influence on peanut and cotton producers.

The great growth in these exports was achieved mainly by a phenomenal expansion of the area of land on which they were cultivated. Realizing the great cash value of peanut and cotton cultivation, an increasing number of indigenous people started to cultivate them, and large areas of bush were cleared for that purpose. Since the Fulbe were the biggest landowners, they reaped the biggest profits. The Fulbe, who themselves strongly disliked agricultural work, hired manpower or forced their former slaves to work for them and so ensured the cultivation of cash crops. This was a typical case in which a precolonial economic resource—land—controlled by the Fulbe was put to a new use to purchase new resources introduced by colonial in-

novations. The Fulbe were certainly not the only ones undertak-
ing cash-crop production; they were not even the major group,
since the Hausa, who were much more populous than the Fulbe
and who in total controlled a greater portion of land, also engaged wholeheartedly in cash-crop agriculture. However, since
the land area controlled by each family was larger among the
Fulbe than among the Hausa, the economic advantage derived
from cash-crop agriculture, per capita, was greater among the
Fulbe. Daryll Forde took notice of this phenomenon when he
wrote that "most of the rights in land, which had been previously acquired by ruling families and lesser members of the
aristocracy, continued to be recognized. Although they commonly affect but a small proportion of the total territory, the
existence of landed estates, formerly worked by slaves and now
farmed by metayage and wage labour, introduce an element in
the northern economy very different in scale and character from
the dominant system of the autonomous household. Such
estates have provided opportunities for experiment with new
crops and farming methods on a large scale."[65]

Table 1   **Peanuts and Cotton in the Nigerian Economy**

	1938	1947	1954	1958
Peanuts:				
Tons exported (000)	180	256	428	513
Value (£ million)	1.3	6.3	29.9	26.9
Percent of Nigerian exports (by value)	13.8	16.9	20.4	20.3
Cotton:				
Tons exported	5.7	5.2	26.0	34.0
Value (£ million)	0.2	0.5	7.3	7.8
Percent of Nigerian exports (by value)	2.6	1.4	5.0	5.9

SOURCES.—Based on K. Buchanan and J. C.
Pugh, *Land and People in Nigeria* (London: Uni-
versity of London Press, 1955), pp. 137, 148; the
Royal Institute of International Affairs, *Nigeria,
The Political and Economic Background* (London:
Oxford University Press, 1960), pp. 92–93, 122.

Besides their role as producers, the indigenous population in
Northern Nigeria participated in the trade of peanuts and cotton. Although with the establishment of marketing boards the
trade was removed from the private market, the indigenous
population continued to work as middlemen between the pro-

ducers and the marketing boards or the private companies acting as the boards' buying agents. Also, African traders controlled some of the crop which was intended for local consumption and which was not bought by the marketing board. Most of those traders were Hausa (though they faced stiff competition from Syro-Lebanese traders). Some of them, based in Kano city (called the "Kano contractors"), were quite wealthy and engaged in large-scale trade, employing their own middlemen who bought the crop directly from the producers or from smaller submiddlemen. The crop generally passed through a long chain of middlemen before reaching the licensed buying agent of the marketing boards. This system was wide open to great abuse; the producers were severely underpaid for their products, the difference going to the middlemen, the contractors, the produce examiners, and the native administration personnel who supervised the whole process.[66]

Besides those two major crops designed for export, the colonial period saw a rapid growth in the production of many other agricultural crops, such as rice, tobacco, sugarcane, etc., which gained cash value and were sold in local markets and in interregional trade within the colonial territory. Sugarcane was also locally transformed into sugar and constituted one of the few local industries before World War II. Finally, Guinea corn, which was the staple diet of most populations in Northern Nigeria, increasingly entered into commercial transactions, since many cultivators who specialized in export crops did not cultivate enough corn or millet and had to buy them in the market.

In North Cameroon, the development of cash-crop agriculture and production for export was much more limited than in Northern Nigeria. There was no economic development worth speaking of during the German period. The few experimental cultivations undertaken by the Germans (in the Pitoa experimental station) were cut short by the outbreak of World War I.[67] The French who replaced the Germans were mainly interested in developing peanut production in the north, and under their guidance (and often insistence) peanuts became the first export crop cultivated in North Cameroon. The French imposed on the local population, under the chiefs' supervision, compulsory cultivation of a yearly quota which was bought at fixed prices by special agencies set up by the colonial administration (the SAP,

Société Africaine de Prévoyance, and later the SEMNORD, Sec-
teur de Modernisation du Nord). Many chiefs knew how to
exploit the compulsory cultivation of peanuts to their advantage. Under the guise of complying with colonial orders, the
chiefs compelled their subjects to produce their quota of
peanuts on land belonging to the chiefs. Thus, most of the
income went into the chiefs' pockets.[68] The resentment of the
population at the compulsory cultivation of peanuts perhaps
partly explains why it declined so rapidly in the 1950s when the
cultivation of cotton became possible.

The cultivation of cotton for export started only in 1951 when
a French company, the CFDT (Compagnie Française pour le
Développement des Fibres Textiles) was asked by the colonial
government to set up a scheme for the development of cotton
cultivation in North Cameroon. The CFDT distributed seeds to
people willing to cultivate cotton at selected locations, trained
them in new techniques of cultivation, supervised their work,
and finally bought their product at fixed prices. The project was
so successful that in a few years cotton cultivation developed
tremendously. By the end of the colonial period cotton exports
had surpassed peanuts in volume and value and had become
the most important export item of North Cameroon.[69] Parallel to
the development of cotton production, cotton ginneries and cotton and peanut oil factories were established in North Cameroon. Before independence there existed one oil factory (in
Pitoa) and four ginneries (in Kaélé, Garoua, Mora, and Tou-
boro), all of them run by the CFDT.[70]

Table 2   **Progress of Cotton Production (in Tons) in
North Cameroon, 1952–66**

	Year							
	Colonial Period					Postcolonial Period		
	1952	1954	1956	1958	1960	1962	1964	1966
Tons	525	7,066	17,413	20,862	20,965	25,100	45,581	57,544

SOURCE.—Adapted from P. Billard, *Le Cameroun Fédéral,* 2 vols. (Lyon: Imprimerie des
Beaux Arts, 1968), 1:111.

The biggest producers of peanuts and cotton in North Cameroon were Fulbe, for the same reasons that we discussed in the

case of Northern Nigeria. The Fulbe were the biggest land-owners and could easily recruit manpower, either by inducing their former slaves to work for them or by hiring people (mainly landless Kirdis descending from the hills). In this way the Fulbe made the best use of their "traditional" control of land and manpower whose value increased with the introduction of extensive cash-crop agriculture. When, after World War II, cotton took the place of peanuts as the most important agricultural source of income, the biggest shift from peanut to cotton cultivation occurred in Fulbe-owned lands. Peanut cultivation persisted in more hilly areas inhabited mostly by pagan groups. The two departments of North Cameroon most heavily populated by Fulbe, Diamaré and Benoué, had also the greatest extent of cotton cultivation. The departments where relatively fewer Fulbe lived, namely, Margui-Wandala, Mayo Danaï, and Logone-et-Chari, had much less cultivation of cotton.[71] Another source of benefit related to cotton cultivation was the premium paid by the CFDT to canton chiefs according to the extent of cotton cultivation in their territory.[72] This policy, devised to get the chiefs' support, again mostly helped the Fulbe since they were so predominant among the canton chiefs.

Because the sale of peanuts and cotton was conducted by special agencies at fixed prices, the role of individual traders was seriously curtailed. However, as in Northern Nigeria, there was a large field of activity for indigenous middlemen who bought the crops from the producers and sold it to the official buying agents. The middlemen in North Cameroon were mostly Fulbe (in contrast with Northern Nigeria, where they were mostly Hausa). Therefore, in North Cameroon the Fulbe dominated the cotton and peanut economy not only as major producers but also as principal traders and middlemen. They also dominated the commerce of other principal agricultural crops of the area, such as millet, sorghum, potatoes, tobacco, onion, whose production and commercialization in local and regional markets sharply increased in the colonial period.

In Futa Jallon the exploitation of economic resources during the colonial period was much more limited than in Northern Nigeria and North Cameroon. Because of unsuitable soil conditions, cash-crop agriculture could not be established on any large scale. Throughout the colonial period Futa Jallon remained mainly a supplier of cattle and meat. Among agricultural products, the greatest success in commercialization was obtained by fresh fruit and vegetables.[73] In the 1930s the planting of orange trees and the collection of oranges gained considerable importance following the establishment in Futa Jallon of a foreign-owned orange perfume manufacturing enterprise, the CAPP (Compagnie Africaine des Plantes à Parfum). The enterprise was highly successful, and in the 1930s Futa Jallon began to export orange perfume to Europe. In 1934, 144 tons were exported and 298 tons in 1939.[74] If we except cattle illegally smuggled out of Guinea, orange perfume manufactured by the CAPP was the only major Guinean item of export that originated in Futa Jallon.

5

Further Impact of Colonial Changes on the Status of the Fulbe in Futa Jallon, Northern Nigeria, and North Cameroon

Commerce, Cattle, Industry

In all three societies studied here, the colonial period brought a phenomenal growth in local and interregional trade which raised the value of commercial activities as resources for wealth considerably. Even in areas where commerce was quite developed in the precolonial period and where standard means of exchange (such as cowry shells) were used, the establishment of the colonial system greatly increased the scope of commercial exchange; the colonial currency replaced earlier types of money, and its use spread to a much wider layer of population.

An important factor of the spread of monetary exchange into the countryside was the colonial policy of collecting taxes in recognized currency. The obligation to raise enough cash to pay taxes forced the indigenous population to produce surplus goods that could be exchanged for cash.[75] As Alhaji Ahmadu Bello pointed out, "When the time for collection [of tax] came, there was often a fearful fuss to get the actual coins required for the tax—it was only a matter of six or seven shillings per taxpayer in those days—and the people rushed to the markets with produce and livestock for sale. Naturally the markets were glutted and prices fell sharply; the rich trader came in and bought at ridiculous prices and did very well out of it."[76] Later, people discovered that colonial currency could also purchase all kinds of new items that became available in markets, some of them locally produced, most of them imported. Increased demand for cash and for new consumption items and increased production of surpluses to meet these demands naturally led to growing commerce. Many new markets were opened, and old markets were greatly expanded. The volume of transactions grew, and the items entering into the transactions were much more diversified. Commerce also started to use the improved communication and transportation facilities brought by the Europeans.[77] While large-scale commerce, especially import-export, was controlled by expatriate elements (European companies or Greek and Syro-Lebanese traders),[78] below them existed a busy sector of indigenous commerce covering local and interregional trade.

In all three territories, indigenous commerce was completely dominated by Muslims.[79] In North Cameroon and Futa Jallon those Muslims were mostly Fulbe, while in Northern Nigeria they were mainly Hausa. In Northern Nigeria the clear dominance of the Hausa in commerce resulted in offsetting the economic advantage that the Fulbe had as the biggest owners of cattle and land (and so cash crops). It therefore reduced (perhaps eliminated) the difference between Hausa and Fulbe in terms of control over sources of wealth. In Futa Jallon and North Cameroon, on the other hand, the unrivaled dominance of the Fulbe in commerce consolidated their economically dominant position relative to other populations.

The entrance of the Fulbe into the sphere of commerce in Futa Jallon and North Cameroon presented a striking example of successful adjustment to change.[80] Although they had despised commercial activities in the past, the Fulbe entered that sphere and succeeded in controlling it as they perceived its rising value as a source of wealth. In Guinea Fulbe dominance in trade spread even beyond Futa Jallon to the coastal zone.[81] In North Cameroon the most important markets, in terms of volume of trade, number of participants, radius of influence, were generally found in areas with relatively heavy Fulbe participation. In areas with a greater concentration of Kirdi people, markets were fewer and smaller. Usually the markets in Kirdi areas were initiated by Fulbe traders looking for new areas of activity. To the extent that non-Fulbe traders existed in those markets, they were small-scale traders with a limited range of activity while the Fulbe concentrated on large-scale, long-distance, interregional trade, which necessitated a more elaborate organization and greater capital, but also provided bigger profits.

In Northern Nigeria, on the other hand, the preexisting Hausa control of the commercial sector was too strong and too independent of political rule for the Fulbe to challenge. Hence, the greatest beneficiaries of the rising value of commerce in Northern Nigeria were the Hausa and not the Fulbe. The Hausa served as principal middlemen and agents for European companies. The expansion of local and regional trade within the north again found them there. When the pacification of hill tribes in Northern Nigeria was followed by the opening of markets in their areas, the Hausa merchants were the first to penetrate into those areas, and they dominated the trade with pagans in a comparable way to the Fulbe in North Cameroon.[82]

One item whose trade developed rapidly in the colonial period was cattle. With respect to ownership, cattle continued to be the almost exclusive domain of the Fulbe.[83] However, an important change occurred, in that its trade took dimensions incomparable with the precolonial period. The Fulbe-inhabited regions became the major suppliers of livestock in their respective colonial territories, answering a growing demand for meat in urban centers. In North Cameroon, the cattle trade was dominated by Fulbe traders, some of whom built elaborate business organizations. They had substantial capital and could make large-scale purchases. The only competition in cattle trade came from a French company, La Compagnie Pastorale, which established itself in Ngaoundéré in the early 1920s. This company pioneered the meat industry in Cameroon by setting up a modern slaughterhouse with refrigeration facilities and later by sending frozen meat by air to the south. In 1954 a second refrigerated slaughterhouse was opened in Maroua and was run by the colonial administration.[84] In Guinea too the Fulbe entered the cattle trade in force and completely dominated it, not only there, but also in Sierra Leone to which they smuggled a great number of their cattle because of the higher prices that could be obtained there. Every major city in Futa Jallon was also an important livestock market from which cattle were brought to Conakry or smuggled into Sierra Leone.[85] In Nigeria, on the other hand, while the Fulbe-inhabited areas were again the main suppliers of cattle to the south, the Fulbe participation in the cattle trade in Northern Nigeria was limited to supplying cattle to the northern markets, where they sold their herds to Hausa traders and served as hired drivers, bringing the cattle to the markets of the south.[86]

The increasing willingness of the Fulbe to enter into cattle trade stood in contrast to their traditional view that owning cattle was an end in itself. It illustrated the Fulbe readiness to alter their use of resources as the value of those resources changed following external events. Nevertheless, owning large herds still had its prestige value, as is shown by the fact that many wealthy Fulbe spent considerable sums buying cattle and raising large herds for no apparent commercial purpose. Cattle therefore played a contradictory dual role, both as a means to acquire more precious wealth resources and as an important prestige resource to which the acquired wealth was in turn converted. The Fulbe, exerting quasi-monopoly over cattle in all three territories, tried to find an optimum balance between the two different uses of cattle that would maximize both the wealth and prestige that could be derived from them.[87]

In addition to the purchase of cattle, some profits of trade activities were reinvested in economic enterprises, thus creating further wealth resources. Such enterprises included opening stores and transporting passengers and merchandise, in which the Fulbe faced stiff competition from expatriate elements, mainly from Syro-Lebanese and Greek traders.[88] Other profits went to supporting Muslim scholars, marrying a new wife, building a new compound, or buying a car or some other western-imported luxury goods, all of which were ways of converting wealth into prestige, some based on traditional prestige resources such as Islamic learning and owning cattle, others based on new sources of prestige derived from the new consumption patterns introduced by colonial innovations. However in this respect a significant difference existed between the Hausa traders of Northern Nigeria and the Fulbe traders of Futa Jallon and North Cameroon. The Hausa were restricted in their conspicuous consumption because they were not supposed to seem to compete for supremacy with the ruling Fulbe aristocracy. No matter how wealthy a Hausa merchant was (some were indeed wealthier than most Fulbe aristocrats), it was not tactful or advisable for him to buy a car that would rival the one owned by the Fulbe chief or to build a compound as imposing as the palaces of the top native administration officials.[89] In North Cameroon and Futa Jallon, to the extent that the Fulbe traders themselves belonged to the aristocratic class (unfortunately, we do not have specific information on what proportion belonged to the aristocracy and what proportion was of commoner origin), they were less inhibited by such considerations. This is an interesting case of interrelationship between power, wealth, and prestige in which the power held by one group dissuaded another group from a full conversion of its wealth into prestige resources so that it would not overshadow the comparable prestige resources of the powerful group. Also, Hausa merchants in Northern Nigeria, more than Fulbe merchants in Futa Jallon and North Cameroon, spent considerable sums in assisting top officials (most of whom were Fulbe) who were in financial trouble. In Northern Nigeria there was a more clear-cut division between the politically dominant Fulbe rulers and the economically strong (if not dominant) Hausa merchants, and the latter found it necessary to spend a large amount of money purchasing the protection and support of the politically dominant group.[90] In other words, they tried to neutralize the power of the ruling group by their own wealth resources. In North Cameroon and Futa Jallon, there was much more correspondence and overlapping between the most powerful and most wealthy groups, and so there was less need to use one resource to neutralize the other.

Among the different patterns of conspicuous consumption, pilgrimage to Mecca (Hajj) provides an especially interesting illustration of interconvertibility between wealth and prestige resources. Although Hajj is one of the five major religious obligations of every Muslim, very few people could afford the expense and hardship of going to Mecca in the precolonial period. In the colonial period, with the improving means of transportation, the time necessary to accomplish the pilgrimage and the hardships involved in the trip were sharply reduced, though the cost of the trip was still beyond the means of all but the wealthiest Africans. For wealthy merchants who could afford it, the pilgrimage was an occasion not only to raise their religious prestige (conversion of wealth into prestige) but also to use that prestige to enjoy better credit in their business (reconversion of prestige into wealth). The merchants who came back with the title *Alhaji* were considered more dependable, and certainly they had proved their affluence. They attracted more customers, could borrow more money when needed, and were more trusted by the local authorities. All that helped them improve their business and become even wealthier.[91] It is not surprising, therefore, to find a great number of merchants among the growing group of Alhajis. In North Cameroon and Futa Jallon most Alhajis were Fulbe, and their Hajj strengthened their control over wealth and prestige resources. In Northern Nigeria, they were both Fulbe chiefs and Hausa merchants. For the latter

the Hajj was the principal way in which they could reduce the
gap of religious prestige between the Fulbe and themselves
while at the same time using their new respectability to further
their business.

One field into which neither the Fulbe merchants of Futa
Jallon and North Cameroon nor the Hausa of Northern Nigeria
tried to enter in the colonial period was manufacture and industry. In all three territories, modern, mechanized industrial
activities remained almost totally controlled by either foreign
companies or the colonial administration. Traditional craftsmanship controlled by Africans (though never by Fulbe) steadily
declined, being severely hurt by the competition of European-
made goods. In Futa Jallon and North Cameroon very few
industries were established in the colonial period, and all
were foreign owned. In Futa Jallon, the only manufacturing
enterprise worth mentioning was the orange perfume manufacturing by CAPP discussed above. In North Cameroon the only
industrial installations were the cotton ginneries and oil mills
run by the CFDT.

Compared to North Cameroon and Futa Jallon, Northern
Nigeria experienced greater industrial development in the colonial period, but African participation in it was minimal.
Before the end of World War II, the only major manufacture undertaken by the indigenous population was the production of
brown sugar out of sugarcane. In Kano, a small factory was also
opened by the native administration in 1934 to produce
clarified butter. Besides that, all other factories existing before
the end of World War II were owned and run by expatriates or
by the colonial administration. (Among them we could cite one
peanut oil mill, some cotton ginneries, and a dairy established
by the colonial administration in Vom on the Jos plateau.) After
World War II, relatively important industrial development
started in Northern Nigeria, mostly with the encouragement
and assistance of the northern regional government and its specialized agencies. Among the most important industries
established in Northern Nigeria between 1945 and 1960 were
textile plants in Kano (1949) and Kaduna (1959), a corned beef
and rice canning factory (1955), three peanut oil crushing plants
(owned by Syrians), and soap, perfumes, cosmetics factories
(1955). Most of these factories were run by expatriates, but there

was an increasing tendency toward partnership with Northern Nigerian government agencies in the supply of capital. [92]

Geographical Mobility, Migration, Urbanization

In this section we shall discuss the changing opportunity to acquire wealth, power, and prestige resources as a result of increased geographical mobility. Many of the colonial innovations which were introduced to Futa Jallon, North Cameroon, and Northern Nigeria contributed to an increase in the geographical mobility of the indigenous people. The building of new towns as administrative and commercial centers attracted a large number of immigrants from the countryside. With the development of commerce, markets became centers of attraction for people from increasingly distant areas. The development of cash-crop agriculture and the rapid expansion of cultivated areas induced people who did not have enough suitable land to migrate to other areas where land was in more ample supply or where hired agricultural workers were needed. Improvement in the means of communication and transportation was another very important factor leading to increased mobility. Finally, the colonial rule brought to the colonial territories a situation of peace and security that encouraged mobility, especially for pagan groups who in the precolonial period could not leave their heavily defended villages for fear of enslavement by the Fulbe.

One of the most important types of migration, which started in the colonial period, was the pagan hill tribes' descent to the valleys and plains. It affected mainly North Cameroon and, to a lesser extent, Northern Nigeria but had little effect on Futa Jallon (with the exception of the hill Bassaris' moving to the plains in northwestern Futa Jallon). [93] In the precolonial period, the tops of hills had provided sanctuaries for many pagans who had fled the Fulbe conquerors. Most of these hills were overpopulated, and the land was not very suitable for agriculture despite the very intensive agriculture on remarkable terraces devised by pagans. [94] When peace came in the colonial period, and as their need for cash and new items of consumption could not be met by their traditional agriculture on their overpopulated hills, many pagan groups started to move down to the plains. Their descent was encouraged by the colonial administration and by the Muslim dwellers on the plains for both political and economic reasons. Politically, pagans who moved down the hills could be more easily governed by the colonial administration and by the Muslim chiefs. Economically, they could help expand the cultivation of cash crops. For the Muslims,[95] the descent of the pagans meant a new available cheap labor force, more customers for their trade, more sharecroppers on their land, and for the chiefs bigger incomes from taxes. The descent of the hill pagans was, therefore, strongly encouraged by the colonial administration with the consent of the Muslim population.

The only problem created by the descent of pagans to the plains was that of land ownership. The Muslim population welcomed the mountaineers to the plains, but they were not willing to allow them ownership of land. They claimed that the land belonged to them (even if uncultivated) and that therefore the pagans had to pay some kind of rent or had to buy the land from them. In general, the Muslims preferred to restrict the rights of pagans on land as much as possible so that more pagans could be forced to work on their fields as hired workers or sharecroppers. Frequent clashes occurred between pagans occupying land and Muslims trying to force payment of rent or expulsion of the pagans.[96] The colonial administration tried to solve these problems by reserving certain areas on the plains for pagan settlement, sometimes buying land from the Muslims who claimed to be the owners.

Despite the problems related to land ownership, the migration of pagans from hills to plains developed steadily during the colonial period. Most of the mountaineers worked as sharecroppers or seasonal hired laborers on fields owned by Muslims. Very few of them succeeded in gaining ownership of land and thus earning economic independence, except when they descended to largely uninhabited plains as was the case with some Jos plateau tribes in Northern Nigeria. Many migrant mountaineers returned to their village in the hills after a certain period of time or during certain months of the year. Even when permanently settled on the plain, they kept intensive contact with their relatives on the hills. They almost always returned there to bury their dead. Most of them retained their traditional religion, at least for one generation; however, toward the end of the colonial period Islamization started to make important inroads. So the political and economic dominance of the Fulbe and other Muslim plains dwellers over pagans spread to the cultural-religious sphere.[97]

In North Cameroon and Northern Nigeria a large part of migration was to areas within the north itself. In a study done in 1954 on the destination of migrants from Sokoto province in Northern Nigeria, it was found that 38 percent were directed to other parts of Northern Nigeria, 25 percent were directed to Western Nigeria, 18 percent to Eastern Nigeria, 17 percent to Ghana, and 2 percent to French territories.[98] If the research had been done earlier in the colonial period, the percentage of migration to other parts of Northern Nigeria would have probably been higher, since there were indications that migration to the south was a recent phenomenon. Unfortunately, we do not have comparable figures on North Cameroon, but the impression received from personal observations in that country was that migration from the north to the south was even less important than in Nigeria. In Futa Jallon, in contrast, the principal trend of migration was out of Futa Jallon, no doubt because of the relative poverty and lack of economic development of Futa Jallon during the colonial period. One major center of attraction was the peanut cultivation areas in Senegal. Every year many people from Futa Jallon went to Senegal during the peanut cultivation season. At the end of the season most of them returned to Futa Jallon, though some remained behind and settled in Senegal for a longer period of time. Unfortunately, we do not know what proportion of those migrants (called *Navétanes*) were of Fulbe origin. Since the non-Fulbe people (mostly descendants of slaves) were on the average much poorer than the Fulbe, it is reasonable to assume that most migrant workers were non-Fulbe. To the extent that Fulbe existed among them, they must have been commoners suffering extreme poverty, since the work in question was most downgrading in Fulbe eyes. For the former slaves, on the other hand, the peanut fields of Senegal provided an important source of income which was totally outside their former masters' control.[99]

A second important center of attraction for migrants from Futa Jallon was the coastal zone of Guinea. These migrants were mainly workers in plantations and in urban centers and traders who penetrated and rapidly dominated the markets opened in the colonial period. A few of them also settled on land rented or

purchased from the local populations and started farming. Toward the end of the colonial period, 4.2 percent of the male
population and about 2.5 percent of the female population living in the Guinean coastal region had come from Futa Jallon. At
first the immigrants were mainly non-Fulbe, but later the poor
Fulbe commoners joined them. Migration from Futa Jallon to
the peanut fields of Senegal was almost ten times as great as to
the coastal region of Guinea, but migration to the coastal region
was more permanent; that to Senegal was more seasonal. About
40 percent of the people of Futa Jallon living in the coastal region had been born there.[100]

A special type of migration that developed during the colonial period was directed toward urban centers. One of the major
changes that occurred in the colonial period was the rapid
growth of cities which, because of their role as economic, administrative, and cultural centers, attracted a large number of
immigrants. The extent of development of urban centers in
Northern Nigeria, North Cameroon, and Futa Jallon corresponded to the general economic development of each territory.
In Northern Nigeria, which showed the greatest degree of economic development during the colonial period, there was also
the greatest development of urban centers. Cities such as Kano,
Katsina, Zaria, which were important urban centers already in
the precolonial period, accelerated their development as centers
of cash-crop agriculture. In 1952 Kano had a population of
130,000, Zaria and Katsina having 54,000 and 53,000, respectively. They were joined by new towns such as Kaduna
(administrative capital of Northern Nigeria) and Jos (headquarters for the tin-mining industry), each with a population of
about 39,000. In North Cameroon the urban centers were much
smaller. In 1958, Maroua had a population of 22,700, followed
by Ngaoundéré with 14,200 and Garoua with 12,000. The first
two were seats of important precolonial chiefdoms, while the
third developed in the colonial period as the administrative
capital of the north. In Futa Jallon, urban centers were even
smaller. The biggest town, Labé, which was the colonial administrative center of the region as well as the seat of an important
precolonial chiefdom, had a population of only 12,000 in 1955.
The second biggest town, Mamou, which owed its growth to
the railroad which passed through it, had a population of only
5,800 in the same year. These two towns of Futa Jallon could not

in any way compete with Conakry, and outside Guinea with
Dakar or Freetown, as points of attraction for immigrants from
Futa Jallon.[101]

The big towns of Futa Jallon, Northern Nigeria, and North
Cameroon remained mainly centers of Islam and were inhabited in large majority by Muslims (the only exception was
the city of Jos, whose population was largely Christian). The
precolonial pattern, according to which the Muslims were concentrated in more urban areas while more pagans were found
in more rural areas, continued in the colonial period too (despite the increasing pagan immigration into cities) as can be
seen in table 3 in regard to Northern Nigeria. Many of the
immigrant pagans adopted Islam soon after their arrival. The
cities were centers of Islamic culture and learning as much as
they were centers of westernization, and pagans were more
affected by their encounter with Islam than by their encounter
with European culture.[102]

Table 3   **Percentage of Muslims, Pagans and Christians
in Northern Nigerian Towns as Compared
with Their Percentage in the Total Northern
Nigerian Population (1952)**

	Muslims	Pagans	Christians
Total Northern Nigerian population	73.0	24.3	2.7
Towns with population:			
Over 80,000	94.0	0.1	5.9
40,000–80,000	90.8	1.5	7.6
20,000–40,000*	74.8	7.7	19.1
10,000–20,000	95.3	1.8	2.8
8,000–10,000	86.1	6.8	5.7

SOURCE.—Adapted from A. L. Mabogunje,
Urbanization in Nigeria (London: University of
London Press, 1958), p. 132.
*The relatively low percentage of Muslims in
this category is due to the influence of the city of
Jos, which had a relatively high percentage of
Christians and pagans.

The urban centers of Northern Nigeria and North Cameroon
also attracted some expatriates and many Africans from the
southern regions. The expatriates were composed of colonial

administrators, merchants, agents of European companies, and a few professionals (doctors, veterinarians, teachers, agricultural experts, etc.). They lived in separate European residential quarters and did not mix with the rest of the population except for business.[103] Between the expatriate community and the local northerners stood the immigrants from the southern provinces of Nigeria and Cameroon (mainly Ibo and Yoruba in Nigeria, Bamiléké in Cameroon). They occupied positions such as low-ranking clerks, apprentice professionals, teachers in western schools, skilled or semiskilled workers. Some of them were also merchants trading mainly with their region of origin. In the eyes of the northerners, they were as much strangers as the Europeans, without at the same time having the prestige accorded to white people. They were disliked and distrusted by the northern populations, Muslim and pagan, Fulbe and non-Fulbe alike. Their different customs were despised by the northerners, and they were accused of blocking the northerners' access to higher positions. They lived in separate quarters called *Sabongari*.[104]

Islamic and Fulbe Identity

The establishment of colonial rule in Futa Jallon, Northern Nigeria, and North Cameroon did not in any way disrupt the position of Islam; perhaps it even strengthened it. On the basis of the colonial duality, Islam remained closely related to the precolonial centers which were founded by the Fulbe and which were allowed to survive in the colonial period. The sedentary Fulbe, being closest to the Islamic center and setting the model of Islamic behavior for all the other populations, continued to enjoy the greatest degree of prestige deriving from proximity to Islam. Where the Fulbe also controlled considerable power and wealth, the prestige received from proximity to Islam helped legitimize that control. The chiefs and officials continued to attribute religious significance to their political positions, and that was widely accepted by the local population.[105] The Fulbe also continued to provide most of the Muslim clerics, teachers, scholars, and judges.

The strong position of Islam as a prestige resource in the colonial period led to its continuing spread to non-Muslim populations. This trend was less visible in Hausaland and Futa Jallon because the great majority of the population was already

Muslim before the colonial period, but it was clearly visible in North Cameroon where Islamization began mainly in the colonial period. By the end of the colonial period some Kirdi populations, such as the Mboum, the Dourou, the Laka, and the Dama, were Muslim in great majority. Among other Kirdis, the proportion of Muslims was greater than that of Christians (two exceptions to that were the Moundang and the Guidar).[106] For most pagan populations in North Cameroon, Northern Nigeria, and Futa Jallon (in contrast with South Cameroon, Southern Nigeria, and parts of the coast of Guinea), entrance into the civilized world was obtained through Islamization rather than westernization and Christianization. The stabilization and consolidation of precolonial Muslim centers and the indirect rule patterns—in which, in Muslim-inhabited areas more than anywhere else, precolonial centers were used as intermediary between the colonial center and the indigenous population—restricted the encounter of the local population with the western Christian civilization represented by the colonial center. The only direct encounter of pagan populations with an alternative to Islam was through Christian missionary activities, which were quite limited in the territories studied here. There were certain areas where missionary activity did enable Christianity to compete successfully with the spread of Islam, such as in the Middle Belt region outside the Fulbe-inhabited area in Northern Nigeria, in the Moundang-inhabited area in North Cameroon, and among the Coniagui in northwestern Futa Jallon, but these cases were exceptional. The Fulbe strongly objected to missionary activities in the areas under their control, and they induced the colonial governments to impose great restrictions on missionary activities in Futa Jallon, North Cameroon, and Upper Northern Nigeria.[107]

Therefore, when, as a result of colonial peace, of the rising need for economic exchange, and easier mobility, pagan populations started to open themselves to the outside world, they also started to adopt some of the outward culture of Muslims. Signs of the alternative European civilization were too distant, too unknown to be desirable. The immediate surroundings of the pagans were dominated by a Muslim civilization which was well organized, enjoyed a very high status, and was also backed by the colonial authorities who saw in it a more developed civilization and a more effective social organization than that of the pagans. So, for the pagans, to become civilized meant to adopt the Muslim way, to act like Muslims, talk like Muslims, dress like Muslims, and be in the company of Muslims. The next step was usually to send children to koranic schools, and that opened the way to full-scale Muslimization.[108]

In North Cameroon and Futa Jallon, but not in Northern Nigeria, Muslimization was also a means of showing closer similarity to Fulbe. Most pagan groups wanted to become Muslim in order to resemble the Fulbe, and immediately after adopting Islam they started to act like them. They spoke Fulfuldé, they dressed like Fulbe, they tried to move to Fulbe quarters of towns and villages; those who could afford it bought cattle. After a generation or so, most of them started calling themselves Fulbe.[109] This eagerness to pass for Fulbe illustrated the great prestige that continued to be attached to the Fulbe identity as a sign of closeness to the traditional center which still dominated the periphery in the colonial period.

In Northern Nigeria, on the other hand, Muslimization led to Hausaization rather than Fulbeization, since the largest group of recognized Muslims were Hausa and not Fulbe. The dominant culture was the Hausa culture, and even the Fulbe were in the process of assimilating it. The difference between the Islamic religious identity and the Fulbe ethnic identity was more clearly drawn. Fulbe identity in Northern Nigeria was a very exclusive identity; it belonged either to the ruling aristocracy or to pastoral herdsmen. This identity provided prestige in itself beyond the prestige of Islamic identity, and only by birth could anybody gain that prestige. Upon Islamization pagans entered into the community of Islam and enjoyed its prestige, which was different from the prestige derived from Fulbe identity. To the extent that they spoke the Hausa language and adopted other external Islamic traits that were considered to be Hausa traits, they came to be considered Hausa.

The prestige derived from closeness to Fulbe identity and the close relationship between Islamic and Fulbe identity, added to the Fulbe predominance in trade and communication centers, strengthened the tendency to adopt Fulfuldé as a lingua franca in all of North Cameroon, spreading it even to areas which were never conquered by Adamawa in the precolonial period and in which very few Fulbe lived. In Futa Jallon the same trends existed, though they were less accentuated in the colonial period because Fulfuldé (or rather *Pular* as it is called there) had already practially completed its spread to all the populations of Futa Jallon in the precolonial period. In Northern Nigeria, in contrast, the same reasons that favored the spread of Fulfuldé in North Cameroon accelerated the spread of Hausa as the lingua franca[110] and caused Fulfuldé to be forgotten even more rapidly. Only the pastoral Fulbe continued to speak Fulfuldé as their primary language. In 1945 Daryll Forde estimated that out of more than 3 million Fulbe in Northern Nigeria, only about 700,000 spoke Fulfuldé.[111] The only area of the old empire of Sokoto included in Nigeria where Fulfuldé was still spoken by all the Fulbe was that portion of old Adamawa which fell under British rule. In that area Fulfuldé continued its expansion and became the regional lingua franca despite a strong challenge from Hausa. In this respect, Nigerian Adamawa followed the trend of the other parts of Adamawa across the colonial boundary rather than that of most other areas of Northern Nigeria.[112]

Islamic and Western Education

In all three territories, Islamic education continued to flourish in the colonial period. The koranic schools functioned normally, and the higher Islamic study centers attracted many students and exerted great cultural influence on the population. In 1900 Lugard estimated that about 250,000 pupils studied in 20,000 koranic schools in Northern Nigeria.[113] Their number rose even more during the colonial period, and the developing western schools did not challenge their position. In North Cameroon 8,630 students studied in koranic schools in 1945, compared to 2,700 students studying in western primary schools in 1948. However, toward the end of the colonial period, in 1958, the total number of western school students had reached 17,853, and that exceeded slightly the 14,273 students studying in koranic schools in 1956.[114] At the end of the colonial period only 1 percent of the population could speak French north of the Benue river and 4 percent south of the Benue. At the same time, literacy in Arabic script averaged 10 percent for the whole of North Cameroon. In Northern Nigeria in 1952, 2 percent of the population were literate in Roman script, compared to 5.4 percent literate in Arabic script.[115] In Futa Jallon Islamic education was even less challenged by western education because of the general underdevelopment of European educational insti-

tutions in all of Guinea. In 1941, 260 Muslim clerics taught
2,466 pupils in koranic schools in the Labé region and 303
clerics taught 4,670 pupils in the Mamou region. These data are
striking when compared with figures showing that the students
enrolled in 1935 in European schools in *all of Guinea* totaled
6,558.[116]

We can see then that Islamic education held its own in the
colonial period. It dominated the educational field in Fulbe-
inhabited areas, overshadowing European types of school.
Even in western schools, some Islamic education was undertaken and Muslim clerics were used by the schools to teach the
pupils religious matters. The Muslim pupils who went to western schools continued at the same time to go to traditional
koranic schools (usually they went half-day to one school and
half-day to the other). Excellence in Islamic learning and knowledge was still one of the most important determinants of prestige in society, and for a long time in the colonial period it was
considered more important than acquiring western skills and
knowledge. Islamic education was considered the only type of
education which had intrinsic value as a source of knowledge,
while western education, when finally accepted, was valued
only for its extrinsic, utilitarian advantages, for promoting
one's chances of acceding to new jobs which required certain
western skills. These jobs provided wealth (in the form of
salaries, share of benefits, or presents from people depending on
their service), and power (controlling people who depended
on their service, decision-making authority), but much less
prestige deriving from inherent qualities attributed to western
knowledge. Some "western" professions (such as those of drivers, tailors, waiters, various kinds of mechanics and repairmen)
could be acquired without formal western education, upon
close personal contact with Europeans and with European enterprises, but most occupations, and especially office jobs, required some western education.

Western education developed very slowly in Guinea compared to other colonial territories, mainly because of the limited
role played by missionary organizations in Guinea. The colonial government, while doing nothing to encourage the
establishment of private, missionary-run schools, did not have
the resources to set up many public schools either. The first
western school was established by missionaries in Boffa (in the

coastal region) in 1878. Between 1878 and 1940, only thirty primary schools were opened in Guinea; the first secondary school was opened only in 1948. At the end of the colonial period, in 1958, the rate of enrollment of school-age children in Guinea was a dismal 9.8 percent.[117]

Within Futa Jallon only a few primary schools were opened by the colonial administration in the biggest towns, and a Catholic missionary school, attended mainly by Coniaguis, was opened in Youkounkoun.[118] There was no secondary education in Futa Jallon. The best students from primary schools were sent for secondary education to Conakry and Kindia, and from there the very best were sent to various higher educational institutions in Senegal. The Fulbe were well represented among the western-educated elements of Futa Jallon, but we do not have data on the relative representation of Fulbe commoners compared to aristocrats. Futa Jallon as a whole was not disadvantaged compared to other regions of Guinea, simply because western education was as little developed in other regions as in Futa Jallon.

In Cameroon and Nigeria, western education developed more rapidly due to the colonial policy of allowing a greater role to missionary organizations, but this policy was limited to the southern provinces of Cameroon and Nigeria; hence the development of western education was accompanied by an ever-increasing gap between the south and the north. Western education in the Muslim-dominated north was undertaken mostly in secular schools established by the colonial administration, but they could not compete in any way with the proliferation of missionary-run schools in other regions.[119]

The government schools opened in Northern Nigeria and North Cameroon were aimed at first toward educating the sons of chiefs and dignitaries. They later evolved into general provincial schools. In 1921 the Katsina Teacher Training College was opened in Northern Nigeria,[120] and later it developed into the only secondary school until World War II. In North Cameroon, in 1931, a supplementary class was added to the Garoua primary school to train pupils for teaching and administrative positions; from that evolved the only secondary school of the north until World War II.

After World War II a greater effort was made to develop western education in Northern Nigeria and North Cameroon, as the local population became more conscious of the great gap that existed in education between them and the southerners. In Northern Nigeria, between the end of World War II and 1958, the number of primary schools rose from 935 to 2,204. In the same period the number of secondary schools rose from one to thirty-one and teacher-training schools from nine to thirty-six.[121] In North Cameroon, compared to twelve schools in 1945, there were 158 public primary schools in 1958 with a total enrollment of 15,376 pupils. For the same year there were also 5,558 pupils enrolled in missionary-run schools which had in the meantime penetrated into relatively non-Muslim-inhabited areas of the north. At the secondary school level, while the school of Garoua became a full-scale high school, a teacher-training school and a missionary-run secondary school were also opened after World War II.[122] Still, these developments could not prevent the gap between south and north from growing even wider after World War II in both countries. In 1956–57 about 2.3 million pupils were enrolled in primary schools in Southern Nigeria, compared to about 185,500 pupils in Northern Nigeria.[123] In Cameroon, while the south, with 85 percent enrollment of school-age children in 1955, showed one of the highest rates in all of French African territories, in North Cameroon the rate was only 6 percent[124] (compare these figures with the average of 9.8 percent for the whole of Guinea in 1958).

The Fulbe were not well represented among western-educated elements in either North Cameroon or Northern Nigeria. They resisted western education and saw in it, as in missionary activities, a direct threat to the Islamic order and to their privileged position in it. The government-run schools established in their area tried to respond to their susceptibilities. For example, the Katsina College was officially proclaimed to be a center for training young Muhammedan men of *birth* and *standing* with the purpose "to teach those boys not only the lessons learned from books which they will here acquire, but the way that *good Muhammedans* should live, the good manners, good behavior and the courteous deportment without which mere book learning is of little worth."[125] In spite of that, it seems that in many cases Fulbe chiefs who were pressed by colonial officials to send their sons to those schools preferred to send their slaves' sons instead of their own.[126] Therefore, among the earliest students in western schools run by the colonial government in North Cameroon and Northern

Nigeria we find both sons of the aristocratic ruling Fulbe groups and sons of their household servitors who were recently Muslimized non-Fulbe. On the other hand, the missionary organizations, whose penetration into Muslim-inhabited areas was curtailed, started to spread in the non-Muslim areas of the north such as the Moundang- and Guidar-inhabited areas in North Cameroon and the Middle Belt region in Nigeria. As a result, the·Moundang and Guidar surpassed the Fulbe in western education in North Cameroon, though most other Kirdi groups, especially those living on the hills, lagged far behind. In Northern Nigeria western education developed more in Middle Belt areas less dominated by Muslims and by Fulbe (see table 4 comparing school enrollment in the Middle Belt and the

Table 4   **Ratio of Primary School Enrollment, Northern Nigeria (6–12 Age Group)**

Province	Primary School Enrollment
Far North	
Sokoto	1 in 35.7
Bornu	1 in 22.2
Katsina	1 in 22.2
Kano	1 in 22.2
Bauchi	1 in 12.0
Adamawa	1 in 9.8
Niger	1 in 8.26
Zaria	1 in 5.25
Kaduna Federal Territory	1 in 1.79
Middle Belt:	
Plateau	1 in 4.5
Benue	1 in 4.3
Kabba	1 in 3.1
Ilorin	1 in 2.76
Province Belonging to Both the Far North and the Middle Belt:	
Sardauna	1 in 14.5

SOURCE.—Adapted, with a reclassification of provinces, from J. B. Grimley, "Church Growth in Central Nigeria," in *Church Growth in Central and Southern Nigeria*, ed. J. B. Grimley and G. E. Robinson (Grand Rapids, Mich.: Eerdmans, 1966), p. 193. Table based on 1952 census and 1960 school statistics as prepared by the Survey Department of Nigeria.

Far North provinces). This development naturally had repercussions on the professional opportunities that were open to
the indigenous population. In many areas western-educated
non-Muslims were more qualified to occupy new positions
than Fulbe. In positions whose appointment was controlled by
the Fulbe, such as in native administration, the Fulbe often
bypassed educational qualifications and preferred less qualified
Fulbe or other Muslims to more qualified non-Muslims. However, we should also note that in Northern Nigeria, unlike
North Cameroon and Futa Jallon, the native authorities were
quite active in financing and running western schools. These
schools, with a more traditional and pro-Muslim outlook,
trained a somewhat different type of western-educated element
than the other western schools. Western-educated people employed in positions controlled by native authorities were pref-
erably recruited from among graduates of native-authority
schools where pupils were almost all Muslim.

Fulbe Participation in the Colonial Center

The discussion that we have had so far on the response of the
Fulbe to various colonial changes and innovations has also par-
tially dealt with Fulbe participation in the colonial center and in
the so-called western sector built around it. To the extent that
the Fulbe learned new professions, entered trade and cash-crop
agriculture, spoke the European colonial language, received
western education, or immigrated to newly built or developed
cities, they did participate in different spheres of the colonial
center. However, discussing this participation, we have compared the Fulbe only with non-Fulbe populations living *within*
their own region, in Futa Jallon, Northern Nigeria, and North
Cameroon. In order to evaluate correctly the extent of Fulbe
participation in the colonial centers of Guinea, Nigeria, and
Cameroon, we should compare them also with people living
outside their own region, in the other areas of Guinea, Nigeria,
and Cameroon.

Comparing Fulbe participation in the colonial center with
that of people outside Futa Jallon, North Cameroon, and Northern Nigeria, we see a significant difference between Guinea, on
the one hand, and Nigeria and Cameroon on the other. In
Guinea the participation of the Fulbe in the colonial center and
in colonial changes was quite intense and started quite early

compared to other Guinean populations. In Nigeria and Cameroon, on the other hand, Fulbe participation in the colonial
center lagged far behind that of Southern Nigerian and South
Cameroonian populations. In Guinea the Fulbe were strongly
represented among the western-educated elements and in
teaching and administrative positions compared to all other
Guinean groups. The only westernized group in which the
Fulbe were not represented was the army, because the Fulbe
always found ways to send their former slaves or the pagan
populations in their area when soldiers were forcibly recruited
in Futa Jallon.[127]

In Nigeria and Cameroon, on the other hand, the Fulbe, together with all northern populations, were very severely underrepresented among the westernized indigenous elements when
compared to the people of the south. The new westernized elite
in the two countries was almost totally made up of southerners,
Ibo and Yoruba in Nigeria, Douala, Bamiléké, Boulou, and
Bassa in Cameroon. We have already seen how much the north
lagged behind the south in western education. Consequently
the great majority of new occupations in Nigeria and Cameroon, those necessitating newly acquired western skills and
knowledge, were held by southerners. Even within the north
most positions which required western skills were held by
people who had migrated from the south. In the military service, populations originating from the north were heavily represented as soldiers, but they came mostly from the pagan
tribes of those areas. However, among the few indigenous
officers, western educational requirements again gave the advantage to southerners.[128] With respect to urbanization and
migration to the coastal centers too, while people from Futa
Jallon formed the largest group of immigrants in Conakry, there
were few northerners or Muslims and even fewer Fulbe among
the immigrants in the southern urban centers in Nigeria and
Cameroon.

In the economic field, compared to people from other regions,
the Fulbe were not prominent in any of the three colonial territories. In Northern Nigeria and North Cameroon, although
the Fulbe were important export-crop producers, they were
surpassed in that by southerners (Yoruba and Ibo producing
cocoa and palm oil in Southern Nigeria, Boulou and Bamiléké
producing cocoa and coffee in South Cameroon). In Guinea, the

main cash-crop production areas were located in the coastal
zone outside Futa Jallon, and the Fulbe did not play an important role in agricultural production compared to the local populations of the coast. In trade the Fulbe occupied a dominant
position within North Cameroon and between the north and
the south. A similar position was occupied by the Hausa in
Northern Nigeria. However, within Nigeria and Cameroon as a
whole, the Ibo and the Bamiléké had a stronger position than
the Hausa and the Fulbe respectively in the new commercial
network established in the colonial period. In Guinea the position of the Fulbe in trade was relatively strong compared to
other Guinean populations, but it was strongly challenged by
the Malinké of Upper Guinea.

The generally greater participation of the Fulbe in the colonial
center of Guinea compared to the Fulbe participation in the
colonial centers of Nigeria and Cameroon could be explained by
some fundamental geographical and cultural factors that differentiated Guinea from Cameroon and Nigeria. Cameroon and
Nigeria both enter into the category of West African countries
(together with Togo, Dahomey, Ghana, Ivory Coast) with a
strong geographical, as well as cultural and economic, division
between southern and northern regions. The southern regions
were closer to the colonial center and were the loci of most
colonial innovations. Northern regions were much more distant
from the colonial center and were affected much less by colonial
changes; they were neglected compared to the south and were
left much more in their traditional precolonial status. Both precolonial Sokoto and Adamawa were located in the northern
parts of their respective countries, and they were much less
affected by colonial changes than the southern regions of
Nigeria and Cameroon. Therefore, the population of Sokoto
and Adamawa, whether Fulbe or not, participated much less in
the colonial center than the natives of the southern regions such
as the Yoruba, the Ibo, the Douala, the Bamiléké.

In Guinea, in contrast, there was no such division between
geographically, culturally, and economically different northern
and southern regions. One could talk only of a slightly more
developed, more westernized coastal zone and a less developed, less westernized interior, though the differences were not
as sharp as in Nigeria and Cameroon and they were not compounded by sharp ethnic, linguistic, and cultural distinctions

between the people of the coast and those of the interior. There were Muslims and pagans on the coast as well as in the interior; the largest coastal group, the Soussou, spoke a different dialect of the same language spoken by the Malinké of Upper Guinea; the forest zone, which in Nigeria and Cameroon corresponded to the most developed southern and coastal zone, was in Guinea southernmost, but also most remote from the coast and from the colonial center. In Guinea the colonial government imposed a much more standardized administrative pattern in all the regions, and there were less differences in the colonial government patterns between provinces than existed between north and south in Nigeria and Cameroon.

Furthermore, Futa Jallon was geographically located in the middle of Guinea, between the coast and the interior. It was much less distant from the Guinean coast, where most colonial changes were concentrated, than were North Cameroon and Northern Nigeria from their respective coast or colonial capital. In Guinea the railroad and highways (hence all trade and transportation) between Conakry and the interior passed through Futa Jallon. In Cameroon and Nigeria, on the other hand, the Fulbe-inhabited areas were at the northern end of the communication network. Northern Nigeria was served by railroads and highways but much less so than Southern Nigeria. North Cameroon had no railroads and only two highways linking it to the south; it was not situated on any important trade route or communication axis and remained largely isolated and detached from South Cameroon. All these reasons together accounted for the difference between the Fulbe participation in the colonial center in Guinea, on the one hand, and in Nigeria and Cameroon on the other.

The extent of initial Fulbe participation in the colonial center, as compared with the participation of the other major ethnic groups of the colony within and outside Fulbe-inhabited areas, gained great importance after World War II, when the colonial center was suddenly opened to much greater indigenous participation, particularly in the political sphere. The groups who were already strongly represented in the colonial center had an important advantage over the others in filling the newly opened positions, including the important political positions. The Fulbe of Futa Jallon were thus in a more advantageous position relative to other Guinean populations than were the Fulbe of

Northern Nigeria and North Cameroon relative to other Nigerian and Cameroonian populations. However, as we shall see in our discussion of decolonization, this preliminary advantage did not play a decisive role in determining which indigenous groups achieved ultimate control of the colonial center at the end of the colonial period.

Part Three   Decolonization and Independence

6

The Opening of the Colonial Center to Indigenous Political Participation

In most West African colonial territories, including Guinea, Cameroon, and Nigeria, the period of World War II was an important turning point in the relations between the colonial center and the indigenous population. The end of the war was marked by radical transformations in the colonial governmental system as a result of which the extent of indigenous participation in the colonial center rose considerably and included the political sphere. Until then, with some notable exceptions in Southern Nigeria,[1] the political activities of the Africans were limited mainly to their role in native authorities. The central colonial government was staffed by European officials and was generally inaccessible to Africans. This was radically changed after World War II when France and Britain, in a series of far-reaching constitutional reforms, opened up the central colonial government to indigenous participation. Gradually an increasing number of Africans were allowed to participate in the political process in the colonial center, and the positions made available to them carried increasingly greater power. This characterized the process of decolonization which ended, about fifteen years after it started, with the achievement of independence, that is, with the completion of indigenous political control over the colonial center.

The opening up of the colonial centers to African political participation started an intense struggle between different indigenous groups, aligned along ethnic, religious, regional, ideological, or economic-interest lines, for the control of those central political positions made available to them. This struggle came in addition to a more publicized struggle between the indigenous population as a whole and the colonial power, the former constantly making new demands for greater political participation in the colonial center, the latter trying to respond to some of them but never catching up with the rising demands and aspirations of the anticolonial movement. We are interested here mostly in the struggle between different indigenous groups vying with one another for the control of the colonial center as it was being vacated by the European colonial power. We shall see how these struggles developed in Guinea, Cameroon, and Nigeria, what role the Fulbe played in them, and how those struggles affected their position within their own region. In this context we shall also examine the relations between the aristocratic and commoner elements among the Fulbe in order to distinguish between a struggle based on ethnicity and one based on class in this new scramble for central political positions.

Guinea

In Guinea, the end of World War II brought a sudden flurry of indigenous political activity, starting with the 1945 election to the French Constituent Assembly and following in quick succession with elections to French National, French Union, and Territorial Assemblies. With this sudden burst of political activity, the various voluntary associations which were in the process of formation by urbanized, mostly western-educated Guineans suddenly gained crucial importance as bases of organization for the first rival political groups and the first candidates for political office. Prominent among them was the first cultural club with political ambitions, founded in Guinea (in 1943), the Amicale Gilbert Vieillard (AGV).[2] It was formed by westernized Fulbe intellectuals, mainly graduates of the William Ponty high school in Dakar. The AGV was an exclusive Fulbe organization and proclaimed its aims to be reforming Futa Jallon. Its members included Fulbe of both aristocratic and commoner origins. Following them, most non-Fulbe groups were also organized along ethnic, regional lines and entered the political arena on that basis.[3] They demanded greater political participation in the colonial center but also wanted to improve their ethnic or regional group's position in the intergroup political balance within the colonial center. This ethnic and regional division of indigenous political forces was most profitable to the Fulbe since they were the largest ethnic group in the country.

The formation of a Fulbe ethnic front was made possible by an alliance between the western-educated elements and traditional elites and between commoners and aristocrats. The Fulbe traditional elite, who lacked the necessary western skills and attributes (knowledge of French, literacy, some basic organization techniques, etc.) to participate in central political positions, needed their westernized kinsmen for that. The westernized Fulbe, on their part, needed the electoral support of the traditional elite; but in order to get it, they had to curb their reformist tendencies, a condition to which not all AGV members readily agreed. A difficult problem in the negotiations that led to the formation of this front proved to be the selection of the common candidate for the Constituent Assembly in 1945. The traditional chiefs were opposed to the radical head of the AGV, Diawadou Barry. Instead, they proposed Yacine Diallo, a Pullo commoner, Ponty graduate, and teacher in his fifties, known as moderate, trusted by the chiefs, yet also a westernized intellectual. Yacine Diallo was also acceptable to most westernized Fulbe. It is interesting to note that the Fulbe traditional chiefs preferred Yacine Diallo, who was a commoner and so was not fit for political office according to traditional criteria, to the radical reformist Diawadou Barry, who was a member of the royal Soriya lineage.[4] The candidate who had the traditional attributes for office was found to be a danger to that traditional order; the candidate without the traditional attributes for office was considered a better guarantee for safeguarding it. The choice of a commoner to lead the front was perhaps also a means to ensure Fulbe commoners' support and defuse any class conflict that might have developed between commoners and aristocrats.

The Fulbe alliance under the leadership of Yacine Diallo worked very successfully for a while. It won all the elections between 1945 and 1954 and dominated the local political scene with the clear support of the French.[5] Diallo himself was elected as Guinean representative to the French National Assembly, and in Guinea he established a branch of the French Socialist party (SFIO), to which he was affiliated. However, the party's early dominance with the support of the French administration made it a prime target of anticolonial attacks, and the Fulbe who controlled it were marked as collaborators of the colonial administration. This was to have very harmful effects on the position of the Fulbe in Guinea in the later years of decolonization.

Strongest opposition to the dominance of the Socialist party, and hence of the Fulbe, in the Guinean political arena came from the PDG (Parti Démocratique de Guinée), formed by a few left-wing intellectuals with the support of some non-Fulbe ethnic associations. At first the PDG failed to make any headway in Guinean politics. It was opposed by many traditional chiefs, by all of Futa Jallon, and by the French colonial administration. Under the administration's pressure, all ethnic associations which had participated in its formation soon withdrew their support. The colonial administration also induced many westernized Guineans who held jobs in the administration to cut all ties with the party. Those who refused were dismissed or sent to distant posts inside or outside Guinea.[6]

In those difficult times, support for the PDG came mostly from some intellectuals in the Conakry area and from regions of Upper Guinea and the forest belt inhabited mainly by the Malinké and the Mandé-speaking Dyula traders.[7] The Fulbe were conspicuously absent among the supporters of the PDG, with the notable exception of Sayfoulaye Diallo, a western-educated intellectual of aristocratic background who later became the second man of the PDG after Sékou Touré. Although the PDG claimed to stand above ethnic differences, it was commonly considered to be the party of the Malinké and the instrument of anti-Fulbe opposition in Guinea. As the content of articles published in the PDG newspapers between 1947 and 1950 shows, in almost every issue of PDG newspapers the Fulbe traditional elite and the Fulbe intellectuals allied with them were singled out for criticism for collaborating with the French and oppressing the people of Futa Jallon.[8]

The fate of the PDG, and consequently of the anticolonial struggle, started to change when it became more closely associated with the leading trade union movement in the country, the CGTG (Confédération Générale du Travail de Guinée), and when the leader of that trade union, Sékou Touré (of Malinké origin), became the secretary general of the party.[9] By associating the political struggle of the party with the professional struggle of the workers, Sékou Touré was able to generate, out of the discontent of the workers, a feeling of anticolonial struggle which no doubt existed in a latent form in a considerable part of the native population. Moreover, linkage with trade unions took place during a period when trade unions were in full expansion and membership in them transcended ethnic and

regional lines. In 1953, a record-breaking sixty-six-day strike in
public services, ending in substantial gains for the strikers,
turned Sékou Touré into a hero and marked the turning point in
the growing popularity of the PDG.[10] At the same time, franchise was also extended to more peripheral groups where the
PDG was strongest.[11] The result was increasing PDG strength
in the 1953 and 1954 elections, at the expense of parties dominated by the Fulbe, and finally victory in the 1956 elections
which brought it to a dominant position in the colonial center.[12]

The PDG brought to the Guinean political scene two elements
which were particularly dangerous to the Fulbe and especially
to the Fulbe aristocratic families. First of all, the PDG espoused
the idea of populism, which was expressed by its becoming a
mass party based on broad popular support and articulating the
wishes and interests of underprivileged peripheral groups. The
PDG fought the fight of peripheral groups against the
centers—both colonial and traditional—which exploited them.
By this attitude the PDG set itself against all traditional chiefs,
including even Malinké chiefs, despite high Malinké representation in the party. Second, the emergence of the PDG broke
down the ethnic polarization of the political scene which had so
far served the interests of the Fulbe. This, in turn, broke the
alliances between westernized Fulbe intellectuals and the traditional elite and between the commoners and the aristocracy.

The period of 1953–56, which saw the upsurge of the PDG,
saw also the beginning of the disintegration of the Fulbe front.
Yacine Diallo died in April 1954. On the question of electing a
successor to him in the French National Assembly, the Fulbe
front broke apart. Surprisingly, the Fulbe chiefs proposed the
candidacy of the once-radical ex-AGV leader Diawadou Barry
who had refused to support Yacine Diallo in the past,[13] but
most of his old friends opposed him and decided to dissociate
themselves from the traditional chiefs. There is no doubt that
this decision was taken as a result of the changing political
atmosphere created by the popular appeal of the PDG's attacks
on the chiefs. Most of the old AGV members supported the
candidacy of Ibrahima Barry (also of aristocratic origin but with
more reformist ideas) and organized themselves around a new
party, the DSG (Démocratie Socialiste Guinéenne). In the election campaign of 1954 Ibrahima Barry openly opposed ethnic
and class differences, backed equality for all, and set himself

against the Fulbe chiefs. His party attacked the Fulbe chiefs much more than it attacked the PDG. Diawadou Barry, on the other hand, broadened his base of support to traditional chiefs of all ethnic groups. His party, the BAG (Bloc Africain de Guinée), had also the full support of the colonial administration.[14]

With open help from the colonial administration, the BAG won a plurality of votes in 1954, but it could not prevent the rising strength of the PDG which, in the following years, became the dominant political force in the country. Only in Futa Jallon did the PDG remain relatively weak, its anticolonial and antichief campaign being carried out by the radical westernized Fulbe of the DSG (we unfortunately do not have data on whether more Fulbe commoners than aristocratic elements supported the DSG). The DSG declined repeated PDG offers for unification, since the PDG was still viewed among the Fulbe as a predominantly Malinké party. As a result the PDG, in fact, remained a predominantly non-Fulbe party, and as the PDG's power rose between 1953 and 1957, Futa Jallon remained conspicuous in its relative lack of support for the PDG (see table 5). However, having captured almost total control of other regions, the PDG could come to power despite its weakness in Futa Jallon and only then start to capture support within Futa Jallon. In the 1957 elections for the Territorial Assembly, the PDG's victory was almost total. It won fifty-six out of sixty seats, including a strong majority in Futa Jallon. Still, three of the four seats which the PDG failed to win came from Futa Jallon, and they were won by the anticolonial, antichief DSG. Of the 650,000 votes cast, the PDG received almost 500,000, the DSG 100,000, and the BAG less than 50,000.[15]

The electoral victories of the PDG in 1956 and 1957 came at the time of the promulgation of the Loi-Cadre reforms, which considerably increased indigenous political participation in the colonial center. The territorial assemblies were given more extensive legislative powers and, for the first time, a territorial government was formed by elected indigenous elements.[16] For the defeated Fulbe this meant the loss of political positions in the colonial center just when the indigenous population was given the effective political control of the territory. Thus they found themselves at the mercy of their triumphant political rivals, who had legal mandate to rule over them and make

Table 5   **Percentage of Votes Received by the PDG,
1951–58**

Electoral Districts	1951	1954	1956	1957	1958
Beyla	52.1	62.3	89.6	96.7	99
Boffa	5.17	86.6	93.0	96.2	99
Boké	3.03	74.3	88.1	85.3	99.9
Conakry	28.3	69.8	83.8	87.7	...
Dabola*	6.57	33.0	68.2	57.4	78
Dinguiraye*	7.17	...	...	61.8	99
Faranah	3.5	...	...	99.8	99
Dalaba*	2.4	6.1	33.2	53.2	57
Dubréka	1.1	38.9	92.3	98.6	99
Forécariah	1.99	76.7	89.5	97.1	99
Gaoual*	2.0	9.9	55.5	50.1	99
Youkounkoun*	15.2	...	...	68.5	98
Guéckédou	30.3	97.4	71.4	67.1	99
Kankan	39.2	59.5	77.2	87.6	93
Kindia	11.2	74.4	82.6	94.6	99
Kissidougou	2.8	9.6	63.6	78.9	89
Kouroussa	56.7	52.2	85.1	93.8	99
Labé*	3.2	...	45.1	69.0	63
Mali*	1.6	19.9	39.1	59.8	99
Tougué*	16.5	...	43.6	60.1	63
Macenta	5.0	60.3	73.4	79.6	99
Mamou*	7.1	19.4	36.3	60.5	59
N'Zerekoré	58.4	39.8	53.1	73.5	75
Pita*	0.6	3.2	8.2	...	54
Telimélé*	5.2	...	28.5	53.8	81
Siguiri	8.7	29.3	67.3	76.6	94

SOURCE.—J. Beaujeu-Garnier, "Essai sur la
Géographie Electorale Guinéenne," *Les Cahiers
d'Outre-Mer*, 11, no. 44 (1958), p. 328.
*Districts in Futa Jallon, three of which—You-
kounkoun, Gaoual, and Dinguiraye—are inhabited by a large majority of non-Fulbe.

crucial decisions concerning their social, political, and economic
destiny.[17]

The PDG's coming to power and the eviction of the Fulbe
parties from their political positions were followed by serious
and often bloody incidents between militants of the two sides,
mostly in Conakry where the Soussou attacked the Fulbe,
burned their houses, and killed and injured some people. In
those incidents Fulbe commoners were certainly not spared.

They sustained Soussou attacks just like aristocratic elements. The dispute was an ethnic one, and it was exacerbated by electoral rivalry between political parties identifying with opposing sides. Indeed, these incidents were, for the most part, organized by the PDG as a campaign of intimidation against the Fulbe, and, since the PDG by then held control of the self-governing colony, very little was done to stop them.[18]

While the incidents that occurred in Conakry pitted the Soussou against the Fulbe on a purely ethnic basis, within Futa Jallon itself something of a "revolution" occurred in which commoners and non-Fulbe populations rose against traditional chiefs at the instigation of the PDG (and to some extent of the DSG). This was part of a general protest against chiefs which took place all over Guinea, but its relative damage was greater to the Fulbe chiefs than to others since the Fulbe chiefs held a stronger position than other chiefs prior to that event.

It is difficult to determine how the antichief elements in Guinea succeeded in arousing the commoners and the peripheral elements against their traditional chiefs. This was attempted in many other countries of West Africa but was nowhere nearly as successful as in Guinea. Regarding Futa Jallon, it is known that the PDG penetrated first into areas inhabited mostly by populations who had resisted the Fulbe in the precolonial period and had been repeatedly raided by them (districts of Youkounkoun, Gaoual, half district of Mali).[19] However, how did antichief protest spread to heavily Fulbe-inhabited areas of Futa Jallon? On this question two explanations have been set forth. Some have claimed that the first people mobilized against the chiefs were the non-Fulbe former slaves.[20] This explanation assumes that the descendants of slaves were all too willing to rise against the Fulbe chiefs, as a result of accumulated past grievances and for promises of political and economic benefit. It is doubtful that such promises, especially when made by outsiders to the region, could outweigh long years of acceptance of Fulbe rule as part of the traditional order and the aspiration to be assimilated into the Fulbe culture. In contrast with this explanation, other people (mainly Fulbe refugees in Dakar interviewed in May 1972[21]) claim that the first to rise against the chiefs were Fulbe commoners and not non-Fulbe former slaves. The former slaves were, on the contrary, the most loyal to the chiefs. According to proponents of this second point of view, the Fulbe commoners were encouraged to rise against their chiefs not by outsiders but by fellow Fulbe who were western educated (both commoners and some aristocrats who betrayed their class) and were organized in either the PDG or the DSG. This explanation has the advantage of accounting for the long-existing cleavage between aristocratic and commoner elements among the sedentary Fulbe of Futa Jallon (in that, Futa Jallon is distinguished from Sokoto and Adamawa), but again it does not explain how those western-educated or urbanized Fulbe succeeded in persuading their rural kinsmen to oppose their chiefs.

It is possible that the commoners and non-Fulbe former slaves might have been simply influenced by the uprising against chiefs which had started earlier in other regions of Guinea. Futa Jallon might well have been taken by the contagion of protests, demonstrations, and organized acts of civil disobedience that were well advanced in other regions as part of the anticolonial struggle and were brilliantly conducted by the PDG which had a strong grass-roots organization.[22] Once popular ferment and uprising developed in other regions, Futa Jallon was not sufficiently insulated from other regions (neither geographically, as were the territories of former Adamawa and Sokoto, nor constitutionally, as was the Northern Region in Nigeria) to be unaffected by the protest movement.

Between 1956 and 1957, the antichief movement grew rapidly and reached a point where chiefs were discredited and the local government apparatus was almost paralyzed. The situation in 1957 is illustrated in reports sent by French colonial officials stationed in Futa Jallon and quoted by Suret-Canale. On Dabola, seat of one of the two precolonial ruling families of Futa Jallon, a local French official wrote, "Actuellemet la situation politique est characterisée par la préeminence totale du RDA [=PDG] sur le cercle, beaucoup plus par haine de l'Almamy et de sa famille que par opinion politique. Le tribunal coutumier ne fonctionne pratiquement plus, les libérations d'esclaves sont des plus nombreuses." On two other important regions of Futa Jallon, reports ran as follows: Labé, "Depuis huit mois je n'ai pas eu affaire à un chef de canton. Pour moi, qu'ils soient là ou pas c'est la même chose." Mamou, "Ces chefs ont commis l'erreur de descendre dans l'arène politique, ils ont lié leur sort à des partis qui ont été vaincus, ils se sont effondrés avec ces partis."[23] Very similar reports came from all other regions of Guinea, showing that the antichief uprising was not limited to Futa Jallon.[24] In Dalaba, in Futa Jallon, on the other hand, an unexpected thing happened just before the territorial elections of 1957. The chief of Dalaba, feeling the danger of being overthrown by his subjects, publicly declared his adherence to the PDG and then was presented as PDG candidate to the elections against the DSG which had championed the uprising against him.[25]

The popular unrest and uprising against chiefs convinced even the French colonial administrators that traditional chiefs had lost control over their subjects. This view was expressed by the governor of Guinea in April 1956, two months after the elections which saw the first PDG electoral victory: "[la chefferie] ... se trouve gravement compromise par le succès d'un parti que les faits présentent comme opposé à elle; il n'est plus admissible que nous maintenions contre vents et marées des chefs qui ne représentent plus rien: leur autorité n'y gagne rien et la nôtre s'y use."[26] Consequently, the French colonial administration started to withdraw its support from the chiefs. The same feeling about the uselessness of the chiefs was expressed also in July 1957, in a meeting of regional colonial administrators with the governor of Guinea and government ministers (all members of the PDG) with regard to a proposed reorganization of local administration. At that meeting, only four out of twenty-two Commandants de Cercle (the highest regional colonial officials) claimed that canton chiefs had any useful role in the territory.[27] Following that meeting, the French acquiesced to the Guinean government's proposal to abolish formally the role of chiefs in local administration. In December 1957, in the context of a reorganization of local government, the office of canton chief and the administrative unit of canton were absolished. New local administrative units not corresponding to cantons were created, and civil servants were appointed by the central government as local administrators.[28] All the political and administrative functions held by canton chiefs were transferred to new nontraditional administrators who usually were loyal PDG supporters and in any case were not natives of the regions to which they were appointed. For the Fulbe aristocracy the loss of political power was tremendous. For the first time since the Fulbe Jihad of the eighteenth century they held no political office beyond the village level. At the village level, chiefs remained, but they had to be chosen directly by the village population. Moreover, the same government decree that abolished the chiefs' role in local administration also abolished the native court system and with it the Fulbe traditional elite lost its dominant position in the native judicial system. European-style mixed courts applying French and Islamic law replaced the native courts.[29]

The dismissal of the chiefs also had economic consequences. With the loss of their administrative office, the chiefs lost their share of taxes and the informal revenues related to officeholding. They could not offer political backing, nor could they appoint people to patronage jobs or dispense administrative services; hence, they lost the gifts received from people subordinate to them or needing their help and service. They could not rely on their political position any more to persuade people to work for them or supply certain kinds of gifts and products.

The reaction of the chiefs to their downfall was to turn for help to the French, though no help could be expected from them. French colonial policy had undergone a deep change in the last years of decolonization. It had transferred political power to the new westernized elite and tried to come to an accommodation with them. It was not willing to provoke a fight with the new elite in order to save the traditional chiefs. The position of traditional chiefs had deteriorated so much that even their ally within Guinea, the BAG, thought it wise to break its ties with them and came closer to the other Fulbe-dominated party, the DSG. In May 1958, the two Fulbe-dominated parties merged to form the UPG (Union Progressiste Guinéenne) headed by Ibrahima Barry, former head of the DSG.[30]

In 1958 the dominant political issue in Guinea, as in all French African colonies, was how to respond to De Gaulle's proposal of a French community in which colonial territories would become fully self-governing states depending on France only in matters of external relations, defense, and monetary policy. The project of "Communauté" was written into the Fifth Republic constitution and submitted to the constitutional referendum of 1958. A "no" vote by colonial territories in this referendum, being considered a rejection of the Community proposal, was to result, as De Gaulle asserted, in the achievement of complete independence and severance of all ties with France.[31] In Guinea, after some hesitation, both the PDG and the Fulbe-dominated UPG decided to call for a negative vote.[32] The UPG's advocacy of a negative vote marked the final break between the westernized Fulbe elite and the traditional chiefs, who preferred to ask their supporters to cast a positive vote. The result of the referendum was an overwhelming "no" majority (about 95 percent of the valid votes).[33] Guinea thus became the only French colony which, rejecting De Gaulle's project of "communauté," attained complete independence. Independence was achieved under firm PDG control at the center, and shortly after the proclamation of independence the opposition party dissolved itself and joined the PDG.

The results of the referendum showed how little influence the traditional elite in general, including the traditional Fulbe chiefs, retained on the Guinean population. Still, Futa Jallon was distinguished from all other regions in registering by far the highest percentage of "yes" votes as advocated by the traditional chiefs. Studying the referendum results (see table 6), two points become immediately clear: First, the "no" vote is overwhelming in every region, including Futa Jallon; in other words, in Futa Jallon too the great majority of the population disregarded the advice given by their traditional chiefs. Second, notwithstanding the fact that Futa Jallon as a whole voted against the wish of its traditional elite, we notice that the very small percentage of "yes" votes came almost wholly from Futa Jallon. If we look closely at the percentage of "yes" votes registered in different districts we note the following: The places where the least "yes" votes were registered were: Farana, zero votes, the birthplace of Sékou Touré, inhabited by Malinké; Gueckédou, one vote, in the forest region; Youkounkoun, one vote, an area of Futa Jallon inhabited by Coniaguis and Bassaris who resisted Fulbe conquest and were subject to repeated slave raids in the precolonial period. The vote in this last place illustrates perfectly the conflict which opposed the Coniaguis and Bassaris to the Fulbe aristocracy of Futa Jallon.

On the other hand, the districts where the "yes" vote amounted to more than 5 percent—that is, more than the percentage of total "yes" votes for the whole of Guinea—were the following: Labé, 40 percent; Dalaba, 22 percent; Tougoué, 18 percent; Mali, 11 percent; Telimélé, 8 percent; Pita, 6 percent. *All* these places are situated in Futa Jallon. In Labé, the heartland of Futa Jallon, were cast more than half of all "yes" votes in Guinea and about half of all abstentions. Even more interesting are the voting results in Dalaba. We should recall that the chief of Dalaba had rallied the PDG in 1957 and had become a high official in the party. He consequently advocated a negative vote

Table 6   **Results of the Referendum for the Constitution of the French Fifth Republic (September 28, 1958)**

			YES		No
Districts	Registered Votes	Number Voting	N	Percentage	N
Beyla	73,401	71,973	37	Less than 1%	71,764
Boffa	33,422	31,544	133	Less than 1%	31,368
Boké	40,476	31,070	99	Less than 1%	30,951
Conakry	44,389	41,514	991	2%	39,232
Dabola	20,349	19,247	8	Less than 1%	19,225
Dalaba	45,128	31,523	6,903	22%	24,676
Dinguiraye	26,537	23,537	76	Less than 1%	23,438
Dubréka	45,479	44,109	23	Less than 1%	44,049
Faranah	35,595	33,835	0	Less than 1%	33,124
Forécariah	42,206	40,309	30	Less than 1%	39,632
Gaoual	31,551	26,771	73	Less than 1%	26,634
Guéckédou	59,771	57,089	1	Less than 1%	57,070
Kankan	79,869	66,358	693	1%	63,590
Kindia	55,213	53,928	1,021	2%	49,904
Kissidougou	71,039	64,017	70	Less than 1%	63,626
Kouroussa	43,476	31,940	643	2%	31,200
Labé	113,349	68,471	27,440	40%	40,143
Macenta	90,622	85,963	97	Less than 1%	85,808
Mali	53,328	41,779	5,701	11%	33,824
Mamou	54,562	44,288	455	1%	43,453
Nzérékoré	104,510	85,312	2,158	2.5%	83,001
Pita	52,586	52,300	3,117	6%	48,634
Siguiri	80,488	71,841	377	Less than 1%	71,514
Tougoué	29,256	21,024	3,905	18%	17,006
Télimélé	52,426	36,584	2,907	8%	34,527
Youkounkoun	26,958	22,906	1	Less than 1%	29,899
TOTAL	1,405,986	1,200,171	56,959	4.7%	1,130,292

SOURCE.—Adapted from Sékou Touré, *L'Ex-périence Guinéenne et l'Unité Africaine* (Paris: Présence Africaine, 1959), p. 190.

in the referendum. Nevertheless, we find in Dalaba the highest percentage of "yes" votes after Labé. This seemingly paradoxical result may be a good illustration of popular opposition to the opportunistic chief who, by rallying the PDG at the eleventh hour, was able to preserve many privileges. Now, by voting "yes" in such a high percentage, the population of Dalaba possibly marked its opposition to its traditional chief and to those who helped the chief retain his privileges at the expense of the local population.

The decline of the Fulbe position at the end of the colonial rule in Guinea was at first limited to the traditional ruling families only. Fulbe commoners were actually the beneficiaries of many of the changes that brought the aristocracy's downfall. As for the Fulbe western-educated elements, to the extent that they supported the PDG (and toward the end of the colonial period an increasing number did), they were treated as heroes. During the summer of 1958, all the western-educated Fulbe organized in the opposition parties joined with the PDG in a common campaign for a "no" vote, and all attacks against them ceased. At the same time, the harassment carried on by local populations (at the PDG's instigation) against Fulbe immigrants and traders in the coastal zone ceased too. During the campaign for a "no" vote in the 1958 referendum, themes of national solidarity and intergroup harmony were stressed and every effort was made to win Fulbe confidence in the PDG regime. As a whole, the Fulbe who supported the PDG and who were not part of the traditional aristocratic elite did not feel a great deterioration in their overall position with the coming of PDG to power in Guinea during the last years of the colonial period.[34] However, as we shall see later, their position was to deteriorate severely in the postcolonial period, especially after the mid-sixties.

Cameroon

The postwar constitutional reforms in colonial government and the new political opportunities that they offered to the westernized indigenous elite were received in Cameroon with the same excitement and rush for political organization that we have seen in the case of Guinea. Here, too, voluntary associations provided the base of support and the organizational framework for westernized Cameroonians, and out of them

emerged Cameroon's political parties. The big difference from
Guinea, however, was that here the Fulbe, like all northern
populations, were almost totally absent from the central political arena until very late in the process. The political struggle in
Cameroon was carried out by different southern groups and
factions, the northerners entering the picture only later, as a
balancing force. The absence of northerners from the central
political arena was largely due to its geographical isolation and
to the fact that very few northerners were westernized and were
counted among the initiators of demand for the political opening of the colonial center. Unlike their counterparts in Futa
Jallon, the Fulbe of North Cameroon (with a few exceptions to
be noted below) felt no immediate need to ensure their continuing dominance in their region by involvement in the central
political arena, as long as they dominated the representation of
the north in the Territorial Assembly and barred the way to
southern ideas or groups who wished to enlarge their field of
action to the north. As late as 1956, ten out of thirty northern
seats in the Territorial Assembly were occupied by traditional
chiefs.[35] Beyond that there was no need to become involved
in the political struggle in the colonial center, in what was
considered to be southern politics.

The first political party of Cameroon was the UPC (Union
des Populations Camerounaises) formed in 1948 by the leading
trade union (the Union des Syndicats Confédérés du Cameroun), a few ethnic unions and some radical anticolonial elements. Its basic demands were two: rapid progress toward
complete independence, and reunification of British and French
Cameroons. The UPC represented the more discontented and
more radical sectors of the southern population. Its greatest
support came from wage workers and poor immigrants in big
cities. In rural areas it possessed some ethnic basis of support,
notably among the Bassa and the Bamiléké, and it was stronger
among Protestants than among Catholics. However, it claimed
and aspired to popular support beyond ethnic, regional, or religious ties.[36] Against the UPC rose a coalition of groups who felt
threatened by it, including cocoa and coffee farmers, moderate
Douala intellectuals and traders, Bamiléké traditional chiefs,
and the Catholic Church in its stronghold in the Yaoundé area.
With effective help from the French colonial authorities, this
coalition succeeded in stopping the UPC's growth. The frus-

trated UPC turned to increasingly violent actions which deteriorated into general uprisings in many areas of the south. As
a result, the UPC was outlawed by the French in 1957, and from
then on it worked as an underground armed guerilla force,
mounting acts of sabotage and terrorism against Europeans and
political opponents.[37] This premature and perhaps unnecessary
military conflict with the French in fact destroyed the UPC's
chances of ever coming to a dominant position in Cameroonian
politics in the course of decolonization.

With the UPC's elimination from the legal political scene, the
anti-UPC alliance broke down to various factions among which
two were prominent. One was organized around the MANC
(Mouvement d'Action Nationale) and was composed of mod-
eratley anticolonial Douala intellectuals, Boulou cocoa farmers,
and other groups coming mainly from the Protestant coastal and
southernmost areas. This group was in sympathy with the
UPC's basic demands of independence and reunification with
British Cameroons; it wanted to achieve a reconciliation with
the UPC that would put an end to the terrorist activities.
Against rapid progress toward independence and reunification
and against any kind of reconciliation with the UPC rose
another southern group, the Catholic-supported Democratic
Bloc (later Democratic Party), which was well established in the
Yaoundé area. At this stage, the northerners made their first
move in the central political area and sided with the Democratic
Bloc.[38]

The beginning interference of the north in the political arena
was the work of a few westernized northerners who, for a long
time, pushed their fellow northerners to a more active role in
Cameroonian politics. Prominent among them was Ahmadou
Ahidjo. He was a Pullo of commoner origin and was one of the
very few northerners sent to study in the south. He was counted
among the anticolonial and reformist elements in the north.[39] In
1946 he was elected to the Territorial Assembly despite the opposition of some traditional chiefs. In 1948 he founded the Association Amicale de la Benoué, which was the first politically
oriented cultural association to be founded in North Cameroon.[40] In 1956 he lost in his bid for election to the French
National Assembly, and he could not unite the different northern political associations into one organization, all because of
the opposition of the traditional Fulbe chiefs who probably re-

sented his commoner origins as much as his reformist ideas. He succeeded, however, in getting their support for the formation of a parliamentary bloc of northern representatives in the Territorial Assembly, and that marked the beginning of concerted northern activity in the central political arena.[41]

When the northerners finally did take a more active role in the central political arena, they did so in the form of a northern Islamic bloc which was dominated by the Fulbe but also included other Muslim groups, such as the Kotoko, the Mandara, the Shuwa Arabs, the Kanuri, and the newly Muslimized chiefs of the Kirdi populations. They were also joined by the Bamoun, the only Muslim group geographically located in South Cameroon. The alliance included aristocrats as well as commoners, conservative as well as reform-minded elements. In order to participate more effectively in the colonial center and protect the common interests of the north against the south, Ahidjo and his friends were ready to curb their criticism of the traditional elite, while the latter were willing to acknowledge the westernized elements' leading role in the central political arena.[42] So, just when the south was breaking up into small hostile factions, the north, under Fulbe leadership (though some of commoner origins), made a forceful entry into the political arena and immediately occupied a position of strength in it as a solid united bloc with the greatest number of members in the Territorial Assembly. Moreover, the formation of the parliamentary bloc came at the most opportune time for the northerners, just when the first self-governing Cameroonian government was in the process of formation, following the Loi-Cadre reform of 1956.[43] The Democrats and the northern bloc, joined by a group of conservative Bamiléké chiefs, formed a coalition government headed by the Democratic leader André-Marie Mbida and seconded by the Muslim Pullo, Ahmadou Ahidjo, as vice-premier. Against them the Movement of National Action formed the opposition.[44]

In 1957–58 the Mbida government took a very rigid stand against independence, reunification with British Cameroons, and reconciliation with the UPC. This not only infuriated the anticolonial opposition, but embarrassed the French, who in those years made great efforts to establish better relations with anticolonial forces all over West Africa and improve their international image tarnished by the Algerian war. They withdrew

their support from Mbida and started to look for ways of replacing him with a person more acceptable to the nationalist forces
in Cameroon.[45] At the same time, the northern leaders were
also growing increasingly unhappy with their Democratic
partners, whom they suspected of preparing to introduce some
important changes in the northern provinces to the advantage
of non-Muslim groups. In 1958 a political pamphlet published
by the Democratic Party asked that the northern regions be
democratized with the establishment of elected municipal
councils as in the south and that the north be required to increase its financial and economic contribution to the country as
a whole.[46] Also, in its objection to unification with British
Cameroons, the Democratic Party often stated that the real unification should take place between the north and the south of
Cameroon by introducing the more progressive southern social
system into the north. The northern deputies feared that, as
soon as it felt strong enough, the Democratic Party and its rigid
leader Mbida would launch a major attack on the northern traditional order and on the dominance of Muslim (mostly Fulbe)
populations over pagans and Christians.

The showdown between the French colonial administration
and Mbida provided the north with a golden opportunity to
cause his downfall. At the secret instigation of the French governor, the northern bloc withdrew from the coalition with
Mbida and caused the Mbida government to fall.[47] By this
move, the northern deputies, led by Ahidjo, suddenly put
themselves at the forefront of the anticolonial movement. They
showed their political strength by causing the downfall of
Mbida, and they were credited for this as an effective anticolonial action. The new coalition government was formed by all
anticolonial forces and was headed by Ahidjo, handpicked by
the French and approved by the southerners who would rather
see a northerner at the head of the government than one of their
rivals from the south. In this way, Ahmadou Ahidjo came to
power at the head of what was regarded as an anticolonial front,
though with the full approval of the colonial power itself.

From his new position of power, Ahidjo could now induce
the other northerners and especially the traditional Fulbe aristocracy to form the long-delayed united political party of the
north. In July 1958, the Union Camerounaise was finally
created.[48] Its top leadership consisted mainly of westernized

Muslim northerners, many of them commoners. But the traditional elite was also well represented among the leaders; many
lamibé and sultans held top positions in the party. Among the
top lieutenants of Ahidjo, Moussa Yaya was a Fulbe commoner,
like Ahidjo himself, while Omaru Sanda came from an aristocratic Fulbe family. Arouna Njoya belonged to the royal lineage
of the Bamoun, while Sadou Daoudou was probably a Fulbeized Muslim Kirdi. Despite the participation of some non-
Fulbe northerners in high positions, the party was, on the
whole, clearly dominated by the Fulbe. The symbol chosen for
the party, cattle, left no doubt about that.[49]

Following the formation of the Ahidjo government, progress
was made in most "anticolonial" issues. The French agreed to
grant Cameroon total independence on 1 January 1960. The
issue of reunification gained momentum with the victory in
British Cameroons of the party favoring it.[50] Steps were taken
also to rehabilitate the UPC. Following a broad amnesty granted
to UPC militants, a large section of them returned to legality
and received political rights. This put an end to the guerilla
activities in the Bassa region, but they continued in increased
intensity in the Bamiléké areas. Against them Ahidjo opted for
repressive measures, and he received emergency powers from
the parliament in order to combat them. In January 1960 Cameroon attained independence under the rule of Fulbe Ahmadou
Ahidjo, in a state of emergency and a wave of terrorism.[51]

Comparing the Fulbe participation in the political arena in
Cameroon and Guinea, we can see that in both cases the Fulbe
kept their dominance as long as they led a united front of all the
population of their region; Fulbe and non-Fulbe, aristocrats as
well as commoners, traditionalists as well as westernized re-
formists, all were united by a common opposition to other
regions' populations. Such a regional front was achieved in
Guinea in the first years after World War II, but it broke down
in the later, crucial stages preceding independence. In Cameroon, on the other hand, such a front was created and entered
the political arena only at the last stage of decolonization. As a
result, while in Guinea the Fulbe were dominant in the political
arena in the first years following World War II but lost their
place to their rivals just before the end of the colonial period, in
Cameroon the Fulbe were absent from the political scene for the
most part of the period of decolonization but came to pre-

dominance just when self-government was achieved. This contrast between the Fulbe in Guinea and Cameroon illustrates the
fact that early westernization and participation in the colonial
center did not necessarily determine which groups held a dominant position in the colonial center at the time of passage to
independence. On the contrary, their early predominance in
the colonial center made the Fulbe targets of the anticolonial
struggle in Guinea, and with its final success came their decline. In Cameroon, on the other hand, the Fulbe were never
targets of the anticolonial struggle, and they were never especially marked for collaborating with the colonial administration,
mainly because they were not visible in the political arena and
occupied no central position for most of the time. The main
groups who were marked as collaborators with the colonial administration were the Catholic Church and the Democratic
Party closely connected with it.[52] The anticolonial struggle was
carried out mainly against them and against some traditional
chiefs in the Bamiléké area. When the Fulbe (together with
other Muslim northerners) finally started to take an active part
in the central political arena, they were able to integrate themselves into the anticolonial current in a way that would not
endanger their traditional position in North Cameroon. At a
crucial period in the development of anticolonial struggle, by
changing southern allies in a seemingly anticolonial move, they
were even able to bring themselves to the leadership position
within the anticolonial movement, and it was under Fulbe leadership that the final anticolonial victory was achieved with
independence.

The discussion of decolonization in Cameroon makes it quite
obvious that no radical social transformation similar to that in
Futa Jallon occurred in North Cameroon during that time. At
first the north was isolated from ideas of change which emerged
in the south. No southern political force had the organizational
strength and ideological motivation to carry its protest activities
into the north (the only organization with such attributes, the
UPC, was banned and was barely trying for a clandestine survival in the south). The few westernized northerners bent on
reform in their region were mobilized instead as representatives and protectors of the north against the south. Toward the
end of decolonization, as the Fulbe became more and more
prominent at the political center, they were in a position to

control the changes that affected their own region and their position in it, and as a result no changes occurred that could challenge the Fulbe dominance in North Cameroon. On the contrary, through their leading role in the political front that represented the entire north, the Fulbe strengthened their influence in all of North Cameroon much beyond the precolonial boundaries of Adamawa. However, at the same time, power started to move from the traditional Fulbe elite to western-educated elements among whom people of commoner origins, such as Ahidjo, were better represented. The central government gradually gained more visibility as the highest decision-making body at the expense of the traditional chiefs. This trend was only in its early stages in the period of decolonization; it developed much more after independence, as we shall see later. Nonetheless, in 1959 Ahidjo had one dramatic opportunity to show his supremacy over the traditional chiefs when he removed the chief of Maroua, one of the strongest Fulbe chiefs in North Cameroon and the only one who had persisted in opposition to him.[53]

Nigeria

In Nigeria, unlike Guinea and Cameroon, political activities of the westernized indigenous elite started long before World War II, but they were limited to only a few locations in Southern Nigeria. In the 1920s and 1930s the first political parties, the NNDP (Nigerian National Democratic Party) of Herbert Macaulay and the NYM (Nigerian Youth Movement), in which Nnamdi Azikiwe made his political debut, were formed. These parties provided the nucleus from which the big southern parties were to develop after World War II. After the war, the colonial government system was greatly modified in a series of constitutional reforms intended to give more political participation to the indigenous populations. The first reforms introduced in the Richards Constitution of 1946 created appointed regional councils in each of the three governmental regions— the north, the east, and the west. The regional legislatures selected among themselves their region's representatives in the central legislative assembly. With that, the Richards Constitution marked the first time that northerners participated in the central legislature and were granted political participation outside the framework of native authorities.[54]

While the participation of northerners in the central legislative council put an end to the complete separation that existed between the governments of the north and the south, the formation of regional legislative councils and the fact that the members of the central legislature were chosen by the regional councils crystallized the separate existence of the three regions, the north, the east, and the west, and created in each region a separate center of power. These centers competed with one another and with the central political institutions of the colonial government. A trend was started toward a weak "national" political center with strong regional subcenters hostile to one another. The two constitutions which in quick succession replaced the Richards Constitution reinforced that trend; they moved progressively toward a loose federal system. As the indigenous population received greater political power within the colonial government system, it received that power not in the "national" central political institutions but rather in regional institutions. Capturing the regional political centers rather than the "national" center became the greatest prize for the rival indigenous groups, since controlling them ensured representation in or influence on the central position. The MacPherson Constitution of 1951 established the principle of 50 percent northern representation in the central legislature (more than half of the Nigerian population lived in the north). The regional assemblies were given more extensive power, and their members were elected. Also, for the first time Africans were included in executive councils in the center as well as in each region. The 1954 constitution pushed further the trend toward more power to the regions and established a federal structure with very strong regional government, although the federal legislature was no longer chosen by regional assemblies, but by separate elections in each region.[55] In 1957 an amendment introduced to the constitution increased the northern representation in the Federal Assembly to more than half by making regional representation proportional to each region's population.[56]

As a result of the devolution of power from the colonial center to the regional subcenters, the struggle of indigenous groups for political control in the colonial administration in Nigeria involved two different conflicts, one at the federal and one at the regional level. While the region was the real arena of struggle for political control between different factions of the region's population, the federal level involved a three-sided fight between the dominant groups of the north, the east, and the west, each trying to outmaneuver the other two in order to bring about those constitutional or other changes that would benefit its own region at the expense of the other two. The extent to which the dominant group of each region could push through constitutional advantages for its own region at the federal level determined the position that it occupied at the federal center.

The first major political party active after World War II was the NCNC (National Council of Nigeria and Cameroons). It was founded in 1944 and was headed by Nnamdi Azikiwe. Although it always claimed to be above ethnic-regional differences and in its first years was the general champion of the anticolonial struggle, the NCNC was, in fact, controlled mostly by the Ibo and was identified as the party of the eastern region. In 1948, fearing that the rise of the NCNC would cause Ibo hegemony throughout Southern Nigeria, some Yoruba led by Obafemi Awolowo created a rival party, the Action Group, which rapidly developed and became the dominant party of the western region. It advocated a more federal structure of government with greater autonomy for each region.[57]

In Northern Nigeria the situation following World War II was more similar to that of Guinea and Cameroon than to Southern Nigeria, in that before World War II there was practically no political activity outside the traditional framework of native administration. Political activities among the western-educated Northern Nigerians started at first in the framework of voluntary cultural associations, alumni clubs, and discussion circles which were formally nonpolitical but provided the organizational basis for action. The first such voluntary association formed in the north was the Old Boys' Association of the graduates of Kaduna College. It was founded in 1939 but was forced to close down two years later because of the opposition of leading emirs. Subsequently, during and after World War II, other cultural associations were founded,[58] most of them critical of the traditional elite and asking for reforms in the native administration system.

After World War II, some of the more radical western-educated northerners contacted the NCNC and in 1950, with its backing, established the first political party of the north, the NEPU (Northern Elements' Progressive Union). This party had unexpected success against candidates of the native authorities in the first round of the 1951 elections. Although its candidates were eventually defeated in the second round, when the emirs and chiefs could appoint 10 percent of the electoral college which tipped the balance against the NEPU, its strong showing at the early stages of the election alarmed the traditional chiefs and moderate westernized elements. They feared the NEPU, not only because of its radical views, but also because of its close association with a southern political party; they were afraid that a NEPU victory might bring southern domination over the north. This fear prompted the creation of the rival political party, the NPC (Northern People's Congress) which developed rapidly and became the dominant party of the north.[59]

The NPC was formed by an alliance of moderate westernized elements and traditional chiefs who decided to play down their differences, alarmed by the prospects of southern domination over the north through the intermediary of radical northern elements who wanted to introduce deep changes in the traditional northern social and political order. Throughout the period of decolonization, the fear of southern domination remained the basic force which directed the actions of the NPC. To prevent such domination it asked for greater regional autonomy and greater power to the regional centers at the expense of the national one. The balance between different forces composing the NPC was well personified by the two top leaders of the party. The first was Alhaji Ahmadu Bello, a Pullo of the royal lineage of Sokoto and a direct descendant of Usman dan Fodio, founder of the Sokoto empire. His grandfather had been sultan of Sokoto in the 1870s, and his father had served as district head in the native administration. He was also western educated and had attended the famous Katsina Teacher Training College, after which he served as teacher and as district head. Ahmadu Bello was a firm believer in the fundamental legitimacy of the traditional order set up by the empire of Sokoto and often publicly stated his desire to become sultan of Sokoto. At the same time, he was also western educated and was in close contact with western ideas and people. The second man of the party, Alhaji Abubakar Tafawa Balewa, on the other hand, was the son of a slave working for the emir of Bauchi. He owed his western education to the fact that traditional chiefs, who were forced to provide children for western schools, often sent the children of their slaves instead. After his graduation, he served as teacher and then as headmaster in the Bauchi Middle School. Abubakar Tafawa Balewa was known as an out-spoken critic of the native authority; in 1950, in a much cele-brated speech at the northern regional council, he sharply criticized the native authority system and proposed the ap-pointment of a commission to study possibilities for reform. This brought him the hostility of many emirs and probably prevented him from becoming the head of the NPC.[60]

Many western-educated northerners who occupied positions in the colonial civil service could not be NPC members since the British law prohibited political party affiliation among civil ser-vants. However, this law did not apply to native administration officials who achieved control of the party organization, thus increasing the influence of chiefs and emirs on the party at the expense of commoners and more westernized elements. The emirs had a very strong influence on the recruitment of candi-dates for party and public offices. In 1959, out of the NPC mem-bers elected to the Northern Nigerian legislature from the Mus-lim emirates, 37 percent were blood kin of ruling emirs, altogether 87 percent belonged to the traditional ruling class, and half of the remaining NPC legislators were lower-ranking employees in the native administration. Of the sixty-eight rural district branches of the NPC investigated in that year, the chairmen of sixty were also the district heads in the native administration.[61] Since the Fulbe aristocrats were dominant in the native administration, they indirectly became domi-nant in the NPC and in NPC-ruled government institutions.

Besides the Fulbe, the NPC represented and was supported by the bulk of the Hausa, the Kanuri, the Nupe, and all other minor Muslim groups. It also represented some (but not all) non-Muslim northern groups who had chosen to join the north-ern bloc against the south even though it was dominated by Muslims. In 1959, the Northern Region Government included two Christians as ministers. Also, one non-Muslim traditional chief, the aku of Wukari, served as minister without portfolio in the regional government, as did three Fulbe chiefs (the sultan of Sokoto and the emirs of Kano and Katsina).[62] Just as in North Cameroon, the beginning of open struggle among indigenous groups for the control of the colonial center caused a unification and alliance of the various Muslim populations living in the north on common basis of Islam and their opposition to the south. In both places, this Islamic front was initiated and dominated by the Fulbe. The prominence of Fulbe among the major party leaders in the NPC compared to the NEPU is shown in table 7.

Table 7   **Ethnic Distribution of Major Party Leaders, Northern Nigeria (in Percentages)**

Party	Fulbe	Hausa	Nupe	Kanuri	Yoruba	Others	Unknown
NPC	32.4	18.9	9.4	6.8	6.8	16.2	9.4
NEPU	14.0	67.1	4.6	3.1	0.0	7.1	3.2

SOURCE.—Data tabulated from members of the National Executive Committee of the two parties in 1958–59; taken from R. L. Sklar and C. S. Whitaker, Jr., "Nigeria," in *Political Parties and National Integration in Tropical Africa*, ed. James S. Coleman and Carl G. Rosberg (Berkeley: University of California Press, 1964), p. 612.

In the Muslim-inhabited areas of the north the main challenge to the NPC came from the NEPU, formed by northerners who refused to ally themselves with the traditional elite. Although headed by Aminu Kano, a Pullo coming from a well-known family of Islamic scholars and jurists, the NEPU was strongly opposed to the ruling aristocracy. One of its proclaimed aims was to unite the commoners in a "class struggle" against the nobility.[63] This was interpreted as a struggle of the Hausa against the Fulbe, since most of the commoners were Hausa while most of the nobles were Fulbe.[64] There was, indeed, a greater proportion of Hausa among the NEPU leadership, as shown in table 7. The NEPU's support came mainly from urban dwellers, petty traders, artisans, and teachers, but not from the traditionalist peasantry or from the native administrative officials.[65]

In the areas inhabited mainly by non-Muslims (the Middle Belt), the dominant political parties were regional parties based on the support of specific ethnic groups. The political parties thus formed were all oriented to serve the interests of the Middle Belt people and assert their separate identity. However, they were divided into rival factions and splinter groups on the

basic question of whether they should cooperate with the NPC
as part of a northern bloc opposed to the south or else oppose
the NPC, ally themselves with southern parties, and struggle
for the formation of a separate Middle Belt region. The most
important party opposed to the NPC was the UMBC (United
Middle Belt Congress) headed by Joseph Tarka and supported
mostly by his kinmen, the Tiv. It formed an alliance with the
Action Group and launched a vigorous campaign against the
Muslim domination of the Middle Belt. Most of the other ethnic
groups in the Middle Belt, and especially those who were
strongly dominated by their traditional chiefs or had traditional
hostility to the Tiv, favored cooperation with the NPC.[66]

Throughout the period of decolonization, the NPC's (and
hence the Fulbe aristocracy's) control of the northern regional
center was not threatened by any of the opposition parties. The
NPC won all the elections by very large margins (see table 8).

Table 8   **Northern Nigeria Election Results (1954–59) in
Terms of Parliamentary Seats**

Year	NPC	NEPU	Action Group	Other
1954	79	...	1	10
1956	107	9	4	11
1959	134	8	25*	7

SOURCE.—C. S. Whitaker, Jr., *The Politics of
Tradition: Community and Change in Northern
Nigeria* (Princeton, N.J.: Princeton University
Press, 1970), p. 374.
*In alliance with the UMBC (United Middle
Belt Congress).

The NEPU's alliance with the NCNC seriously hurt its chances
of acceptance in the north, since it was portrayed as a collaborator with the south. In the cities, in order to take away part
of the NEPU constituency among commoners, the NPC enlisted
popular wealthy merchants of commoner origins and gave them
high political positions in the party. One of them, Alhaji
Ahmadu Dantata, even beat Aminu Kano in his own fief in Kano
in the 1956 elections.[67] The NPC met with a stronger challenge in
the Middle Belt area inhabited mainly by non-Muslims, but
even there it won by a substantial margin. Nevertheless, unlike
the UC in North Cameroon which faced no opposition in the

north, the NPC in Northern Nigeria had to reckon with established opposition parties.

Turning now to the federal arena, we see that the whole period of decolonization was characterized by continuous struggle and bargaining between three foci of power represented by the three parties, NCNC, AG, and NPC, each dominant in its region (though in the west the AG was strongly challenged by the NCNC) and supporting minority parties in the other regions. At the "national" territorial level, political control allowed to the indigenous population was held either by all three parties jointly or by two of them forming a temporary alliance against the third. As the alliances changed, so changed the parties which dominated the central political institutions. However, generally speaking, as the share of power accorded to the northern region increased with its population size, so the NPC's power at the federal level gradually rose at the expense of the other parties.[68] Until 1951 the NCNC was the dominant political force in Nigeria, but then it lost its predominance and became a regional party like the other two. Between 1951 and 1953, the AG, NPC, and dissident members of the NCNC held federal executive positions against the opposition of the NCNC. In 1953, on the question of demanding early self-government from the British, the AG and NCNC were temporarily united against the NPC, creating for the first (and only) time a clear north-south cleavage. While the AG and the NCNC demanded early self-government, the NPC fiercely opposed it, fearing that this could bring the more advanced southerners into political control over the whole country. The debate caused great tension between Southern and Northern Nigeria. In the north, leaders seriously considered the possibility of secession from the rest of Nigeria, and disturbances occurred in Kano where mobs of northerners attacked southerner (mainly Ibo) inhabitants.[69] The crisis was resolved by the constitution of 1954, which established a loose federal structure and accorded to each region the right to demand self-government separately. Between 1954 and 1959, the usual trend toward three separate regional powers continued to assert itself, each party retaining decisive supremacy in its own region and helping opposition parties in the other regions. In 1957, self-government was granted to the two southern regions, while the north decided to receive self-government on 15 March 1959, the fifty-sixth anniversary of the fall of Sokoto to Lugard's troops.[70] The choice of the date, by inferring continuity between the Sokoto caliphate and Northern Nigeria, was a clear symbol of Fulbe dominance in the north. In the meantime, the northerner Abubakar Tafawa Balewa became Federal Prime Minister. At first he formed a national government with ministers from all three major parties. After the 1959 elections, however, he headed a coalition government of the NPC and the NCNC while the AG remained in opposition. The top leader of the NPC, Ahmadu Bello, preferred to remain prime minister of the Northern Regional Government, thus showing again that in the loose federal structures of Nigeria, the regional offices were not considered in any way inferior to the federal ones.[71] Finally, in October 1960, Nigeria attained independence as a loose federation with a weak and unstable federal government resting on short-term arrangements by three political parties, each entrenched within its own region and enjoying the support of the local dominant ethnic group.

It is more difficult to compare the participation of the Fulbe in the struggle for control of the colonial center in Nigeria with that of Cameroon and Guinea because of the more complicated political structure in Nigeria due to federalism. Nevertheless, it is clear that Fulbe participation in the Nigerian political center resembled more that of Cameroon than that of Guinea in that the Fulbe were not the initiators of political action but rather reacted to initiatives started by other groups outside their region. Their involvement in the central political arena came much earlier than that of their Northern Cameroonian counterparts, but it took a very similar shape, namely, the formation of a regional front, on the common basis of Islam and opposition to the south, which transcended the ethnic and class boundaries of the northern population. In Guinea such an Islamic front could not be formed by the Fulbe against the other regions because most other groups living in other regions were also Muslim. Just as there was no north-south division in Guinea, unlike Cameroon and Nigeria, there could be no Muslim–non-Muslim cleavage either since Muslims were spread all over Guinea and constituted close to 70 percent of the population.

Once the Fulbe entered the newly opened political arena in Nigeria, they concentrated their efforts on capturing the regional center, which they did without much difficulty. Then, basing themselves on their dominant position in their own re-

gion, they started to press for a regional quota representation at
the federal level. When they received that (50 percent of the
seats reserved for the northern region in the central legislature,
for instance), their dominance in their own region made them
by definition the strongest force participating in the federal
center. Thereafter, they consolidated their position at the federal level and at the same time weakened that level so that, no
matter what happened at the federal center, it would not have
any great effect on the region where their domination was much
more solid. However, even at the federal level no concentrated
challenge against them was mounted by their southern rivals,
except for a brief period in 1953. (From that confrontation the
north emerged strengthened, because the outcome was the
establishment of a loose federal structure in Nigeria.) The two
dominant southern groups, the Ibo and the Yoruba, were as
hostile to each other as they were to the Fulbe-dominated north,
and often one of the southern parties preferred to ally itself with
the north against the other southern party rather than ally together against the north. After 1954 the northern region, and
hence the Fulbe-controlled NPC which dominated it, increasingly consolidated its position at the federal center, and it
was under NPC-dominated government that Nigeria attained
independence in October 1960. As in Cameroon, but unlike
Guinea, the Fulbe-dominated party occupied a dominant position in the colonial center when political power in that center
was transferred to the indigenous population.

The increasing political strength of the northern region compared to the south toward the end of the colonial period was
reflected also in the tangible advantages that it brought to all
northerners over southerners who lived in the north. In accordance with the NPC's goal of safeguarding northerners' interests
against southern competition, an explicit policy of "northernization" was put into effect, under which people of northern
origin were given priority in education and employment in the
northern region.[72] In 1957 the Public Service Commission of the
northern region stated that "it is the policy of the regional government to Northernize the Public Service: if a qualified Northerner is available, he is given priority in recruitment; if no
Northerner is available, an Expatriate may be recruited or a
non-Northerner on contract terms."[73] In its actual application,
this policy was carried out more vigorously against southerners

than against expatriates. British officials were kept in their offices until such time as a northerner was trained and ready to take their place, so that the place would not be occupied by a Southern Nigerian in the meantime. Southerners already working in the north were encouraged to find employment in their own region; they were not given promotions, and some of them were actually laid off. The northernization policy was pursued with such vigor that, while in 1955 the percentage of northerners in the civil service was negligible, a year after independence it already exceeded 50 percent.[74] In order to train the northerners who would take up administrative posts, an Institute of Administration was created in Zaria in 1954 and was open only to persons of northern origin.[75] This policy, initiated during decolonization, spread rapidly to other spheres of life after independence and became an official measure of discrimination against Southern Nigerians living in the north. It played an important role in the growing tensions and hostility between the north and the south in the postcolonial period.

Reaching ruling positions also provided important control over the allocation of economic and financial resources, a subject which has not been dealt with so far. In Northern Nigeria this was reflected in the NPC's control of the Northern Regional Development Corporation (NRDC) and the Northern Regional Marketing Board. The NRDC was founded in 1956 with the objective of financing projects designed to promote the economic development of the region. As part of its function the NRDC made loans at favorable interest rates to small businessmen for various agricultural, industrial, and commercial projects. It also participated in the financing and administration of major economic projects, including the Kaduna textile factory. The NRDC was partly financed by the Northern Regional Marketing Board, which also had a monopoly on buying peanuts and cotton at fixed prices and supervised the quality grading of the products.[76] Although in theory the NRDC and the Regional Marketing Board were autonomous bodies, most of their top officials were appointed by the northern regional government and hence were either NPC stalwarts or heads of native authorities. For example, in 1958, of a total of 144 members of provincial loans boards who made recommendations on the allocation of loans, 8 percent were emirs and chiefs, 12.5 percent were district and village heads, 37.6 percent were other native authority officials, and 15 percent were legislators. Of the twenty-three people who at one time or another sat on the board of NRDC between 1950 and 1958, 26 percent were emirs and 17 percent were district heads. Not surprisingly, native authorities and merchants closely associated with the NPC were the greatest beneficiaries of NRDC and Marketing Board funds.[77] Unfortunately, we do not have corresponding information on Cameroon and Guinea which could show the influence of the ruling parties on the allocation of financial resources. Perhaps the ruling parties in Guinea and Cameroon had less control over those matters because the French tended to maintain closer financial supervision on the colonial territories up to the end of the colonial period and in many cases even later.

Obviously, no radical social transformation occurred in Northern Nigeria as a result of decolonization. The traditional Muslim elite, and the Fulbe aristocracy in particular, maintained their dominant position and even consolidated their supremacy over non-Muslim-inhabited areas (with the possible exception of Tivland). Nevertheless, some changes did occur as a result of political innovations in this period. In order to form a united northern front and recruit westernized elements to their side, the Fulbe noblemen had to give up their monopoly of top positions and allow some commoners among the westernized elements, some non-Fulbe Muslims, and more rarely a few non-Muslims to occupy top political positons. People of servile status, like Abubakar Tafawa Balewa and Maitama Sule, or non-Fulbe merchants, such as Musa Gashash, occupied some of the highest-ranking positions in the party and in the government. While some precedent could be found in the traditional system for persons of servile origin serving in administrative positions as delegates of the chiefs, the participation of Hausa merchants at the top political positions was a truly new development. In 1958, 27 percent of the Executive Committee members of the NPC were entrepreneurs of non-Fulbe and nonaristocratic origin.[78] Also, the political alliance with other ruling groups of Northern Nigeria which had never lived under Fulbe rule necessitated a fair representation of them in the top political posts. However, by far the more serious loss of power for the Fulbe chiefs (though not necessarily the whole aristocratic class) was caused by the gradual transfer of political supremacy from native authorities to new central or regional political institutions occupied by their western-educated representatives. There was no abrupt change and very little formal modification of functions, but the regional government gradually gained more visibility as the ultimate decision-making body at the expense of the traditional chiefs. We have seen a similar trend in North Cameroon. In Northern Nigeria, the leader of the NPC and head of the northern government, Alhaji Ahmadu Bello, being himself a Pullo of royal origin, was much more favorably disposed toward the chiefs than his Cameroonian counterpart. However, he too, without changing the general traditional style of government, tended gradually to transfer to the Northern Regional Government many prerogatives held by the emirs. The latter were aware that power was gradually slipping away from them, and they tried to stop this as best as they could. During the formation of the regional Executive Council, the emirs strongly objected to the creation of a ministry of local government which would have put the native administration affairs under the supervision of a member of the Northern Regional Government. Upon their insistence the proposal was withdrawn, and responsibility for local government was left in the hands of the British governor. The emirs preferred the disinterested British officials' supervision to that of a native African member of the regional government, even if of aristocratic origin, because in accepting the latter's supervision they would have formally accepted the supremacy of the regional government over them. However, in 1954, despite the emirs' objections, the ministry of local government was created and Ahmadu Bello became the first minister.[79]

The emirs tried to keep their power by retaining close control over recruitment to party positions and to legislative assemblies. By fusing the party grass-roots organization with the native administration, they were in a position to control the party organization closely. However, in 1955, an NPC convention voted to freeze for five years the slate of party officers, and so in the five most crucial years of transfer of power from the colonial administration to the federal and regional government there was very little recruitment to party offices that the emirs could influence.[80] They could still exert their influence on the electorate and, as a last resort, turn it against the NPC (as did the emir of Zaria in 1955 and the former emirs of Yola and Dikwa in 1959). But at that stage open confrontation with the

NPC could be costlier to the chiefs than to the party. Between 1954 and 1960, several traditional chiefs who clashed with the Northern Regional Government were forced to resign. Among them were two very important emirs, those of Bauchi and Yola. The emir of Zaria was also threatened with dismissal. The emir of Dikwa who refused to resign was formally deposed.[81]

The chiefs' power was weakened also by some formal changes introduced in the native authority system in Northern Nigeria. With the Native Authority Law passed in 1954 (after the NPC came to power in the north), the form of "Sole Native Authority" (that is, the native administration held by the traditional chief alone with a council accountable to him only) was officially abolished, and all native authorities were forced to have recognized councils participating in local government. At the chiefs' insistence, a distinction was maintained between "chief-and-council," where decisions were taken by the majority of the council members and could not be vetoed by the chief, and "chief-in-council," where the chief could veto the council's decision but had to submit to the regional government the reasons for his action and the regional government could, in turn, override the chief's veto. In the biggest emirates the "chief-in-council" system was maintained. Another change was in the way the council members were selected; reformist circles pressed for the election of council members. In some native authorities, generally of less importance and outside the Fulbe areas, the councils had a majority of elected members by the end of the colonial period. In most councils there was a minority of elected members, and a few had no elected members.[82] In 1957, further reforms which would have seriously curtailed the power of the native administrations were proposed by the Hudson Commission, sent to study the provincial administration in Northern Nigeria, but its recommendations were shelved by the northern legislature because of the strong opposition of the emirs.[83]

7

The Fulbe Role in the Postcolonial Centers

The Formation of the Postcolonial Center

The formation of the postcolonial center differed from that of the colonial center in that it was not established as a separate center in rivalry with its predecessor but evolved from within it as a result of increasing participation and then control by indigenous elements. The achievement of independence formalized the completion of the process by which the colonial power which had built the colonial center transferred its political control to a group of indigenous people who claimed to represent the entire population of the colonial territory. At that point, the colonial center formally ceased to exist and in its place was born the postcolonial center.

Although originating from within the colonial center, the postcolonial center owed its legitimation to being distinct from it. The political control that was achieved by indigenous elements had to be used to introduce such changes as would make the postcolonial center distinctive and independent from its colonial predecessor. At the symbolic and cultural level, illustrations of this ranged from "Africanizing" names of streets, rivers, and towns to efforts at rewriting African history, glorifying the precolonial past, and disclosing hidden signs of "African civilization." In more instrumental fields this led to great efforts to achieve rapid and thorough Africanization in essential services in the country, to build impressive industrial, educational, and other development projects, to exert closer control on foreigners and foreign enterprises, and in international affairs to steer a so-called neutralist line, trying to give the appearance of being unaffected by the wishes and interests of the excolonial power.

The postcolonial center also tried to remove the alien nature of the center and the relative lack of contact with the indigenous populations that it had inherited from its colonial predecessor.

In doing so, the occupants of the postcolonial center introduced changes which had important implications for the structure of the center and its relationship with the periphery. Unlike the European builders of the colonial center, the new African elite which occupied the center claimed to represent the native population and to be in direct contact with it; it was less tolerant of autonomous traditional chiefs who claimed the same role. The new elite was eager to assert the postcolonial center's direct authority over the whole population and, in the process, to reduce the importance and autonomy of traditional subcenters which had been allowed to exist in the periphery. This trend was perceptible everywhere, though it was not carried out with the same vigor and to the same extent in every country. It was much more advanced in Guinea than in Cameroon and even more than in Nigeria. However, in each case, colonial duality declined significantly with the passage to independence, and the center increased its direct control over the periphery. It became much more difficult for a certain region or society within the periphery to be insulated from the center, to maintain its isolation and autonomy; hence the position occupied by a certain group in the center became all the more important in determining its position within the periphery. In the case of the Fulbe, it became more important than ever for them to be well represented in the center in order to ensure their continuing dominance or superiority within their own region.

The attainment of independence is formally considered as the point at which the postcolonial centers were formed, but in reality they were far from being fully crystallized at that point. The degree of consolidation of the postcolonial center is measured by its degree of visibility and independence from its colonial predecessor, by its gaining legitimacy from the population at large, and by its ability to express elements of the culture of the population that it claims to represent. In this sense the consolidation of the postcolonial center only started after independence. In the process, it involved important changes in the relationship between different sectors, or subcenters at the periphery. Independence marked the formation of the postcolonial center only in a narrow political sense, and that formed a precondition for its formation in a broader sense. Here we shall focus on the narrow political sphere, since that was the sphere whose occupation gave to the incumbents ruling power over the whole country, that is, power to introduce changes that could deeply affect the social, political, economic, and cultural destiny of all the populations in society. In our discussion of the three countries we shall see that the struggle which had started among indigenous populations for the control of political positions at the center during decolonization continued after independence, and, because of the greater direct influence of the center on the periphery, the outcome of this struggle had a stronger impact on the position of each ethnic or other social group in its own region within the periphery.

Major Political Developments after Independence

Guinea

In Guinea independence was achieved in a state of euphoria and overwhelming support for the PDG, which had led the anticolonial struggle. Even most of Futa Jallon seemed to have been won to the government side, and the two opposition parties merged with the PDG. However, in a few years popular support declined drastically. The political leadership was deeply divided, plots to overthrow the government started to appear, and a small clique around Sékou Touré barely clung to power by brutal repression of all signs of opposition within the center and in the periphery.

A principal reason for this political deterioration was the government's inability to cope with the economic and administrative difficulties caused by the abrupt termination of French presence in Guinea. Two days after independence, Guinean exports ceased to be admitted to France under the "favored nation" treatment accorded other French African territories. All French investments were canceled. French financial assistance to the Guinean treasury was suspended. After 1 October 1958, almost all administrative and judicial services handled by French officials were stopped. Within two months, all French functionaries were repatriated and many local French business enterprises stopped their activities or at least repatriated most of their capital.[84] The Guinean elite suddenly found itself alone at the center, forced to perform every function and fill every post, for most of which it had no adequate training. This situation was faced at a time when peripheral aspirations were running high, in a spirit of liberation and agitation against central authority which the PDG itself had cultivated during the last year of anticolonial stuggle. The periphery's aspirations had to be curbed now, and its mobilization had to be used not against the center but as a means of control by the center in what was called a continuing stuggle against internal and external enemies. A new mobilization system was then established. Party militants filled all the posts vacated by the French, and the party set up a close surveillance of the population at every level. Gradually the party took over all government functions. In 1962, local party committees replaced village councils and chiefs in the administration of villages. In the 1970s the whole regional government passed to party sections reconstituted as "Local Revolutionary Governments." Party committees were implanted in every service and enterprise, and they incorporated all the intermediary associations, including youth movements and trade unions.[85] Only the army remained for a while outside the direct control of the party, but being distrusted by the civilian leadership, it was kept intentionally weak, inadequately armed, and stationed at points far away from big urban centers. In the late 1960s and in the 1970s, accused of fomenting plots against the regime, the army was all but destroyed. Its leadership was completely eliminated and military power and all police functions passed to the party militia, the army being used mostly in rural development projects in outlying districts. In the 1970s even the ministry of defense was abolished, since it clearly had no practical function to perform (it was reestablished in May 1975).[86]

Meanwhile, partly conditioned by ideological considerations, partly as a way to find a solution to pressing economic problems, great radicalization occurred in economic policy. Between 1958 and 1961, banks, insurance companies, the diamond industry, and most foreign trade companies were nationalized. Guinea withdrew from the *franc* zone and created its own currency (called *Silly* since 1972). The government opened state-owned trade stations which monopolized most of the internal and external wholesale trade. They bought products from local merchants at a fixed price which was generally lower than market prices. This naturally opened the way to a flourishing black market and to smuggling of goods to the neighboring countries where higher prices were received. In 1964 stiff controls were established on retail trade as well, requiring that every shopowner and merchant deposit a very large sum in order to be entitled to engage in commerce. This law aimed at consolidating private trade in fewer private hands, and it succeeded in reducing the number of registered traders by four-fifths in Conakry and Kindia and by two-thirds in Mamou.[87] As a result, the distribution of goods was severely disrupted and smuggling grew more than ever. The basic consumption goods became impossible to find, while prices skyrocketed in the black market.

Total economic breakdown was averted, however, by the one bright spot in the economy, the rapid development of bauxite export conducted by foreign companies. Starting in 1958 with the large-scale extraction of bauxite deposits in Fria, Guinea became a major mineral exporter. By the mid-1960s bauxite and alumine accounted for about 61 percent of the total legal exports of Guinea. Not surprisingly, this sector was the only one not touched by nationalization (with the exception of the Franco-Canadian Bauxite du Midi, nationalized in 1961) and which enjoyed fairly liberal conditions of repatriation of profits, advantages in taxation and royalties, good conditions of work for its expatriate personnel. The mining sector was truly a foreign enclave on Guinean soil, left there because it supplied the Guinean government its only sizeable income, which saved it from bankruptcy. Until the early 1970s the bauxite sector was dominated by the Fria enterprise (which in 1973 provided 75 percent of Guinea's foreign earnings), but in the last years the sector expanded to other foreign enterprises which started to exploit other bauxite deposits in Boké, Kindia, and Dabola, the last one situated at the fringes of Futa Jallon.[88]

The Guinean population as a whole was deeply disappointed by postcolonial developments which brought to it unforeseen economic hardships and political oppression. The reaction at the periphery was the loosening of ties with the center to reduce political pressure and also as a means of economic self-protection. Based on traditional subsistence economy and some illegal trade, the periphery could survive economically in isolation from the center. However, this worsened the situation of those at the margin of the center, who, integrated into the modern economy and hence having no access to the resources of the periphery, did not hold top political positions and thus had no access to their spoils either. Among these groups, urban shopkeepers, lower-ranking civil servants, teachers, professionals, and students showed the first signs of discontent, which grew continuously, countered by increasingly harsh repression. Starting in 1961, several attempts were made to overthrow the government. All of them failed and provoked purges among people suspected of opposition to the regime. A frightened political leadership, seeing the constant narrowing of its base of support, reacted by further closing itself to the outside and purging itself inside. With every purge fewer and fewer people were left in power positions, and they were more and more isolated from the rest of the population. The purges and repression reached their climax in 1971–72 following the alleged "Portuguese invasion" of Guinea. Scores of people, including army officers, government and party officials of all levels, intellectuals, and professionals, were executed or imprisoned. The party and government were reorganized at all levels and filled with new people.[89]

The reorganization of regional government was also a desperate attempt to regain control of the periphery, which had cut itself off from the center. By 1969–70, the government was unable to enforce any law in the countryside beyond the elementary maintenance of order. It was common knowledge, as many refugees now jokingly tell,[90] that laws and decrees in Guinea had a maximum life span of two weeks. People paid attention to them only as long as they were mentioned on the radio. However, if the enforcement of a particular decree was in the interest of a local executive official, it was strictly enforced and those unaware of it could pay dearly. This naturally created great abuses, and arbitrary rule by local law enforcers made life quite difficult in the periphery too.

The rapidly deteriorating economic and political situation in Guinea affected all regions and ethnic groups and could not be portrayed as the result of interethnic or interregional struggle. However, the Fulbe were hurt more severely than other groups, being singled out as a group of questionable loyalty to the regime. During the first years of independence, while the regime still enjoyed wide popular support, some efforts were made to gain Fulbe support. The melody of an old Fulbe folk song praising Alfa Yaya, chief of Labé, who had tried to organize opposition to the French, was selected for the Guinean national anthem. Alfa Yaya himself was proclaimed a national hero together with the Malinké warrior Samori Touré, and their faces appeared on Guinean money.[91] However, beyond those symbolic gestures, the Fulbe were not well represented in government and party positions, and their position deteriorated further when opposition to the regime started to rise and appointments were made on a more political basis. Estimating the proportion of the three largest ethnic groups in the population as Fulbe, 34 percent; Malinké, 29 percent; Soussou, 20 percent,[92] we see in table 9 that the Fulbe were underrepresented among the officeholders, the Soussou were almost proportionately represented, and the Malinké were overrepresented in every field. This ethnic imbalance among high officeholders increased with time. Among the administrative personnel the Fulbe had a representation of 32 percent, compared to 31.6 percent Malinké, in 1959, while in 1965 Fulbe representation fell to 26 percent compared to 33 percent by Malinké. The more powerful the office, the smaller was the representation of the Fulbe. In the Political Bureau of the party, according to Charles, the ethnic distribution of members between 1958 and 1966 was as follows: Malinké, 47 percent; Soussou, 28 percent; forest-zone people, 14 percent; Fulbe, 11 percent. The imbalance between Fulbe and Malinké was most clearly marked in the regional and local administration where Malinké, with 43–51 percent of the positions, held almost twice as many positions as the Fulbe.[93] Since

Table 9   **Ethnic Affiliation of Surveyed Top Officeholders in Guinea, 1958–66**

	Administrative Personnel (%)	Political Personnel (%)	Trade Union Personnel (%)
Fulbe	23	26	29
Malinké	40	36	33
Soussou	17	17	19
Forest zone people	8	9	8
Others	4	5	3
Unknown	8	7	8

Source.—Based on Bernard Charles, "Cadres Guinéens et Appartenances Ethniques" (Doctoral diss., Université de Paris, Sorbonne, 1968); adapted from Claude Rivière, *Mutations Sociales en Guinée*, (Paris: Rivière, 1971), p. 68, where Charles's table is reproduced.

in the colonial period the Malinké were underrepresented in the civil service compared to the Fulbe and the Soussou, the change to Malinké dominance after independence was clearly related to the change in the ruling power. The privileged position that the Malinké occupied in independent Guinea, compared to the position of the other two major ethnic groups, the Fulbe and the Soussou, was illustrated in a very popular anecdote which compared the achievement of independence in Guinea to the slaughtering of a fat cow: the Malinké took the meat of the cow, gave the hide to the Fulbe, and left the bones to the Soussou.[94]

While underrepresented in central political positions, the Fulbe were overrepresented among opponents of the regime. The alleged antigovernmental plot of 1961 (the first of a long series of alleged plots, not all of them substantiated) came from the town of Labé, heartland of Futa Jallon.[95] Later, in the long series of conspiracies, attempted coups, and various forms of opposition to the regime, the Fulbe were always very salient. Possibly at first the Fulbe were really more active than other groups in their opposition to the regime, but after 1965–66, when opposition spread all over the country, they were intentionally singled out in order to justify harsher repression against them. With opposition growing within the center and in the periphery, the top leadership increasingly fell back on primordial affiliations (ethnicity and kinship) as the only guarantee of loyalty. Therefore, the predominance of the Malinké in the postcolonial center increased even more, and the Fulbe as an ethnic group were increasingly put into the role of villain and associated with opposition to the regime. It is not surprising, therefore, to find the two Fulbe former opponents of the PDG, Diawadou and Ibrahima Barry, among the first to be dismissed from their ministerial posts (in 1962 and 1964, respectively), then arrested (1968), and later allegedly executed (1969 and 1971, respectively).[96] Between 1965–70 great purges of Fulbe occurred in the administration and the army. The reorganization of the army after its first attempted coup in 1965 all but eliminated the Fulbe presence in it. Between 1969 and 1972, the Fulbe were far more numerous than other groups among the many people who were arrested and executed. The repression of would-be pockets of opposition to the regime was somehow always carried out with more vigor and brutality in Futa Jallon than in any other place.[97] The campaign against the Fulbe gained new dimensions in summer 1976, after Sékou Touré explicitly denounced Fulbe racialism in a radio broadcast and linked it to the latest antigovernment plot in which the former secretary general of the Organization for African Unity, Diallo Telli, was allegedly implicated.[98]

One Pullo who formed an outstanding exception to all that was Sayfoulaye Diallo. He not only preserved his position within the party and government but, at a certain period, seemed to be heading the activities directed against fellow Fulbe. Fulbe refugees with whom we discussed this question tended to think that Sayfoulaye Diallo had lost his power by the mid-1960s and that he had become a pawn at the hands of Sékou Touré, who intentionally made him the agent of the worst actions undertaken against Fulbe in order to discredit him in the eyes of other Fulbe and so weaken his position.[99] In any case, Sayfoulaye Diallo lost his post as foreign minister, as well as his seat in the Political Bureau of the PDG, in April 1972. He disappeared from public sight for a while and was said to be in poor health. He surfaced again in December 1973 when he was made head of an enlarged ministry of social affairs, though he probably did not retain his former powers.[100]

During the fifteen years that followed Guinean independence, the Fulbe were, therefore, totally eliminated from the central political positions, with the exception of a few (and constantly changing) people kept for symbolic purposes in ministerial posts devoid of any power, while large numbers of them were severely persecuted for their opposition to the regime. The result was a rapidly increasing emigration of Fulbe to neighboring countries, especially to Senegal, which was added to the more voluntary economic emigration that had existed since the colonial period. According to unofficial Senegalese estimates, about 350,000 Guinean refugees lived in Senegal in May 1972, and 90 percent of them called themselves Fulbe (they were either Fulbe or former slaves of the Fulbe). If these figures are accurate, it means that about one-fourth of the total population of Futa Jallon lived in Senegal, an increasing number of them having had to take refuge there for political reasons.[101]

Cameroon

Cameroon attained independence in a state of emergency under the shadow of violence and terrorism and headed by a coalition government that many considered weak and ephemeral. In great contrast with Guinea, where the government enjoyed almost unanimous and enthusiastic popular support in the first years of independence, in Cameroon large sectors of the population were actively opposed to the government to the point that some of them took up arms against it. Even those who supported it did so by calculation of short-term profit and not out of deep-seated commitment. However, despite these very shaky beginnings, the Ahidjo government scored a striking success in consolidating itself, extending its authority over the whole population, winning its fight against armed opposition, and broadening its basis of popular support. With a mixture of energetic action against the guerillas, great flexibility and reconciliatory gestures toward the legal opposition, including the legalized UPC, and also some shrewd manipulation of divisions between different southern political factions, Ahidjo succeeded in a remarkable way in strengthening his positon in the political center; this indirectly strengthened the authority of his government and consolidated the postcolonial center's position as a whole.

In Cameroon, unlike Guinea, independence was not achieved as a result of a popular uprising of peripheral groups against the colonial center. On the contrary, passage to independence was accompanied by the utter failure of the only real popular uprising that occurred during the period of decolonization. When independence was achieved, the Cameroonian people were weary of terrorist activities and eager for some kind of peace and order. The very consolidation of the center responded to the wishes and aspirations of the population. Once it assured its survival by militarily defeating the armed opposition of the UPC, [102] the political elite found itself in a relatively comfortable position enjoying broad support from a relatively undemanding periphery.

At the same time, unlike Guinea, passage to independence caused no discontinuity in the French presence in Cameroon, and no disruption occurred in vital technical, economic, and administrative matters. Even the fight against terrorism was carried out partly by French troops and advisors stationed in the country. [103] After independence, French advisors, technicians, and economic interests remained in Cameroon and contributed to greater economic development and prosperity. The population, therefore, received not only peace and order but also unexpected prosperity. Exports developed rapidly and so did industry; new large-scale development projects were undertaken, foreign investment flowed into the country, new job opportunities were opened to young Cameroonians, and many local people developed highly profitable business enterprises.[104]

These favorable conditions were well exploited by Ahidjo to consolidate his power and become a national leader. His party, the UC, having already united the entire north, started to penetrate into southern provinces. In the first general elections held after independence, in April 1960, the unity achieved in the north around the UC, compared to the fragmentation of southern political forces, was illustrated by the fact that for the forty-four northern (including Bamoun) constituencies there were just forty-four candidates, while for the fifty-six southern constituencies there were more than 400 candidates. But even more important was the fact that for the first time the UC captured seats (seven of them) in non-Muslim southern constituencies. With these seats it won the bare absolute majority, fifty-one seats out of 100.[105] Following the elections many southern political groups started to join the UC. The period of 1961–62 witnessed a great rush of opposition deputies getting on the UC bandwagon. Between 1960 and 1962 the number of UC members in parliament rose from fifty-one to seventy-seven out of a total of 100, only two of them captured in by-elections in the south, the rest won by other parties' deputies joining the UC.[106]

Encouraged by this success, Ahidjo became more aggressive in demanding the elimination of all organized opposition to his rule. Opposition parties' meetings were broken up, their candidates were harassed, they faced various obstacles in registering for elections, in campaigning, etc. In 1962, four opposition leaders (Mbida, Mayi-Matip, Okala, Beybey-Eyidi) who published a manifesto opposing the one-party idea were arrested and sentenced to prison terms on charges of disseminating news prejudicial to public authorities, inciting hatred against the government, and inciting conflict between ethnic and religious communities.[107] In the 1964 elections, the only party which presented candidates against those of the UC was the Democratic Party, and it won 6.5 percent of the votes as against 93.5 going to the UC, which won all the seats.[108] After 1964, all the opposition parties were dissolved or quietly faded away. In 1966 the three existing political parties of West Cameroon (the ex-British mandate which had joined Cameroon in 1961[109]) also joined the UC and together formed a new national party called the Union Nationale Camerounaise (UNC).

Between 1966 and 1968 opposition leaders were released from prison and either retired from politics or joined the ruling party. Other pockets of opposition to the regime—in the Catholic Church, among some labor leaders, students, and radical intellectuals—also gradually reconciled themselves to the regime or faded away. In opposition to the government remained only a small hard core of UPC terrorists who continued some activity in the Bamiléké region until their leader, E. Ouandié, was captured and put to death in 1971. Finally, the last place to escape complete direct control by Ahidjo, ex-British West Cameroon, was also put under direct control of the central government in May 1972 when the federal arrangements that had been made between ex-British West Cameroon and ex-French East Cameroon were abolished, the territory of West Cameroon forming two of the seven provinces of the unitary state of Cameroon.[110]

The consolidation of Ahidjo's rule after independence and the monopolization of power by his party naturally strengthened the political position of Muslim, northern elements, and especially of the Fulbe, at the postcolonial center. However, since Ahidjo's rule was enabled by southern groups' rallying to him, first in coalition governments, then by joining his party, many important government and party positions were necessarily held by southerners. In the first government formed after independence there were six northerners, including Ahidjo himself, among the nineteen cabinet members. In successive governments, after that, the northern strength was about one-fourth.[111] However, there was a much greater turnover among officeholders of southern as opposed to northern origin. In the regional administration some division was kept between the north and the south. Very rarely was a northerner appointed to a top regional administrative post in the south, and even rarer was the case of a southerner being appointed to a high administrative post in the north.[112]

Fulbe predominance in the postcolonial center in Cameroon did not necessarily strengthen the position of the traditional

Fulbe aristocracy. Paradoxically, just as with the extension of UC control to South Cameroon the Fulbe increased their influence over regions which until then were completely beyond their sphere of influence, the traditional Fulbe elite lost its ascendancy and control over its westernized representatives at the center, some of whom were of commoner origins. Now the traditional chiefs were the ones who needed the support of their westernized kinsmen in order to keep their authority within their region. Traditional chiefs who opposed Ahidjo were quickly punished, as we have seen with the removal of the powerful lamido of Maroua in 1959. In 1963, another powerful Fulbe lamido, of Ngaoundéré, was deposed for openly opposing Ahidjo's policies.[113]

The predominance of Fulbe elements in the postcolonial political center had an obvious influence on Fulbe representation among administrative personnel. At the time of independence there were very few Fulbe in the administration. In 1961, one year after independence, only 3 percent of the higher- and middle-ranking administrative personnel were Muslims,[114] and most of them were Bamoun. After independence the number of Fulbe and other northerners in the central administration started to rise rapidly, though not to the extent that they could challenge the overwhelming southern supremacy. Interestingly, the Fulbe and other northern officeholders in central positions were mostly concentrated either in the highest ranks (ministers, their personal secretaries, and top aides) or in the lowest ranks (drivers, messengers, guards, etc.). They were found less in the middle ranks where the technical executive work was done which required more specific professional abilities.

The great gap between the northern and southern populations in western education and professional skills also explains the fact that, despite their preponderance in the highest political positions, the Fulbe and other northerners were almost nonexistent in other sectors of the center. There were no northerners among leading Cameroonian businessmen, and very few were employed in specialized economic agencies of the government. Among the seventy-five largest private and semipublic companies of Cameroon, only two were established in the north, none of them owned or run by northerners (they are the textile company, CICAM, and the French meat company, Com-

pagnie Pastorale, ranked twenty-fourth and fifty-sixth respectively).[115] In 1971 not one of the judges or one of the secondary school principals in Cameroon (including those serving in
the north) was Muslim, and probably none were northerners.[116]
The top political leadership was aware of this, and northern
leaders made great efforts to reduce the gap between the south
and the north. The north was systematically advantaged in the
allocation of financial resources by the government; this was
openly admitted and justified as giving priority to the development of the least-developed regions of the country. One of
the greatest development projects undertaken by the government with the help of foreign investment was the building of
a railroad from Yaoundé to Ngaoundéré in the north (completed
in 1974). Projects for the large-scale exploitation of bauxite
mines in Adamawa awaited the completion of the railroad.[117]
In the sphere of education, emphasis was put on the development of education in the north, and northerners were
entitled to lower standards of academic achievement for eligi-
bility to certain jobs or to institutions of higher learning. A
crash program was devised to increase the number of Fulbe in
the administration through studies in the National School of
Administration (Ecole Nationale de l'Administration), which
was the western educational institution with the highest proportion of Fulbe and other northern students. However, despite
strenuous efforts by Fulbe political leaders, Fulbe representation in central administrative, economic, and educational positions was still insignificant in comparison with that of
southerners.

One institution where the northerners were relatively well
represented was the army (and gendarmerie). Among the military, the northerners, but mainly non-Fulbe elements, were
already dominant during the colonial period, and they maintained their position after independence under the firm control
of the minister of armed forces Sadou Daoudou (who, incidentally, is the only member of government who has served
in his post without interruption since 1960). The officers' corps,
for a long time headed by French officers after independence, is
now gradually passing into Cameroonian hands, and there the
representation of southerners is relatively higher than in the
other ranks where northerners clearly predominate. The police
force, in contrast, is mostly in southern hands, probably serv-

ing the purpose of ethnic and regional balance and somewhat
concealing the political predominance of the north.[118]

Nigeria

The trends seen in the discussion of decolonization in Nigeria
continued and were accentuated until the civil war of 1967–70.
The federal center could not assert itself as the supreme national
center for the whole country. It was rather seen as the platform
or battleground for the different regional centers fighting each
other. However, it became increasingly clear in the postcolonial
period that the tripod was not balanced, that one of the rival
regions, the north, dominated the federal center by virtue of its
greater population. The ruling party of the north, the NPC,
increased its domination of the federal political center between
1960 and 1966. Southern parties, whether in coalition (NCNC)
or opposition (AG), watched helplessly and in mounting frustration as the federal center slowly passed to northern control.
Their frustration and bitterness were compounded by the fact
that at the same time they considered the north economically
and culturally backward, much less worthy than the south of
holding a controlling position within the postcolonial center.
The north was privileged also in the allocation of federal funds
and economic facilities, and this was bitterly resented by the
southern regions since the north, unlike the south (especially the
east and midwest after the discovery of oil in their territory), had
never been a net contributor to the federal revenues.[119] This
unbalanced situation took on very serious proportions when
the NPC used the powers of the federal government not only to
maintain its supremacy at the federal level but to interfere in
and indirectly control the southern regions, especially the west.
An important attempt of this nature was the decision to create
the midwest region out of the non-Yoruba-inhabited areas of
the western region.[120] In 1962, an even more serious interference was made when the NPC-dominated federal government encouraged a rift within the Action Group, supported
dissidents led by S. Akintola against the party leader Awolowo,
and ensured by all means (including steps verging on illegality)
Akintola's control of the western regional government while
Awolowo was brought to trial and sentenced to ten years in
prison for an alleged conspiracy to overthrow the federal
government.[121]

The uneasy partnership between the north and the east at the federal level broke down in the aftermath of the incidents related to the 1962–63 census. Because the results of the census would have decided the proportional representation of each region in the federal legislative assembly, each regional government did its best to inflate the results in its own region. When it became apparent at the end of the first count that the east would have considerable gains and that the north would lose its absolute majority, the federal government stepped in and ordered a recount in which the initial northern loss was ingeniously recuperated and the precensus ratio of 54–46 percent between the north and the south was restored.[122] The eastern and midwestern regions refused to accept the validity of the revised figures. The north and the west (ruled by Akintola) accepted them. After the census incident, the NCNC, the AG, and the two opposition parties of the north (NEPU and UMBC) formed a united front, the UPGA (United Progressive Grand Alliance), against which the NPC and Akintola's group formed a counteralliance which had the upper hand until the military coup of January 1966 put an end to the NPC's rule in Nigeria.[123]

In the period of NPC rule, between 1960 and 1966, a great effort was made to raise the proportion of northerners among the army officers. In 1961 a strict quota system was introduced according to which 50 percent of all cadets had to be selected from the north. The quota system resulted in a significant increase of northern representatives among officers (table 10), though mostly at lower levels. The higher levels still reflected the period of recruitment by open competition of all Nigerians, and in them the southerners (especially the easterners) continued to be more strongly represented than northerners.[124]

In the federal civil service and in specialized economic and professional agencies there was no significant rise of northern elements. Within the north, on the other hand, the process of northernization in the civil service was carried out with great vigor and even spread to the private sector, where southerners faced increasing difficulties in conducting business, opening stores, renting land, etc.[125] As a result, the northerners clearly dominated civil service jobs held by Nigerians within the north, though by 1962 expatriates still held a high percentage of senior posts.[126] However, this northernization policy helped the Middle Belters more than other northerners (including the

Table 10   **Ethnic-Regional Background of Combat Offi-
            cers in Nigeria**

	North	West & Non-Ibo from Mid-West	East & Ibo from Mid-West	South Cameroon
Pre-independence	8	10	37	2
	(14%)	(17%)	(65%)	(3.5%)
Pre-quotas	21	12	29	3
	(32%)	(18%)	(45%)	(5%)
Post-quotas	104	46	66	
	(48%)	(21%)	(31%)	. . .
TOTAL	133	68	132	5
	(39%)	(20%)	(39%)	(2%)

SOURCE.—N. J. Miners, *The Nigerian Army,
1956–1966* (London: Methuen, 1971), p. 118.

Fulbe) because western education was more advanced in the
Middle Belt than in the Far North. Only in purely political positions were the Fulbe dominant in the northern regional center.

The military coup of January 1966 put an end to the supremacy of the Muslim north and of its party, the NPC.[127] It also
opened the way to the emergence of a stronger all-Nigerian
political center which clearly transcended the various regional
centers. In the few months following the January 1966 military
coup this center was controlled by the Ibo. They were prominent among the instigators of the coup and also among the
military who, suppressing the early coup, took control of government at the end. Major Nzeogwu, who was regarded as the
chief organizer of the early coup, was an Ibo who had lived
most of his life in the north. Out of the thirty-two officers who
were later imprisoned for having taken part in the coup, only
five were not Ibo.[128] On the other hand, the two top men of the
NPC, Ahmadu Bello and Abubakar Tafawa Balewa, and their
ally in the west, Akintola, were killed in the January coup attempt. So were most of the high-ranking army officers of northern origins; as a result the highest ranks in the army became
even more heavily dominated by Ibo. The chief of staff, General
Ironsi, who finally seized power, was Ibo too and surrounded
himself mainly with Ibo advisors. He failed to free the imprisoned Yoruba leader Awolowo and turned down collaboration offers by northern opposition leaders Aminu Kano and

Joseph Tarka. All this created great suspicion of Ibo rule among northerners, including Middle Belters, and to some extent also among westerners. The suspicions and fears turned into great alarm and anger when Ironsi abolished the federal structure of government, thereby eliminating what the northerners considered an essential constitutional safeguard against southern domination. The same decree also created a single civil service and a single civil service commission, which meant for the northerners that they would have no protection from fierce Ibo competition in civil service jobs even within the north. In the northern eyes the southern domination that they feared ever since the beginning of the period of decolonization was finally about to be realized.[129]

At the regional level, Ironsi appointed a Pullo of aristocratic origin, Lt. Colonel Hassan Katsina, the son of the emir of Katsina, as military commander of the north. In the person of Hassan Katsina the Fulbe aristocrats still held the highest political position in the north, but now, in contrast with the past, this position was effectively, as well as formally, subordinate to the federal center where the Ibo were dominant. After a while even Katsina's position was put in jeopardy when Ironsi announced that the military governors of each region would be periodically rotated,[130] thus creating among northerners a dreadful vision of having an Ibo as military governor in the north.

The deep resentment against Ibo domination had its first violent expression in May 1966 in riots in which many Ibos living in the north were killed. In July 1966 a second military coup occurred, this time conducted by northerners against the Ibo. Many Ibo officers, including Major General Ironsi, were killed, and a new military government was formed to rule the country, headed by Lt. Colonel Yakubu Gowon, a non-Fulbe, Christian native of Northern Nigeria.[131] In September 1966 violence against Ibos in the north erupted again in a larger scale. From 10,000 to 30,000 Ibos were killed, and the rest had to be evacuated to the east. During all the tragic events of July–September 1966, the northerners—soldiers and civilians alike—acted as a united bloc. Attacks against Ibos were carried out in the Middle Belt cities as well as in the Far North, and they were more extensive in economically more developed and more westernized cities such as Jos, Kaduna, and Kano, where the northerners faced the strongest competition from the Ibo.[132] In any event, the attacks resulted in the complete alienation of the Ibo from the new military regime. The eastern region, ruled by Colonel Ojukwu, started preparations for an eventual secession.

While the Ibo were irrevocably set against the new regime, the other groups were gradually united in support of it. One of the first acts of the new military regime was to restore the federal structure abolished by the previous military regime. Another early act was to liberate the AG leader Awolowo, who was given a prominent political role in the new regime, together with the two prominent leaders of the anti-NPC opposition in the north, Aminu Kano and Joseph Tarka, and a few leading members of the NPC such as Shatima Kasim and Maitama Sule. So the Ibo of the east, who counted on other southern groups' joining them against the north, found themselves instead faced with a coalition of all other groups and regions of Nigeria.

With the second military coup of July 1966, the north regained a position of dominance in the political center. But this time the dominant element among the northerners was the group representing the Middle Belt and other minority elements within the north and not the Fulbe, Hausa, or any Muslim population of the Far North.[133] A striking illustration of that was the abolition of the four-regions federation in May 1967 and the formation of a new federal structure with twelve states, most of them formed by breaking up the former northern and eastern regions. The increasing number of regions eliminated the disproportionately strong position of the north in the federation, and it ended the Fulbe (or other Muslim) control of the Middle Belt area of the north. The reorganization followed a reversal in the northern position which, at the constitutional talks of 1966–67, had first demanded a loose confederal structure with the existing regions but then advocated a stronger, more centralized federal structure and the breakup of existing regions into a greater number of units. These demands were long-standing Middle Belt ideas and had been strongly opposed in the past by the people of the Far North and by the NPC. Their adoption reflected the rising power of the Middle Belters within the northern group and in the military government.[134] The formation of new states was accepted with resignation in the Muslim north, which had most to lose from it. It was received with jubilation in the Middle Belt area of the north and with general satisfaction in the west, the region least touched by the new fragmentation of the regions. The twelve-states federation was flatly rejected by the Ibo majority in the east. In this case too, quasi-unanimity was reached among most other ethnic groups against fierce Ibo opposition. This deepened the schism between the Ibo and the other Nigerians and precipitated the secession. On 30 May 1967 the eastern region finally broke away from Nigeria, declaring itself the independent republic of Biafra. This started the civil war which lasted until 1970, at the end of which the Ibo were defeated and forced to remain within Nigeria.

The Gowon regime, which reunited Nigeria and asserted the supremacy of the federal center, was overthrown in July 1975 by another military coup on the charge of corruption. The new head of state, Murtala Muhammed, was a Muslim northerner from Kano, probably of Hausa origin, but having blood ties with the Fulbe aristocracy. He had been active in the anti-Ibo coup of July 1966 and had emerged as the chief protagonist of far-northern and Muslim interests in the period which led to the civil war.[135] However, his coming to power did not seem to tip the balance toward the Muslim Far North again, as many thought it would.[136] Murtala Muhammed's rule was marked by two important political decisions. First, a widespread purge was conducted in the military, civil service, and university, and corruption and abuse-of-power charges were brought against some civilian political leaders and all the state governors of the previous regime. All but two of the governors were found guilty, but since they covered all the regions, this did not have repercussions on interregional relationships. Second, and more important, the twelve states were broken up into a nineteen-state federation, but again since the breakup covered most states in all the regions, its immediate effect on interregional balance was not clear.[137] In any case, Murtala Muhammed's rule did not last long. He was assassinated in an abortive coup attempt in February 1976, allegedly instigated by supporters of Gowon. The second man in Murtala's regime, the chief of staff, Lt. General Olusegun Obasanjo, a Yoruba, became the next head of state. A large number of officers were subsequently executed for their part in the attempted coup.[138]

The Fulbe have not returned to a position of dominance at the federal center ever since the fall of the NPC in 1966. Most of the

officers who have risen to prominence since then were not
Fulbe. None of the military governors of the six northern states
created in 1967 were Fulbe, and the governors of only three of
the ten states created in the north in 1976 carried a Fulbe name.
Muslim names abounded in the Supreme Military Councils and
Executive Councils under all regimes since July 1966, but we
have no data on the proportion of Fulbe among them. Hassan
Katsina, the son of the emir of Katsina, who reached a high
position under Gowon, was later dismissed from the army (a
relation of his, Chief of Police Yessufu, on the other hand, entered the Supreme Council). Among civilian leaders, a prominent Fulbe figure was paradoxically Aminu Kano, the long-
time opponent of the Fulbe-dominated NPC.[139]

However, beyond their loss of representation among top
political officeholders, the greatest blow to the Fulbe position in
the political center after the military coups was no doubt the fact
that the regional center where the Fulbe were strongest never
regained its strength of the days of civilian rule. The new military regime that was formed after July 1966, although restoring
the federal structure that was abolished by its predecessor,
nevertheless kept greater power at the federal level. The supremacy of the national center over the regions increased with the
breakup of the four regions into twelve and then nineteen
states, each headed by a military commander appointed by the
Supreme Military Council and accountable to his superiors at
the federal level. Under Murtala Muhammed's rule most of the
military governors did not originate in the states that they governed, and they were not members of the Supreme Military
Council. This trend seemd to be reversed in December 1976,
with the reform brought to the local government system, installing a majority of elected members to local government councils,
since it gave greater power to elected local elements at the expense of those appointed by the central military government.
However, we do not know to what extent the Fulbe chiefs profited from the reform to reassert their local power through the
newly elected council members.[140]

Generally speaking, the very existence of military rule, where
hierarchical chain of command and centralized authority were
the most important principles, did not allow a multiplicity of
concurrent centers of power. Moreover the military, more than
the civilian politicians who preceded them, had a feeling of

Nigerian identity and a common approach to the structuring of the new political center. The long civil war helped to form among all the Nigerians, except the Ibo, a sense of national unity that they had not experienced before.

After the war, signs of interstate bickering and antagonism surfaced again around such issues as the creation of new states, the system of federal revenue allocation (mainly oil revenues) to the states, and the census figures of 1973. On the last issue, northern figures were bitterly contested in the south and the federal government had to backtrack, eventually canceling the results under Murtala's rule.[141] But the importance of this issue faded when plans to return to civilian rule in 1976 were postponed indefinitely (census figures would have determined each state's strength in the elected federal parliament). On the other two issues, measures taken by the successive military governments clearly strengthened the federal government as the center of gravity. By increasing the number of states and reducing their size, the federal government increased its predominance over the states. In the issue of reallocation of federal revenues, the principle of allocating according to population size was given preference over allocating according to each state's contribution to that revenue. This decision no doubt favored the poorer northern states compared to the oil-rich states of the south; however, its general effect was to strengthen the principle of unity and equality between states and to prevent the creation of enclaves of privilege in one state against the others. The proposed draft of the constitution which was to prepare the return to civilian rule, published in October 1976, was also directed toward strengthening the national center against forces of regionalism within the federal framework. For example, the draft stipulated that political activities would not be allowed to bear ethnic or religious labels, and their Executive Committe would have to be composed of members from at least two-thirds of the nineteen states.[142] As a result of all that, while one could not claim that the federal center gained political stability, it did emerge as the supreme national center, the political and cultural focal point for all of Nigeria, far overshadowing any regional or sectoral center.

8

Status of the Fulbe in Postcolonial Futa Jallon, Northern Nigeria, and North Cameroon

Having examined the general transformations that occurred after independence in Guinea, Cameroon, and Nigeria and having seen what role the Fulbe played in those postcolonial developments, we will now turn to the Fulbe-inhabited regions within each country and examine the effect of those developments on the dominance of the Fulbe there. As in our discussion of the precolonial and colonial periods, the analysis will focus on a number of commodities, attributes, or activities which serve as resources for wealth, power, and prestige and which, in turn, help to determine the relative dominance of the Fulbe in their own region.

Political and Administrative Offices

In all three territories, after independence traditional native authorities became increasingly subordinate to the central and regional governments as the new elites became less willing to tolerate autonomous alternative loci of power at the periphery. However, beyond that general tendency, there were great differences among the three territories in the extent to which the Fulbe occupied local government positions within their own region, whether within or outside the native authority framework.

In Guinea, we have seen that the reorganization of local government in 1957, one year before independence, completely abolished all official administrative positions occupied by native authorities. With the formal abolition of the institution of chiefdom, the Fulbe aristocracy lost its official position within the local government which had enabled it to maintain a ruling position in Futa Jallon. The new local government positions were filled by PDG militants, among whom few Fulbe, and even fewer aristocratic Fulbe, were found. Many heads of local party branches were Fulfuldé-speaking descendants of former

slaves. Occasionally a few Fulbe chiefs or other Fulbe of aristocratic origin did occupy high-ranking positions in the local government because they had rallied in time to the ruling party, the
PDG. One such example was the former canton chief of Dalaba,
who had adhered to the PDG on the eve of the 1957 elections
and was rewarded with the high office of "governor of region"
after the reorganization of local government. However, in these
cases, following a general rule set by the Guinean government
according to which local government officials above village level
could not serve in their native region, they served outside their
own region and probably outside Futa Jallon altogether. Within
their own region, the traditional ruler-subject relationship was
broken. They were cut off from their own power base and were
entirely dependent on their superiors in the party and government hierarchy.[143]

In North Cameroon, in great contrast with Futa Jallon, the
Fulbe continued to dominate local government both because
the traditional native authority system was maintained and because the Fulbe also dominated the new local government
which was formed outside and above the traditional native authorities. Of the twenty-four people serving as governor, prefects, and subprefects in North Cameroon in 1972, half were
Fulbe, less than a quarter were Kirdi, and about a quarter belonged to non-Fulbe groups who were Muslim before the Jihad
and who lived outside the boundaries of precolonial Adamawa.
When we look only at the governor and prefects, that is, the
highest ranking regional administrators, the proportion of
Fulbe increases. Of the six people serving as governor or pre-
fect, four were Fulbe, one was Kirdi, and one (the governor)
was Kotoko (a Muslim people living outside precolonial
Adamawa). This shows a very strong representation of Fulbe in
the regional governmental apparatus, considering the fact that
the Fulbe make up only about 25–30 percent of the total population of North Cameroon.[144]

It is interesting to compare Fulbe representation among prefects and subprefects who hold positions of real power within
the region with Fulbe representation among deputies of North
Cameroon in the parliament, a position which gives them more
prestige than power since in Cameroon, as in most one-party
states, the power of the government (including local government) eclipses that of the legislative assembly. Comparing the

figures in table 11, we see that in the politically more powerful regional executive positions, Fulbe representation was 67 percent at higher ranks (governor and prefects) and 50 percent including lower ranks (governor, prefects, and subprefects). In the politically less powerful but more prestigious and more visible position of parliamentary deputy, the proportion of the Fulbe dropped to 25.8 percent of the Federal Assembly and even less in the East Cameroon Assembly (the figures on the East Cameroon Assembly are not very accurate because of the large number of people on whom no information was available). Among the Kirdi, on the other hand, the opposite trend is observed. Their representation reached 50 percent in the Federal Assembly and somewhat less in the East Cameroon Assembly, while in the regional executive positions their proportion dropped to 20.8 percent and to 16.5 percent when only higher ranks are considered. We can see, therefore, that in the legislative assemblies, where membership had more visibility, more symbolic value, but less political power, ethnic arithmetic was more scrupulously observed: The Kirdi population of the north was given large representation to give them and other Cameroonians the impression that the northern political scene was not monopolized by the Fulbe and that the Kirdi also participated in high political office. However, in the key political positions of regional administration, which had less visibility, the Fulbe strongly dominated top offices.

Table 11 also shows that Muslims virtually monopolized all political positions, both those with more symbolic value and those providing more power. The smallest percentage of Muslims recorded is a high 87.5 among northern region deputies of the East Cameroon Assembly (only 43 percent of the total population of North Cameroon is Muslim[145]), and it rises to 100 percent among the politically most powerful prefects and governor. These figures show beyond any doubt that Muslims completely controlled the North Cameroon political scene and that a person had hardly a chance of acceding to any political position, even of symbolic value, if he was not Muslim. The ethnic balance that the Ahidjo regime tried to keep among North Cameroon representatives in the parliament was not extended to any kind of religious balance. The Ahidjo regime acknowledged and respected the ethnic diversity of the people of North Cameroon and tried to give some political representa-

Table 11 Ethnicity and Religion of North Cameroonian Political Leaders

	Governor and Prefects of the Northern Region, 1972		Governor, Prefects and Subprefects of the Northern Region, 1972		North Cameroon Deputies, Federal Assembly, 1970		North Cameroon Deputies, East Cameroon Legislative Assembly, 1970	
	N	(%)	N	(%)	N	(%)	N	(%)
Ethnicity:								
Fulbe	4	(67.0)	12*	(50.0)	5	(35.6)	10	(25.0)
Kirdi	1	(16.5)	4	(16.6)	7	(50.0)	17	(42.0)
Others	1	(16.5)	6	(25.0)	2	(14.4)	4	(10.0)
Unknown	0	(0)	2	(8.4)	0	(0)	9	(22.0)
TOTAL	6	(100.0)	24	(100.0)	14	(100.0)	40	(100.0)
Religion:								
Muslim	6	(100.0)	23	(95.8)	13	(92.8)	35	(87.5)
Others	0	(0)	0	(0)	1	(6.2)	4	(10.0)
Unknown	0	(0)	1	(4.2)	0	(0)	1	(2.5)
TOTAL	6	(100.0)	24	(100.0)	14	(100.0)	40	(100.0)

SOURCES.—Victor Azarya, "Dominance and Change in North Cameroon: The Fulbe Aristocracy," Sage Research Papers in Social Sciences, Studies in Comparative Modernization Series, no. 90-030 (Beverley Hills, Calif.: Sage, 1976), p. 54; data received at the ORSTOM Center in Yaoundé, Cameroon, 1972.
*Includes the chiefs of Bogo and Mindif, who performed the function of Subprefect although they were not formally Subprefects.

tion to each group. But it did not recognize any religious diversity; it asked, on the contrary, that the people of the North all unite around Islam, and so it did not give any political representation to any religious group other than Muslims.

The data presented so far have compared the Fulbe in general with non-Fulbe populations of the north. Comparing the Fulbe of commoner and aristocratic origins, however, we get a somewhat different picture. While the Fulbe occupying native authority positions were all of aristocratic origin, many of those who headed the new local and regional government units were commoners. Our data on top regional administrators and the northern deputies in the legislative assemblies (see table 12) show that, among the politically powerful regional administrators, people of commoner origin were clearly dominant, while in the more symbolic posts of legislative assembly membership, people of aristocratic background (both Fulbe and non-Fulbe) were more strongly represented. Among the top-ranking regional administrators (the prefects), for example, all four of the Fulbe who held that position were commoners, while in the Federal Legislative Assembly four of the five deputies known to be Fulbe were of aristocratic origin. So, this time, the positions of real political power were held by commoners, while positions of greater visibility, more symbolic but less political value were left to the traditional aristocracy, in order to show a façade of unity between aristocrats and commoners within the Fulbe, just like the unity between the Fulbe and non-Fulbe elements of the north. The dominance of commoners in new local government units was all the more important because, with a few exceptions,[146] the regional administrators, the subprefects and prefects, had superior power over traditional chiefs. Thus, regarding the continuing Fulbe domination in political and administrative posts in North Cameroon, an important change did occur in that for the first time most of the highest political and administrative positions were held by Fulbe commoners and not by aristocrats. In comparison with the non-Fulbe populations of the north, on the other hand, the Fulbe as a whole continued to be the ruling element.

In Northern Nigeria between 1960 and 1966, the Fulbe dominated the local political and administrative positions both within the native authorities and, through the ruling NPC, in

Table 12   Traditional Status of Cameroonian Political Leaders Known to Be Fulbe

	Prefects of the Northern Region, 1972		Prefects and Subprefects of the Northern Region, 1972		Federal Assembly Deputies, 1970		East Cameroon Legislative Assembly Deputies, 1970	
	N	(%)	N	(%)	N	(%)	N	(%)
Traditional								
Noblemen	0	(0)	4*	(33.3)	4	(80.0)	4	(40.0)
Commoners	4	(100.0)	6	(50.0)	1	(20.0)	2	(20.0)
Unknown	0	(0)	2	(16.7)	0	(0)	4	(40.0)
Total	4	(100.0)	12	(100.0)	5	(100.0)	10	(100.0)

Source.—Azarya, "Dominance in North Cameroon" (see table 11), p. 57. Data received at the ORSTOM Center in Yaoundé, Cameroon, March 1972.
*Includes the chiefs of Bogo and Mindif, who informally performed the functions of Subprefect.

the new local government structure. Within the native authorities, the Fulbe held much more autonomy and more broadly defined political functions than their counterparts in North Cameroon. However, as we have already seen at the end of the colonial period, power began to shift from the native authorities to the regional government. The regional government extended its local administrative network and supervised the native authorities more closely. In 1962, for example, the regional government established its own provincial administration headed by Provincial Commissioners whose work necessarily reduced the autonomy of native authorities. In 1961 a much-publicized government inquiry into the financial affairs of the emirate of Zaria resulted in great changes in the Zaria native administration structure and in the dismissal of many high-ranking traditional officeholders.[147]

The gradual shifting of power from traditional rulers to the Northern Regional Government did not occur without clashes between the emirs and the regional government. In the most celebrated of these cases, the emir of Kano, openly defying the Northern Prime Minister Ahmadu Bello, urged the Kano NPC members in the northern legislative assembly to vote against two government bills which he regarded as a threat to the authority of emirs. One of them dealt with land registration, and the second established the controversial provincial commissioners mentioned above. The reaction of the northern government was to open an inquiry on alleged financial irregularities in the emirate of Kano at the end of which it forced the emir of Kano to resignation and exile.[148] In the precolonial period even the sultan of Sokoto, although having the legal right to do so, was never able to force down an emir of Kano. So the incident was seen as a striking illustration of the regional government's power at the expense of native authorities. In the eyes of the northerners, the prime minister of the North was in the process of becoming a "Grand Emir" of the whole region. In fact, by 1963, he was widely referred to as "Sarkin Arewa" meaning "Emir of the North."[149]

The shift of power from the native authorities to the regional government did not modify in any way the political dominance of the Fulbe aristocracy in Northern Nigeria, because the regional government too was controlled by Fulbe aristocrats. Unlike North Cameroon, where many of the Fulbe controlling the

new administration were commoners, in Northern Nigeria the
new administration too was controlled by aristocratic elements.
The dominant position of the Fulbe and of all aristocratic elements can be seen in tables 13 and 14 showing the ethnic
group and traditional status distribution of the members of the
Northern Legislative Assembly and of the Northern Regional
Government ministers between 1961 and 1965. From these tables
we see that the Fulbe, who formed less than 20 percent of the
total population of Northern Nigeria, occupied 54.8 percent of
the parliamentary seats and 46.9 of the ministerial positions in
Northern Nigeria. At the same time 87.9 percent of the parliament members and 90.9 percent of the government members
belonged to the traditional aristocracy.

It is interesting to compare the great dominance of the Fulbe
and of people of aristocratic origin among the parliament members and government ministers within Northern Nigeria with
the relatively small representation of Fulbe and aristocratic elements among the northern members of the federal government
(table 15). The Fulbe and people of aristocratic origin were still
overrepresented relative to their proportion in the northern

Table 13   **Ethnicity and Traditional Status of Members of
the Northern Nigerian Legislative Assembly,
1961–65**

	Ethnicity							
	Fulbe	Hausa	Nupe	Kanuri	Yoruba	Other	Unknown	Total
Numbers	57	19	4	12	2	10	34	138
Percentage of known cases	54.6	18.3	3.8	11.5	1.9	9.6	. . .	100

	Traditional Status		
	Traditional Noblemen	Commoners	Total
Numbers	102	14	116
Percentage of known cases	87.9	12.1	100

SOURCE.—Adapted from C. S. Whitaker, Jr.,
*The Politics of Tradition: Community and Change
in Northern Nigeria, 1946–1966* (Princeton N.J.:
Princeton University Press, 1970), pp. 322, 324.

Table 14   **Ethnicity and Traditional Status of Northern Nigeria Regional Government Ministers, 1961–65**

| | Ethnicity | | | | | | | |
	Fulbe	Hausa	Nupe	Kanuri	Yoruba	Other	Unknown	Total
Numbers	15	2	4	7	1	3	6	38
Percentage of known cases	46.9	6.3	12.5	21.9	3.1	9.4	. . .	100

| | Traditional Status | | |
	Traditional Noblemen	Commoners	Total
Numbers	30	3	33
Percentage of known cases	90.9	9.1	100

SOURCE.—Adapted from C. S. Whitaker, Jr., *The Politics of Tradition: Community and Change in Northern Nigeria, 1946–1966* (Princeton, N.J.: Princeton University Press, 1970), pp. 322, 324.

populations as a whole, but they certainly did not occupy a dominant position among the northern federal ministers. This was probably done intentionally to convey the idea that at the federal level the north (or its dominant party, the NPC) functioned as a united front of all northern elements, Fulbe and non-Fulbe, aristocratic and commoner alike. When the confrontation was with other regions and the north had to act as a united front, non-Fulbe, nonaristocratic elements were given great representation in the highest political positions. However, when the confrontation was with other groups within the north, and the government of the north itself was at stake, then the Fulbe and the aristocratic elements retained close control over political positions and fewer concessions were made to other groups.

Things changed considerably after the military coups of 1966. The NPC was banned, and with it the Fulbe aristocracy lost its principal means of access to the regional government structure. Some Fulbe of aristocratic origin did continue to hold high-ranking positions within the regional (later the new states') governmental structure; however, both among the military and among the civilians holding top governmental positions in the

Table 15   **Ethnicity, Religion, and Traditional Status of Northern Nigerian Ministers in the Federal Government, 1959–64**

Group	Number
Ethnicity:	
Fulbe	3
Hausa	2
Kanuri	2
Nupe	1
Yoruba	1
Other	1
Total	10
Religion:	
Muslim	9
Christian	1
Pagan	0
Total	10
Traditional status:	
Traditional noblemen	5
Commoners	5
Total	10

SOURCE.—Adapted from C. S. Whitaker, Jr., *The Politics of Tradition: Community and Change in Northern Nigeria, 1946–1966* (Princeton, N.J.: Princeton University Press, 1970), pp. 475–76.

north, the Fulbe were far outnumbered by non-Fulbe elements and their almost organic ties with the regional government through the NPC were dissolved. Now the traditional elite was firmly subordinated to military governors and the states' governments were staffed by many progressive, reform-minded northerners who had resisted the authority of the emirs in the past.

Furthermore, some reforms introduced into the regional and local administration system by the military regime weakened the position of all native authorities. In February 1966, shortly after the first military coup, it was announced that native courts, police forces, and prisons were to be removed from the control of native authorities. With that, the three most important elements of the chiefs' political authority were taken away from them.[150] Furthermore, in April 1966 all elected members of native authority councils were removed and were replaced by persons nominated by the military regime. Since most of the elected councilors were members of the NPC, which was in close association with the chiefs, the effect was again a loss of political influence for the chiefs. The breakup of the northern region into different states was another important blow to the Fulbe chiefs' power. It removed from Fulbe control some areas where very few Fulbe lived (Ilorin, Kabba) and areas such as the Jos plateau which entered under Fulbe control only through the Fulbe control of the Northern Regional Government. In addition, the very division of the regional government into smaller territorial units brought regional government supervision closer to the native authorities. Later the state governments took measures which further weakened the traditional chiefs. In the Kano state, in November 1968, the huge emirate of Kano was divided into five separate native administration areas, each having its own council (one-third of the members appointed by the emir and two-thirds by the military governor) which took over many of the functions held by the Emir's Council. Similar new administrative areas with separate councils were created also in the emirates of Zaria and Katsina in the North Central State (now called Kaduna State) and, in December 1968, native authorities were renamed "local authorities" to stress the change from the past system. In the Benue-Plateau and Kwarra states located outside the boundaries of precolonial Sokoto, native authority councils were abolished completely and replaced by new "local administration councils" (or "local authorities") composed of members nominated by the military state government. New local authorities in some cases cut across old native authority boundaries. Part of the territory of the emirate of Ilorin, for instance, was attached to another local authority.[151] We do not know how the latest reforms introduced in local government in December 1976 have affected the Fulbe traditional elite. It is possible that the electoral apparatus installed in the selection of local government council members has, paradoxically, increased the power of local chiefs and notables, compared to the situation where the majority of council members were appointed by the military government. This might be especially true because in most Fulbe-inhabited states (unlike most other parts of Nigeria) the council members were elected in indirect elections and not directly by the population.[152]

In any case, we should stress that, despite their significant political losses following the military takeover, the Fulbe aristocrats still remained the local ruling group in areas they inhabited. Even though their political power was more restricted, their administrative functions more narrowly defined and more closely supervised by the military regime, the traditional ruler-subject relationship between the Fulbe aristocracy and other populations was, on the whole, preserved. So even after its political losses, the position of the Fulbe aristocracy in Northern Nigeria remained much closer to that of its counterpart in North Cameroon than to that in Futa Jallon.

The Military and Police

With independence, supreme control of military and police forces passed from the colonial power to independent governments which were even less willing than their colonial predecessors to tolerate any organized means of coercion outside their own direct control and therefore further restricted the military and police forces controlled by native authorities.

In Futa Jallon, since already in the colonial period the Fulbe chiefs were left with no military or police force of their own, no important change occurred in this field after independence. Having no military power, the extent of Fulbe influence was limited to participation in the national army and police force and in these the Fulbe were severely underrepresented compared to their proportion of the total population. In Cameroon, shortly after independence most traditional chiefs lost the small local police force and prisons that they still controlled. The prisons were put under direct governmental control. The chiefs were allowed only to keep a very small number of personal guards for ceremonial purposes, to impress onlookers and symbolize the chiefs' authority.[153]

In Northern Nigeria, until 1966 native authorities continued to have their own police forces. In 1965 the total native authority police forces numbered 7,000 men, but they were scattered among sixty-one independent forces the largest of which, in Bornu and Kano, numbered about 600 men.[154] They were not, therefore, a significant factor at the regional level, but at the local level they were very effective as instruments of coercion.

The status and functions of these forces continued along the lines set up in the colonial period. They enforced traditional authority orders, assisted the Nigerian Police Force in keeping law and order, and were frequently used to intimidate and harass the opponents of the native authorities and of the ruling party. Their partisan use by the native authorities and the ruling NPC against their opponents aroused such widespread criticism that one of the first acts of the military regime in 1966 was to remove them from native authority control and to put them under the control of the Nigerian Police Force pending their complete integration with it later. At the same time all prisons run by native authorities were brought under the control of the federal government.[155] With these changes, the native authorities, and with them the Fulbe traditional aristocracy, lost all hold over the military and police force, with the exception of a few bodyguards chosen from among their most loyal servitors.

Traditional Justice

In Guinea, the abolition of all the administrative functions of traditional chiefdoms by the PDG government one year before independence was accompanied by the abolition of all native courts. In their place was formed a new network of courts whose judges were appointed by the central government completely outside the control of traditional chiefs. The new judges came mostly from loyal PDG militants among whom very few were Fulbe of aristocratic origin.

The Islamic law, which was maintained in the 1957 reform, was abolished shortly after independence and was replaced by a series of new codes. Little effort was made to accommodate the new codes to Islamic law, as is illustrated by the fact that in 1959 civil marriage was made compulsory and in 1968 polygamy was legally abolished, though one cannot imagine that such a law would be enforced.[156] In a more general sense, as mentioned earlier, Guinea has fallen into a state where laws, decrees, and ordinances are utterly ignored, often by the highest government officials themselves. The judicial system has fallen into complete disrepute by being used for partisan purposes or bypassed altogether. In view of the total collapse of the state's judicial system, many people in Futa Jallon, as well as in other areas of Guinea, tend to turn to traditional forms of justice in order to settle their differences. This increases the influence of Muslim judges who had really never ceased to function despite the official abolition of native courts. The former chiefs, although politically powerless, are still approached to give advice on various questions, to arbitrate, and to settle differences between local people. These functions tend to increase the influence of Fulbe traditional elites and enhance their prestige, which had fallen to its lowest level during the few years that preceded and followed independence.[157]

In Cameroon, a govenment ordinance enacted a few days before independence introduced a great reorganization of the judicial system that could have drastically reduced the judicial powers held by native court judges. The 1959 decree declared that all native courts would eventually be abolished but that the native courts in their traditional format would continue to function until the time when sufficient new judges were trained to take over judicial functions from traditional judges. In the meantime, all matters concerning land tenure were taken out of the native courts' jurisdiction.[158] By making the abolition of the native courts conditional on the formation of qualified new judges, the government could postpone the dissolution of native courts indefinitely while at the same time keeping this possibility as a constant threat over the heads of traditional judges and chiefs in order to ensure their obedience to the government. As of spring 1972, traditional Islamic courts were still functioning in North Cameroon and almost all the judges were Fulbe. They were appointed by the canton chiefs with the approval of the government, and their field of jurisdiction extended to all noncriminal matters that fell under customary law with the exception of land tenure.

In Northern Nigeria, just before independence some important reforms were introduced in the judicial system. Those who have studied these reforms are in disagreement as to whether their net effect was to weaken or strengthen Islamic law and Islamic courts. According to these reforms the native Islamic courts were required to try all criminal cases in accordance with a new regional code of law which did not derive exclusively from Islamic law. Also the reforms provided for the first time the possibility of appeal from a native court to a provincial court in matters not concerning Islamic personal law. (For Islamic personal law appeals had to remain within the Islamic native court system at whose top stood the Sharia High Court of Appeal.) However, at the same time, the code of law, which was very strongly influenced by Islamic law, was extended to all the populations of Northern Nigeria, Muslims and non-Muslims alike.[159]

Whether we consider these reforms as weakening or consolidating Islamic law and the judicial system, native courts remained under the control of the Fulbe who were predominant among Muslim judges as well as among chiefs who appointed them. The judicial power of the native courts was widely used for partisan purposes against the opponents of the ruling NPC and of the traditional chiefs. Between 1956 and 1966 native courts became the symbols of the repressive rule of the native authorities and of the ruling NPC; their partisan functioning and their abuse of power became an important issue of public protest.[160]

The control of the native authorities over the judicial system was abolished by the military regime in what was considered the heaviest blow dealt to the native authorities after the military takeover. The highest native courts (emir's courts and grade A and B native courts) were completely abolished, while lower native courts were put under direct control of the Northern Regional Government.[161] With the loss of control over native courts, the Fulbe traditional aristocracy lost its most important means of pressure on the subject population. However, Islamic law continued to be used as the basic legal framework and continued to provide the usual advantages in prestige to Muslims and especially to the Fulbe, who were seen as the pacesetters of Islamic orthodoxy.

Taxes and Other Economic Returns of Political Officeholding

When all administrative functions of traditional chiefs were abolished in Futa Jallon in 1957, the chiefs and their councilors also lost their share of taxes. This was the most important immediate economic loss incurred by the Fulbe chiefs with the abolition of chiefdoms. Besides that, having lost their administrative position they also lost the various unofficial or indirect incomes received from people who needed their services or support in the administration.

In North Cameroon and Northern Nigeria, on the other hand, with the continuing functioning of traditional chiefdoms in local administration, Fulbe chiefs and traditional officeholders continued to receive official and unofficial revenues derived from their administrative positions, in the form of tax shares, salary, various fees and dues, and customary gifts or other unofficial revenues from people depending on their help and services. In North Cameroon, the Ahidjo government tried to curb some of the unofficial revenues of traditional chiefs. It tried especially to forbid their receiving the zakaat, a Muslim almsgiving obligation which was supposed to be given to the needy, but which in the past was paid to chiefs, ostensibly on a voluntary basis. Despite the central government's efforts to stop this practice, zakaat was still paid to chiefs in most North Cameroonian chiefdoms in 1972.[162]

In Northern Nigeria, the system of taxation was slightly changed between 1960 and 1966. According to a Personal Tax Law passed in 1962, the regional government received 12.5 percent of the two basic taxes (the kharajj and the jangali, or community and cattle tax) collected by the native authorities, the rest going into native treasuries. The regional government also collected a new tax from self-employed wealthy Nigerians and from salaried people from whose salaries deductions were made by the employer in a new "Pay as You Earn" scheme. This new tax was in effect the first income tax enacted in Northern Nigeria. The native authorities received 20 percent of it for their assistance in collecting the tax. In urban areas native authorities earned some revenue also from land leasing to strangers (including Nigerians from outside the north).[163]

The development projects and other activities entered upon by native authorities in Northern Nigeria continued to expand after independence. Native authorities built schools, conducted literacy programs, maintained printing presses, participated in trade and industry, conducted agricultural experiments, initiated settlement schemes, etc. In 1964 the Northern Nigerian native authorities employed 42,000 people, or about half of the total number of people employed in organizations employing more than ten people in the region.[164] Entering into such a wide range of activities meant that the top native authority officials, most of whom were Fulbe of aristocratic origin, controlled either employment or essential services needed by many people, and they could capitalize on their position through various gifts and services provided to them by people who depended on them. The more activities were conducted by the native authorities, the larger the number of people that the Fulbe native authority officials could control and the greater their unofficial revenues.

Furthermore, the Fulbe's domination of the northern regional government enabled them, as seen already at the end of the colonial period, to control such bodies as the Regional Marketing Board, the Northern Nigerian Development Corporation, and the Northern Nigerian Investment Board which allocated substantial funds in the form of loans to merchants and industries and financial participation in various enterprises. This whole network of loans and grants was often used to bring side benefits to those who controlled it.[165] The situation changed somewhat after the military coups of 1966, which put an end to the close association between the regional governments, native authority functionaries, and leading entrepreneurs. Soon after the first military coup, the military governor of the north, Hassan Katsina, set up a commission of inquiry to look into the affairs of the Northern Nigerian Development Corporation and of the Northern Nigeria Marketing Board. Although nobody was prosecuted, many leading merchants, contractors, entrepreneurs, and leading NPC politicians were understandably nervous about the inquiry. During the second military regime, in 1967, the results of the inquiry were published in a White Paper in which the Northern Nigerian Development Corporation was accused of serious malpractices. In the same period the Marketing Board exhausted all its funds and had to be saved by emergency bank loans. In 1973, the federal government took over from marketing boards the responsibility for fixing the price of products bought by them, thus greatly reducing the influence that the marketing boards had over farmers.[166]

With the breakup of the northern region into several states, the financial status of the native authorities was harmed when most state governments raised their share of the taxes at the expense of that of native authorities (in part as a remedy to the serious financial difficulties faced by all northern states except Kano). In 1975 native authorities incurred another serious loss of revenue when the jangali (cattle tax) was abolished in order to help pastoralists who had lost large herds during the big drought. However, this time the state governments cut the native authorities' loss with a capitation grant and by reducing the state's share of the community tax to 1 percent. Besides the decline in direct revenues, the shrinking of the native authorities' range of activities (with the removal of police, prisons, native courts, and also of secondary schools previously run by them) caused a further loss of indirect benefits (in the form of fees and gifts) that native authority officials could derive from them.[167]

Slaves

During the postcolonial period full emancipation of former slaves occurred only in Futa Jallon at the initiative of the government. A new land-tenure law enacted in 1959 ended the former slaves' economic dependence on their former masters by abolishing landowners' rights on land on which one did not live and work oneself.[168] Land on which former slaves worked no longer belonged to their masters, hence the slaves could not be expelled from the land and had no more economic obligations toward their former masters. This changed the free labor of former slaves in their master's fields into wage labor, which became increasingly difficult to find. It also sharply reduced the payment, by former slaves, of a share of their products to their former master, though some of them still continued the old practice in the 1970s, unaware of or unwilling to accept their newly acquired economic independence.[169]

Economic emancipation was accompanied by political emancipation. People of slave origin, as well as free Fulbe commoners, were freed from the traditional chiefs' control following the abolition of chiefdoms in 1957. On the contrary, people of slave origin who were active in the PDG during decolonization were given government and party positions that brought them to ruling positions over their former masters. This brought them considerable power but not prestige. The Fulbe called them by the derisive name of "Fulbe of 28 September," that is, people who came to the position of Fulbe (= ruling or privileged positions) only on September 28, the date Guinea achieved independence.[170] The "Fulbe of 28 September" were feared and obeyed, but they were also despised, ostracized, and ridiculed for their lack of education, their ignorance in matters of Islam, and their general lack of finesse in their style of life. The traditional prestige resources deriving from the proximity to Islam and to the Fulbe identity and way of life were not destroyed after independence, and since their distribution created incongruence with the distribution of power, the interconvertibility between power and prestige was sharply curtailed.

The Guinean government tried to combat this incongruence by removing the prestige element of Fulbe identity. As part of its campaign to ensure the full emancipation of former slaves in Futa Jallon, the PDG government tried to persuade those of them who had adopted Fulbe names to renounce those names, detach themselves from their Fulbe master's family, and develop their own separate identity (alleged to be that of some Mandé-speaking group). This effort had little success since the descendants of slaves who had adopted Fulbe names and were more or less accepted among the Fulbe were not willing to forsake this important cultural and social security for uncertain short-term political benefits. The Guinean government also tried to erase all the linguistic distinctions between free persons and persons of servile status. For example, it forbade the use of the word *matchoudo*, which in Fulfuldé means "person of servile status." The word *runde* used for villages inhabited by former slaves was also forbidden, and all the runde were called *fulasso*, like the hamlets inhabited by the real Fulbe.[171]

In contrast with Futa Jallon, in North Cameroon and Northern Nigeria little changed occurred in the position of former slaves after independence. They remained dependent on their masters, who remained the political chiefs and the landowners. The respective governments did not oppose the "voluntary" labor of former slaves on their masters' land, a practice which continued in both countries, though less in Northern Nigeria than in North Cameroon.[172] In the cultural field, former slaves were more than ever bound to their old masters in North Cameroon, trying, like most other non-Fulbe, to be assimilated within the Fulbe group. In Northern Nigeria, on the other hand, the impossibility of assimilation into the Fulbe group put a certain limit to former slaves' cultural fusion with their masters. By becoming Muslim, former slaves were assimilated instead into the Hausa group.

Land and its Products

In our preceding discussion, we have already touched upon the question of Fulbe ownership of land, and we have seen the big difference that occurred in this respect in the postcolonial period between Futa Jallon, on the one hand, and North Cameroon and Northern Nigeria, on the other.

In Futa Jallon the new land-tenure law enacted in 1959 proclaimed state ownership of all land but left usufruct and inheritance rights to the people who lived on it and cultivated it. The sale of land was allowed only through special government permission, and all collective tribal or community property on noncultivated land was abolished.[173] With this law the Fulbe aristocrats not only lost the land cultivated by their former slaves and a share of the products of that land, they also lost the means to force their former slaves to work on their other fields. Wage labor still existed, but it was expensive and was opposed by the government which threatened to take away land on which extensive hired labor was used. So, even though they still controlled more land[174] than the former slaves did, the Fulbe suffered a considerable decline in income derived from land. Fortunately for them, this loss was mitigated by the fact that Futa Jallon was not an important cash-crop cultivation area and agriculture provided only a small part of their income compared with commerce and cattle.

In North Cameroon and Northern Nigeria no significant redistribution of land occurred in the postcolonial period. The Fulbe continued to be the biggest landowners and the major recipients of income derived from the land.[175] In North Cameroon, a law passed in 1959, shortly before independence, reinforced the property rights of local communities or tribal-ethnic collectivities on vacant land. With the exception of very limited parcels of land proclaimed to be public and owned by the state (about 0.2 percent of the total land area), the rest of the vacant land in rural areas was considered to be owned by the ethnic or tribal collectivity of the area.[176] This new land-tenure system, which stood in sharp contrast to that of Guinea, gave to the heads of collectivities—chiefs of cantons and villages, most of whom were Fulbe—the right to decide on allocation and usufruct of vacant land. Moreover, the new law made it impossible for immigrants to settle on any land that they thought vacant, clear the bush, and claim ownership of it. They were now forced to recognize Muslim (mostly Fulbe) ownership of most of the vacant land on the plains and to pay the landowners some kind of rent in cash, crops, or labor. This was exploited by Fulbe who welcomed pagan settlers on the plain on the condition that they become sharecroppers or part-time workers on the Fulbe's land.

In Northern Nigeria, a new land-tenure law, enacted in 1962, declared all land in Northern Nigeria, whether occupied or vacant, as being "native land," that is, land owned by "native" individuals or collectivities. A "native" was defined as a person whose father was a member of a tribe indigenous to Northern Nigeria. It thus excluded the Southern Nigerians.[177] When land was considered owned by a collectivity, the local chief, as head of the collectivity, was recognized as custodian of that land and could decide on its allocation and usage. Thus, as in Cameroon, collectivities were accorded rights of ownership over land that was not occupied by any individual family. This prevented immigrants from settling on land that seemed unoccupied and claiming ownership over it. They had to rent or buy it from the collectivity which owned it (buying and selling had some restrictions which were controlled by the regional government). The land ownership of nonnatives (i.e., foreigners or Southern Nigerians) required permission from the northern ministry of land and survey, and this permission was not easily granted.[178]

In both countries the Fulbe's control of land, as chiefs controlling collective land and also as the biggest private landowners, made them the principal beneficiaries of the continued development of cash-crop production. The greater the amount of land owned, the greater was the share of cash crops grown on it. The Fulbe owned large farms, and they could afford more than other people to hire or force other people to work for them and to expand their area of cultivation.[179] In Northern Nigeria the production and export of peanuts continued their rapid growth in the first years after independence, even though an increasing quantity of peanuts was processed into oil and cake within Northern Nigeria. The quantity of peanuts exported rose from a yearly average of 415,000 tons in 1954–58 to 907,000 tons in 1969–70, but then, following drought conditions, it fell disastrously to less than 300,000 tons in 1973–75 as a result of which, for the first time since its export began, the Nigerian government was forced to ban all peanut export in order to meet the needs of the local peanut-crushing industry.[180] The export of cotton, which was far less important than peanuts, increased slowly until 1963, but since then it has declined because of the rapid growth of the domestic textile industry. In 1975, Nigeria had to import 40 percent of its raw cotton requirements.[181] In North Cameroon, while the export of peanuts did not rise greatly after independence, the value of exported cotton more than quadrupled between 1958 and 1970 but had a precipitous drop after 1971, following drought conditions, inducing some farmers to return to more drought-resistant peanuts.[182]

9

Further Developments in the Status of the Fulbe in Postcolonial Futa Jallon, Northern Nigeria, and North Cameroon

Commerce, Cattle, Industry

In our discussion of colonial change we saw that indigenous commerce which developed then was dominated by the Fulbe in Futa Jallon and North Cameroon, while in Northern Nigeria it was dominated by the Hausa. After independence little change occurred in the development of commercial activities in Northern Nigeria and North Cameroon. The Hausa in Northern Nigeria and the Fulbe in North Cameroon consolidated their control on indigenous commerce and benefited from its rising wealth value. In Futa Jallon, on the other hand, although the Fulbe remained in control of private commercial activities, they were not permitted to enjoy their position fully because of central government policies which severely restricted private commerce and limited its economic returns. The price controls following the nationalization of wholesale commerce in 1960 were the first restrictions, and they encouraged the development of black market and smuggling. However, the real blow to private commerce came with the 1964 controls which severely hit retail trade with the obligation to deposit a large sum as capital in order to be legally entitled to conduct business. In March 1975, Radio Conakry announced the abolition of all private trade and the creation of state monopolies to conduct commerce at all levels. However, one cannot imagine that this decision was implemented, any more than were others before. Usually local authorities shut their eyes to illegal trade, either because they were bribed or because they knew that such trade was the only way to prevent a complete breakdown in the distribution of goods. However, this situation made the traders very vulnerable to pressures of all sorts on the part of local officials.[183] In short, the Guinean government's trade policies caused very serious economic losses to the indigenous merchants as a whole among whom the Fulbe were prominent in Futa Jallon.

The Guinean government's intervention in commerce hit the Fulbe especially hard in cattle trade. After independence, faced with an alarming scarcity of meat due to increasing smuggling of cattle across the borders, the government imposed a yearly quota of cattle (about 10 percent of registered animals) to be sold for slaughtering at fixed prices. This decision, although theoretically applicable to the whole country, was in fact directed against the Fulbe, since they owned almost all the herds in the country.[184] The result was a rapid depopulation of cattle in Futa Jallon. The cattle which were not smuggled across the borders had to be marketed at such a rate that many smaller herds could not reproduce themselves. Many Fulbe lost their herds completely either by selling them precipitously to smugglers or being forced to sell them in official markets at lower prices. Many others had their number of cattle severely reduced. Beyond the obvious economic loss that they incurred, they were also ashamed and humiliated by the rapidly declining size of their herds. On the other hand, smugglers (many of whom were Fulbe) made big profits out of the illegal cattle trade across the borders.

In North Cameroon and Northern Nigeria, in contrast, the cattle trade, conducted openly in a free market, continued to develop rapidly and the Fulbe continued to receive most of the profit from it, in Northern Nigeria as owners of cattle, in North Cameroon as both owners and traders. In North Cameroon about 5 percent of the total number of cattle (approximately 2–2.6 million herds of cattle[185]) were sold each year, almost all by Fulbe, and mostly to Fulbe traders. Fréchou's research on the destination of cattle sold there showed that when the buyer was Fulbe its destination was mostly for further commerce, while when the buyer was Kirdi, its destination was mostly dowry or slaughter for ceremonial consumption.[186] Furthermore, in both countries other activities developed, such as the opening of canned meat factories (in Kano and Bauchi in Northern Nigeria and Maroua in North Cameroon) and the building of new slaughterhouses with refrigerated storage facilities (Ngaoundéré and Maroua in North Cameroon), that increased the demand for cattle and raised their price, thereby increasing the income of Fulbe cattle owners. However, the drought that hit all of West Africa in 1972–74 had severe effects on the herds even though Nigeria and Cameroon were only marginally affected by it. Many head of cattle died (about 70,000 in Cameroon), the trade of cattle declined precipitously, and with it declined the earnings of the Fulbe. Cameroon had to halt all export of meat, and in Nigeria, which had always been a meat importer, the scarcity of meat reached alarming proportions.[187]

Besides providing considerable income, cattle continued to be an important source of prestige in both countries, and again the Fulbe were the principal recipients. The importance of cattle as a prestige resource was illustrated by the fact that all the wealthiest people and those occupying top political positions invested large sums of money in raising large herds.

In other fields of commerce, developments which had started in the colonial period continued without great modification in North Cameroon and Northern Nigeria. The commercialization of major export crops was monopolized by special agencies which also regulated their price, but beyond that, indigenous commerce was left in private hands, mostly Fulbe in North Cameroon and Hausa in Northern Nigeria.[188] Private business expanded and generated considerable wealth. Profits were either reinvested in the business or were converted into prestige through conspicuous consumption of various sorts, buying new consumption items, building new compounds, raising cattle herds, supporting Muslim scholars, etc. Pilgrimage to Mecca, by which wealthy merchants acquired prestige and then reconverted it into further wealth, continued at an accelerated pace after independence. In Northern Nigeria, Hausa traders added to their prestige also by intermarrying with the Fulbe aristocracy. After 1966, with the political weakening of the traditional elite, they were also less inhibited from competing with the traditional elite in conspicuous consumption. In short, all that happened in North Cameroon under Fulbe control occurred to a much greater degree in Northern Nigeria under Hausa control.

In the field of industry there was little development worth mentioning in Futa Jallon after independence. The only industrial enterprise that had been established in Futa Jallon in the colonial period, the orange-perfume-extracting enterprise run by the French, continued to function in association with the state, but production steadily declined from 300 tons before World War II to 136 tons in 1960 to only 56 tons in 1966.[189] After independence, the most important industrial enterprise under-

taken in Futa Jallon was the opening of a canned fruit and
vegetable factory in Mamou in 1963. This factory, owned by the
state and run by Russian experts, was designed to produce
canned meat too, but its meat section never functioned because
of the great scarcity of meat in the country. Its vegetable and
fruit sections too had great difficulty in receiving sufficient
supplies of raw material and had catastrophic results in marketing the products. Instead of bringing economic relief to the
area, the Mamou cannery, in fact, created more economic problems: The local population was forced to provide the cannery
with fruit and vegetables at a very low price and then they were
asked to buy the processed canned products at a much higher
price. As the PDG's newspaper *Horaya* frankly admitted in its
criticism of the management of the Mamou factory, peasants
had to sell their fresh tomatoes at 25 Guinean Francs per kilo
and then had to pay 400 Guinean Francs per kilo of canned
tomatoes.[190]

In North Cameroon, industry still remained in the hands of
expatriate firms or the government, out of the reach of indigenous entrepreneurs. It included cotton ginneries and oil mills
run by the CFDT (the French company developing cotton in
North Cameroon), the CICAM textile plant built in Garoua in
1966 and owned by foreign companies and the government of
Cameroon and Chad, a cement plant in Figuil, a soft drink
factory in Garoua, and the canned food factory in Maroua. In all
these industrial activities the North Cameroonian population
supplied only raw materials and the labor force.[191]

In contrast with North Cameroon, in Northern Nigeria indigenous entrepreneurs, mostly Hausa, started to enter industry,
banking, and similar activities which until independence had
been the exclusive domain of Europeans and southerners. In
these fields the northern entrepreneurs were strongly supported, both financially and politically, by northern regional
governmental agencies. In banking, the Bank of the North,
owned by Northern Nigerian interests, was closely associated
with, and supported by, the northern region government. In
1972 a new Agricultural Credit Bank was opened in Kaduna
with federal government help.[192] In industry, although most of
the large-scale mechanized plants remained under the control of
public corporations or foreign companies, a few wealthy local
entrepreneurs started to participate financially in industrial ac-

tivities together with government agencies and foreign companies. The list of industries, developed in Northern Nigeria after independence, with or without the participation of northern entrepreneurs, is too long to be reproduced here.[193]

Geographical Mobility, Migration, Urbanization

The most important change that occurred in the postcolonial period in patterns of migration in Futa Jallon was the sharp increase in migration to neighboring countries. To the already important migration in the colonial period, inspired mainly by economic motives, was now added a new wave of politically motivated migration of people opposed to, and persecuted by, the Guinean regime. Also, while colonial migrations were mainly temporary, the postcolonial migration was permanent; very few of the emigrants ever went back to Futa Jallon. Most of the new emigrants lived in great poverty in the neighboring countries. They were not allowed to work in many types of jobs in order not to provide competition for the native citizens of those countries. They formed great concentrations of refugees along the Guinean borders, many of them unemployed or with bare means of subsistence. They were a vocal opposition group against the Guinean government, were implicated in several attempts to overthrow it, and caused considerable embarrassment to the countries that hosted them.

Migration within Guinea was directed mainly toward bauxite mining areas, where the income level and conditions of employment were incomparably better than in other areas. The capital city of Conakry apparently continued to attract immigration too. The population of the city showed an increase of more than 300 percent, from 50,000 in 1955 to 170,000 in 1965,[194] but we do not know whether this great increase occurred mostly between 1955–58, during the great economic boom experienced by Guinea in the last years of the colonial period, or whether it was evenly divided before and after independence. Nor do we know whether the proportion of Fulbe among immigrants changed. Guinean refugees in Senegal, asked about this matter, generally indicated that migration from Futa Jallon to other areas of Guinea was hindered by the economic and political insecurity felt by migrants outside their home region.[195]

In North Cameroon and Northern Nigeria, with better transportation and communication facilities and better prospects for

employment and trade, the geographical mobility of the population continued to increase after independence. The descent of
pagan hill tribes to the plains continued at an accelerated pace
and was strongly encouraged by the respective governments
which, like their colonial predecessors, perceived the economic
and political advantages of that migration. Many government
plans existed for the resettlement of hill tribes willing to move
down to the plains, mostly continuing schemes that were
started in the colonial period.[196] The Muslim populations living
on the plain, mostly Fulbe and Mandara in North Cameroon
and Hausa in Northern Nigeria, continued to favor the descent
of hill tribes since they knew that they could exert closer political, economic, and cultural influence on mountaineers who
moved down to the plain. As in the colonial period, the only
serious conflict arose over land ownership. The Muslims
claimed property rights over land on which hill pagans wanted
to settle. In these conflicts in North Cameroon the Fulbe were
even more favored after independence than they were in the
colonial period, because they now held political supremacy
both within native authorities and in the central government.
Moreover, in North Cameroon the new land-tenure law enacted
in 1963, stipulating that land could be owned by a collective
group even though it was not cultivated, reinforced the claim of
Fulbe and other plains dwellers that even land that seemed
empty, in fact, belonged to their collectivity by virtue of its
being their tribal land.[197] We do not have comparable information on possible conflicts over land ownership in Northern
Nigeria between Muslims and pagan immigrants. One can advance the hypothesis that, if indeed such conflicts did occur,
the Muslim population received favorable treatment from the
northern government until 1966, but that this has stopped since
1966, with the establishment of a military regime in which the
position of Fulbe has been weakened while the position of
Middle Belters and other non-Fulbe, non-Mulsim elements in
the north has been strengthened.

The general development of cities as economic and administrative centers continued in North Cameroon and Northern
Nigeria after independence. Cities continued to offer greater
employment and educational opportunities and attracted many
immigrants. They also continued to be centers of Islam. Many
pagans who came to the cities as immigrants soon adopted

Islam. Podlewski found, for example, that among the Matakam, Islamization was much more advanced among those who migrated to urban centers than among those who moved down to settle in small villages on the plains.[198] For the pagans, urbanization, like other types of opening up to the outside world, was generally a prelude to Islamization.

The most important change that occurred within the city population in Northern Nigeria as a result of postcolonial developments was the disappearance of a large number of southerners, especially Ibo elements, following pogroms conducted against them in 1966. Until the massacre of the Ibos, more than a million southerners lived in the north, mostly in urban centers, and provided tough competition for northerners in business and in skilled work.[199] The place vacated by the Ibos after 1966 was filled partly by northerners (Hausa in trade and mostly Middle Belters in professional and administrative services) and partly by other southerners, mainly Yorubas. After the Ibo exodus, the north experienced an influx of Yoruba immigration and tension mounted between them and the northerners who directed toward them their general hostility to southerners. During the civil war years, despite all the talk about "One Nigeria," there were rumors of impending attacks on Yorubas. Though these rumors did not materialize, many northern state governments preferred to employ Europeans rather than Southern Nigerians if suitable northern elements were not available.[200] Among the northern elements, too, important changes in employment occurred after the formation of the separate northern states. Most northern civil servants were required to return to their state of origin and serve there. This caused the return of many Middle Belters from other regions of the north to the states created in the Middle Belt. More administrative positions were then opened in the Far North to the local Hausa, Kanuri, and Fulbe people.[201]

Islamic and Fulbe Identity

In the postcolonial period little change occurred in the prestigious position occupied by Islam in Futa Jallon, North Cameroon, and Northern Nigeria. In each territory, the Fulbe continued to set the model of Islamic behavior for most of the other populations and to provide most of the clerics, Islamic judges, teachers, and scholars. In Northern Nigeria and North

Cameroon, where the Fulbe also controlled considerable power and wealth, the prestige received from proximity to Islam helped them legitimize that control. Where they incurred great economic and political losses, as in Futa Jallon, prestige deriving from closeness to Islam and from the memory of their past glory was the only basis on which the Fulbe still enjoyed a high standing and which enabled them to maintain some superiority over the non-Fulbe. The economic and political emancipation of former slaves in Futa Jallon paradoxically increased the importance of the Fulbe's superiority in the religious ritual and educational spheres, since, as a sign of their rising social standing, the former slaves wanted to adopt an increasingly Islamic and Fulbe life-style in which the Fulbe of aristocratic origin served them as teachers, guides, legitimators. Former slaves insisted on providing their children with a good Muslim education which could be received only from a Fulbe teacher. The Fulbe's presence was deemed necessary in life-cycle ceremonies (circumcision, marriage, etc.), sacrificial offerings, or any other religious ritual without which the ceremony did not seem to receive full religious legitimacy. Public prayers were never led by former slaves; good-luck amulets, medicine against witchcraft, advice on suitable time for risky endeavors could be received only from the Fulbe. In short, the more Muslim the former slaves became, the more "functional" became the Fulbe's superiority in religious matters, and that enabled the Fulbe to maintain a prestige much higher than that of non-Fulbe people.[202]

Pilgrimage to Mecca continued to develop after independence, and the title "Alhaji" conferred great Islamic prestige. The postcolonial governments, especially those of Nigeria and Cameroon, encouraged the Hajj and accorded many facilities to the pilgrims in obtaining passports, visas, and air transportation at reduced rates. In Guinea, too, in the first years after independence the government encouraged and facilitated pilgrimage, but in later years it suddenly modified its attitude, canceled the facilities, and restricted the number of people allowed to go on Hajj to 800 per year, chosen by the political party from among a much greater number of candidates.[203] Among people who went on the Hajj in all three countries, wealthy traders continued to dominate, but they were joined by an increasing number of politicians who wanted to strengthen their political position by increasing their religious prestige, thereby legitimizing their control over power resources. In Nigeria, the premier of the northern region, Ahmadu Bello, and the federal prime minister, Abubakar Tafawa Balewa, had already gone to Mecca before independence. In Cameroon, President Ahidjo went on the Hajj in 1966 and thereafter insisted upon being called by his new title, "Alhaji Ahmadou Ahidjo." In Guinea, President Sékou Touré and most of his cabinet ministers did not go on the Hajj, but interestingly one of the few cabinet ministers who did go was the most important Fulbe member of government, Sayfoulaye Diallo. Although he did not go on pilgrimage, Sékou Touré chose to stress his Islamic identity by adopting the name of Ahmed and insisting upon being called Ahmed Sékou Touré.

In Northern Nigeria and North Cameroon, the Islamization of pagan populations continued at an increasing rate after independence. (Futa Jallon was already almost entirely Muslim when independence was achieved.) With the continuing opening up of pagan populations to outside influences, with their increasing migration to population centers and their increasing contact with other regions and populations, Islamization made rapid progress among them. In his study of Matakam migration in North Cameroon, Podlewski noticed that the Matakam and other pagan migrations were never directed toward areas inhabited by other pagans but always toward areas inhabited by Muslims. In Muslim areas there was a civilization which claimed to be universalistic and in which they hoped to gain acceptance that they could not expect from other pagan groups strictly limited by blood ties.[204]

The trend toward Muslimization was strongly encouraged by the NPC government in Northern Nigeria and by the Ahidjo government in Cameroon. Both governments regarded the Islamization of pagan elements in the north as the best assurance for their domination in the region and in the country as a whole. In Northern Nigeria between 1963 and 1965, widely publicized campaigns of Islamization were carried out in pagan areas, at the instigation and with the participation of the northern premier, Alhaji Ahmadu Bello, but they were discontinued after the military coup of 1966 and the death of Ahmadu Bello.[205] In Cameroon, no overt Islamic proselytism took place, but the propagation of Islam among pagans accelerated with the

tacit encouragement of the government. In both Northern
Nigeria and North Cameroon, Christian missionary work was
obstructed in various ways. Difficulties were made in issuing
visas to expatriate missionaries, in granting building permits,
and in approving land acquisitions. Northern Christians and
pagans faced discrimination in employment and promotion.[206]

So in postcolonial Northern Nigeria and North Cameroon,Is-
lamization of pagans was not only a passage to "civilization,"
but also a passage to the ruling side and to becoming entitled to
all the spoils that derived therefrom. This situation changed in
certain areas of Northern Nigeria after 1966–67 when the NPC
lost power and non-Muslim Middle Belters came to powerful
positions within the military government. After the formation
of separate states in the north, the feeling of supremacy of Islam
over Christianity apparently came to an end in the Middle Belt
states, but in the other states it has probably continued up to
the present.

The close relationship between Islamization and adopting
Fulbe culture and identity continued in North Cameroon after
independence. Pagan populations, starting with their chiefs,
considered Islamization an opportunity to raise their social
status by assimilating within the Fulbe ethnic group. This situation is well described in a letter from a Dutch anthropologist
who has done fieldwork among the Kapsiki, a pagan hill tribe
living on the Mandara hills:

> The Fulbe that I was speaking about are almost exclusively
> Fulbeized Kapsiki, with a few Fülbeized Matakam, Bana,
> Daba, Mousgoy. Real Fulbe are very rare; some school-
> teachers for instance. Some Fulbeized Kapsiki seem to be a
> little ashamed of their Kapsiki background, especially when
> they do not live in Kapsiki territory. The photographer of
> Mokolo [Mokolo = administrative center of the department
> to which Kapsikis are attached—author's comment] is a case
> in point. He is a Kapsiki (even a kamazé, a possible chief)
> grown up in Mogodé. He became Fulbeized, learned his
> profession in Guider [another northern town] and settled in
> Mokolo as the only photographer in town. He is one of the
> richest men in Mokolo right now. People are dependent upon
> him for identity cards and so on. He refuses to speak Kapsiki
> and speaks only Fulfuldé and French. Nevertheless the
> people of Mogodé like him (admire him a little bit) and do not
> seem to have bad feelings about his rejection of his Kapsiki-
> ness.

In Mogodé the Fulbeized Kapsiki speak about half Kapsiki, half Fulfuldé. The Lamido speaks only Fulfuldé (only with me Kapsiki) but acknowledges that his mother still lives in the Wula mountains (one of the most traditional Higi villages just across the Nigerian border) and that he is a real Kapsiki. Once a Kapsiki is Islamized he almost immediately starts calling himself Fulbe, and the others do too. . . . In the beginning I was struck by the easy relations between the two groups (pagans and Fulbeized). Fulbeization is accepted as a matter of fact and not in the least are the Fulbeized Kapsiki considered as traitors to Kapsiki life. Fulbeization is dependent on opportunity, becoming a merchant, having many contacts with the outer world and especially with various functions in the Lamido's court.[207]

This Fulbeization of Muslimized pagans is at present very strongly supported by the Fulbe in the central government. They see this as the best way of consolidating the northern united front under Fulbe leadership. However, since this trend reduces the Fulbe's distinctiveness from other populations and in the long run threatens to eliminate their separate identity within the northern population, most of the "real" Fulbe are not very pleased by the proliferation of Muslimized Kirdi calling themselves Fulbe. They welcome them into their ranks, not so much as Fulbe, but as Muslims, and they are quick to point out that the genealogy of the Kirdi and their ignorance of the subtleties of the pulaaku (the Fulbe moral code and style of life) betray the falsity of their claim to Fulbe identity. Thus, even after they become Muslim and call themselves Fulbe, the Kirdi enjoy less prestige than the people considered to be "genuinely" Fulbe.

In Northern Nigeria, Islamization did not lead to Fulbeization in the postcolonial period any more than it did in the colonial period, and for the same reason: the existence of the large non-Fulbe Muslim majority of Hausa whose language and culture dominated the territories of the old Sokoto empire. Islamization in these territories led to Hausaization, which granted all the prestige and other advantages that pagans could expect from becoming Muslim.

Islamic and Western Education

In the postcolonial period Islamic education started to decline gradually under the challenge of rapidly developing western education. The decline was greatest in Futa Jallon and least in Northern Nigeria. In 1961 there were still eleven times more koranic schools than western schools in Northern Nigeria, and literacy in Arabic script was higher than literacy in English. In North Cameroon in 1960–61, about 10 percent of the population was literate in Arabic script while less than 1 percent was literate in French.[208] Nevertheless, the professional opportunities that western education provided started to attract pupils away from koranic education. The number and quality of koranic schools, and especially the number of people willing to pursue higher Islamic studies, declined.[209]

In Futa Jallon Islamic education, as well as other organized Islamic religious activities, was considered by the government as a source of conservatism which stood in the way of its revolutionary ideas; hence it tried to restrict or closely supervise them. In mosques the Imams were ordered to preach on themes chosen by party officials. Clerics and scholars were forbidden to go on tours for preaching, teaching, and alms receiving. Clerics from other countries were not allowed into Guinea. In 1961, for a short time koranic schools were closed when the Guinean government decided to close all private schools, but they were soon after reopened again.[210] The closing of private schools was a measure directed mainly against missionary-run schools as part of the government's campaign against Christian missions, which it considered as agents of continuing French cultural colonialism.[211] Islam, in contrast, was considered part of the country's precolonial heritage, and hence no strong measures were taken against it despite its being seen as a source of conservatism.

Generally speaking, in all three territories, western education developed rapidly after independence. Governments made great efforts to build schools, train teachers, and raise the level of literacy. Statistics on the level of education became a matter of regional and national pride. By developing western education, each region or country increased the number of indigenous people who were qualified to occupy positions requiring western skills and knowledge. After independence the wealth and especially the power provided by those positions increased rapidly, since many political positions previously held by Europeans were handed over to the indigenous population. Moreover, beyond the professional outlets it opened, western education began also to have some intrinsic prestige value as a source of knowledge in the eyes of new generations of Africans. All this greatly increased the overall value of western education compared to Islamic education.

In Northern Nigeria and North Cameroon the development of western education received special attention because of the effort to reduce the gap between the north and the south. In Northern Nigeria, it was the basic precondition for the whole "northernization" program. Between 1959 and 1965 the percentage of children enrolled in northern primary schools more than doubled, a large part of that expansion being undertaken by native authorities themselves. Whereas in 1958–59 native authority capital expenditure on primary education was only 8.7 percent of their total capital expenditure, it rose to 28.1 percent in 1962–63, the second largest item of their capital expenditure for that year.[212] At the same time great emphasis was laid on the development of secondary and higher education. In 1962, the first university of Northern Nigeria—Ahmadu Bello University of Zaria, named after the prime minister of the north—was opened, incorporating in itself also the Institute of Administration of Zaria which had been founded in 1954. Even though one of the major goals of the establishment of the Ahmadu Bello University was to promote northernization by providing more opportunities for higher education to northerners, in 1964–65 almost half of the students enrolled at the university were still strangers to the region.[213] Generally speaking, despite great governmental efforts and the important progress registered after independence, there still existed a very wide gap between the north and the south in western education. While almost universal primary schooling was achieved in the south, in the north only about 10 percent of primary-school-aged children enrolled in school.[214] Similar differences existed also in secondary and university education.

In North Cameroon, although no official northernization policy existed, there was a special emphasis on education in order to reduce the imbalance between the north and the south. The central government put the north in a privileged position in allocating funds for education, and lower educational standards were required from northerners than from southerners in recruitment to office. After independence, western education developed rapidly in North Cameroon. The number of students in western schools increased from 23,754 students in 1959, a year before independence, to 63,581 students in 1965–66, more than doubling the number.[215] Nevertheless, differences between the north and the south in western school enrollment remained very great. In the north the enrollment in western schools of 6–14-year-old children in 1970 was only 22 percent, compared with the average 60 percent enrollment for the whole of Cameroon and more than 80 percent for each southern province (except former British Cameroon). In secondary education only 4 percent of all Cameroonian students were from the north, compared to about 27 percent of northerners within the total population.[216]

In Guinea too there was rapid development in western education, and even the strongest opponents of the Guinean government acknowledged that this was one field in which the government had been successful.[217] As to Futa Jallon's share in that development, the only data available to us show that with a 10.8 percent rate of enrollment, compared to 28.2 percent in the coastal zone and 25 percent in Upper Guinea and the forest zone, Futa Jallon was the region with the lowest rate of schooling.[218]

Within Northern Nigeria and North Cameroon, the Fulbe did not occupy a prominent position among western-educated elements. In Northern Nigeria, western education was most developed in the Middle Belt where missionary schools were concentrated. The distribution of primary school population enrolled in school in the six separate states of Northern Nigeria in 1967 shows clearly that the two Middle Belt states, Kwarra and Benue-Plateau, with the greater number of non-Muslims and non-Fulbe population had a great advantage over the four states of the Muslim Far North (table 16). In 1964, in a move to restore some balance in educational development between the Middle Belt and the Far North, the northern government decided that no new school buildings would be built in provinces where a 28 percent level of schooling had been attained so that more schools could be built in provinces with lower levels.[219] This was clearly discriminatory against provinces with highest schooling which happened to be also those where most non-Muslim and non-Fulbe people lived. It was strongly opposed by the Middle Belters and was abolished after the military coups of 1966.

Table 16 **Primary School Enrollment in the Six Northern States of Nigeria, 1967**

Region and State	Number of Pupils	Enrollment Percentage of 6–12 Years Age Group
Middle Belt:		
Kwara	112,094	33.07
Benue-Plateau	118,935	21.00
Far North:		
North Central	74,881	12.93
North Eastern	102,393	9.30
North Western	51,377	6.34
Kano	47,138	5.78

SOURCE.—Adapted from *Northern States of Nigeria, Local Government Yearbook* (Zaria, Nigeria: Ahmadu Bello University, Institute of Administration, 1968), p. 98.

With respect to the representation of Fulbe among the western-educated elements in North Cameroon, we unfortunately do not have a very clear picture. In research done on the territories north of the Benue river, Podlewski found the Fulbe to have the second highest rate of schooling (32 percent) after the Moundang (46 percent).[220] However, it is not clear whether that rate also includes enrollment in koranic schools. The importance of this point is shown in a second research done by Podlewski in the North Cameroon territories south of the Benue river, where he shows that the Fulbe had a general schooling rate of 36 percent but when only western schools were taken into consideration, it dropped to 8 percent and in that the Fulbe lagged behind the Mboum and the Dourou.[221] In another research, Martin showed that in the departments of Diamaré and Mayo Danaï the Fulbe were ranked third in schooling after the Moundang and Toupouri but before the Guisiga, Massa, and other populations.[222]

It is clear in any case that, as in the colonial period, the Fulbe did not occupy a particularly strong position among the western-educated elements of North Cameroon. The greater conservatism of the Fulbe in matters of education was illustrated by the fact that the Fulbe were the only group of northerners among whom enrollment in koranic schools was higher than in western schools. Even among students in western schools, the Fulbe were most strongly represented among students in Franco-Arabic schools where more emphasis was put on Islamic education but very poor results were obtained in terms of preparation for western occupation or higher western education.[223]

The relatively low rate of western schooling among the Fulbe in Northern Nigeria and North Cameroon put them at a disadvantage in competing for occupations requiring western education. Many non-Fulbe elements, such as the Moundang, the Toupouri in North Cameroon, the Middle Belters in Northern Nigeria, were better qualified than the Fulbe for these occupations. On the other hand, the Fulbe held the political supremacy (both within native authorities and in the central or regional government) which they could use to their advantage in recruitment. In consequence, we find that the top positions where appointments were made on political basis were occupied mostly by the Fulbe while the intermediate and lower ranking positions where the daily executive work was done and most technical professional skills were needed were held by more educated but less powerful non-Fulbe groups. In Northern Nigeria, as Dudley pointed out, "While the 'far North' have so far tended to predominate in the top ranks, the new crop of administrative grade civil servants are more likely to come from the 'lower North'. . . . In other words, Northernization is creating a situation in which the upper reaches of the administrative class are dominated by N. A. type men largely from the far North with relatively poor education but long administrative experience, while the bottom ranks of that class may soon be filled by younger graduates from lower North."[224] The situation has probably changed in Northern Nigeria since the establishment of separate states and the priority given in each state to the recruitment of natives of the state. At the same time, with the decline of the political power of the Fulbe, many non-Fulbe people—and, in the Middle Belt states, many non-Muslim people—acceded to highest political positions formerly closed to them.

The professional opportunities open to Fulbe and other local people in the modern sector depended also on the extent of competition provided by people of other regions immigrating to Fulbe-inhabited areas. In Futa Jallon there was no immigration of populations originating from other regions. In Northern Nigeria and North Cameroon, on the other hand, very serious competition was provided by southerners settled in the north. We have seen that in the 1950s in Northern Nigeria the regional government launched a policy of northernization to help the northerners combat southerners in recruitment to western occupations. After independence, northernization was expanded and developed into a general policy of favoring northerners over southerners in every possible field. Southern Nigerians living in the north were systematically discriminated against in all kinds of employment and promotion, governmental contracts, education, scholarships, loans and grants. They were also barred from land ownership in the north and could only rent land for a determined time period. Moreover, a law enacted in 1962 determined that in any urban center southerners could not hold more than 20 percent of the land.[225] All this created great difficulties for southerners who wanted to establish businesses in northern cities, and it ruled out any permanent southern settlement in the north.

After the military coups of 1966, the northernization policy was denounced and officially abolished and the most obvious discriminatory measures against southerners were removed. In 1968 most northern states abolished all restrictions on land ownership by southerners.[226] However, while abolishing the northernization policy of the previous civilian administration, the military regime could not in fact prevent its final success as a result of the massacre of thousands of Ibos living in the north and the exodus of the survivors. By the end of 1966 there were practically no Ibos and few southerners in Northern Nigeria. At first that created great shortages of skilled manpower, and many services came to a standstill. Railways were virtually paralyzed with the loss of 6,000 Ibo engineers; the mail lost 80 percent of its personnel, the electricity corporation, losing 50 percent of its manpower, functioned at half capacity.[227] However, after the initial shock, the north started to adapt to the new conditions. Jobs vacated by the Ibo were taken over partly by other southerners (mostly Yoruba), but mainly by northerners, Hausa in commerce and transport, mostly Middle Belters in professional and administrative jobs. After the civil war, the northern states officially asked the Ibo to return to the north and guaranteed that they would be welcome and protected. Many Ibos have indeed returned to the north, but their numbers are very far from the pre-civil war concentrations.

In North Cameroon there was no official policy of northernization, though the Cameroonian government did make some efforts to give priority to northerners in recruitment to administrative posts and tried to restrain the influx of southerners into the north. But despite the government's displeasure, southern immigration to the north has developed since independence, and southern competition for jobs in the north has been stronger than ever. Most skilled professional jobs in northern cities are handled by southerners. This strong southern presence has created considerable tension between northerners and southerners in northern towns, but fortunately no violence has erupted so far between the two groups.

Conclusion

In this book we tried to examine in a comparative framework the transformations that occurred in three precolonial West African societies, Futa Jallon, Sokoto, and Adamawa, as a result of their encounter with a process of far-reaching social change starting in the colonial period. The first phase of this process was the establishment of colonial rule in their territories and the many innovations that it introduced, including the incorporation of the three societies in larger colonial units called Guinea, Nigeria, and Cameroon and the building of a new colonial center in each of these territories. The second phase of change was the gradual withdrawal of the European colonial power from that center and the takeover of the center by indigenous elements in the process of which the colonial center was transformed into a postcolonial, politically independent center. In dealing with the many facets of these changes, our main interest was to see whether and how the groups who were dominant in the precolonial period held their position in the radically changing conditions. However, the identification of the dominant group necessitated intermittent moving between two different levels of analysis. On the one hand, we had to deal with those groups, almost all of whom were Fulbe, who monopolized ruling positions as a result of the Jihads and emerged as an aristocratic group over all the other populations of all ethnic groups. On the other hand, we had also to deal with the Fulbe as a whole (though we disregarded the nomadic groups) as an ethnic group holding dominant positions over the non-Fulbe populations. The study of dominance was, therefore, both a study of interethnic relations and of relations between aristocrats and commoners, no matter what their ethnic origin. It should be also pointed out that this study's focus was not the position of "chiefs" or "rulers" as holders of specific governmental or political offices, but rather a wider stratum of people,

not all of whom were actual rulers but who were usually related
to one of the ruling dynasties by blood ties, were legitimate
candidates to ascriptive political office, and whose dominance
was based also on nonpolitical resources. Hence, many of the
conclusions reached in this book should not be automatically
applied to the position of "chiefs" facing change but rather to
that of a larger group of aristocratic families among whom actual chiefs were chosen.[1]

To identify our basic concept of dominance, or superiority,
we defined a dominant group as that which controlled more
than any other the resources that maximized its power, wealth,
and prestige. We then examined what were the commodities,
activities, or attributes which served as such resources in the
three societies, how were they modified with colonial and postcolonial change, and how were they distributed among the different groups of people in the three societies before, during,
and after the colonial period. On the basis of our study of the
Fulbe history and of the changes that occurred with the formation of Fulbe states in the three areas, we identified the following major sets of resources: (1) political officeholding, (2) military force, (3) position in the Islamic judicial system, (4) taxes
and other revenues received by political officeholders, (5) slaves
or free manpower, (6) land and its products, (7) cattle, (8) trade
and craftsmanship, (9) Muslim identity, knowledge, and piety,
and (10) Fulbe identity and style of life. We have seen that with
the exception of trade and craftsmanship the Fulbe controlled all
these resources in the precolonial period, and this determined
their general dominance in society. We cannot determine in any
definite way a one-to-one correspondence between these resources and power, wealth, and prestige. Cattle, for example,
brought both wealth and prestige, slaves brought both wealth
and power, Muslim identity brought both power and prestige.
Moreover, power, wealth, and prestige could also be converted
into one another. Tax income was clearly the expression of the
conversion of power into wealth, and judicial positions expressed the conversion of prestige into power. Needless to say,
the resources that we have enumerated above are not valid for
the study of distribution of power, wealth, and prestige in any
society. Some of them, such as cattle, slaves, or Muslim identity, are specific to the societies discussed here. However, the
use of wealth, power, and prestige resources to determine pat-

terns of social inequality is a general scheme that should be applicable to any society.

We have seen that in precolonial Futa Jallon, Sokoto, and Adamawa the great control that the Fulbe exerted over most of the resources enumerated above, especially those closely related to power and prestige, derived from the fact that the Fulbe controlled the "central" positions in each society. In all three societies, after the successful Jihads, the Fulbe formed new "centers" and occupied most central positions. The nature of power and prestige resources was such that they were, almost by definition, distributed among the population according to their proximity to the center. Wealth resources, on the other hand, were not so closely related to centrality, and some peripheral groups could amass wealth, especially as a result of trade which was considered an activity of peripheral groups, though supervised and taxed by the "center." However, the wealth that peripheral groups could achieve through independent economic activity did not match the economic payoffs from political positions occupied by the Fulbe at the center (slaves, land, taxes, gifts, etc.). Thus the politically superior Fulbe also became superior in the economic sphere. In other words, since prestige and especially power resources were easily convertible into wealth resources, the great superiority of Fulbe over other populations in power and prestige deriving from their greater proximity to the "center" made them superior in wealth, too.

Our survey of the precolonial situation showed us that basic similarities existed between the three societies prior to the colonial period. In all three we found states that were formed by the same people, the Fulbe, in the name of the same religion, Islam, as a result of Muslim holy wars (Jihad) that brought them into a ruling position over non-Fulbe people. The economic changes that followed state formation in the three areas, including the trend toward Fulbe sedentarization and the growing importance of agriculture based on slave labor, also bore striking similarities. In all three societies a process of restratification occurred, and a new Fulbe aristocracy was formed and occupied a privileged position in society.

However, besides those striking similarities between the three societies, we also found some differences. Some of these were related to minor structural details and were not of great importance to our analysis in that they did not affect in any significant way the dominance of the Fulbe in each society or their adjustment, as a dominant group, to colonial and post-colonial change. Because the three societies were not identical, such differences were inevitable. However, there were also some differences that had an important effect on the extent of Fulbe dominance in their respective societies and their sub-sequent adjustment to change. One such difference, which in my view far surpassed all the other factors in importance, was found between the Hausa-inhabited areas of Sokoto, on one hand, and Futa Jallon and Adamawa, on the other. Hausaland was significantly different from both Futa Jallon and Adamawa in that:

1. In great contrast with Futa Jallon and Adamawa, Hausa-land, before the Jihad, had a flourishing civilization with elaborate political and economic structures, a very rich and developed commercial and communication network, important centers of trade and of Islamic learning, and close ties with the Islamic world. Moreover, probably influenced by its cosmopoli-tan nature, its strong ties with the outer world, Hausa culture and civilization were relatively universalistic, open to anybody who wanted to integrate into it by speaking its language and adopting its basic customs and patterns of social organization.

2. Attracted by this flourishing pre-Jihad civilization, the Fulbe who assumed ruling positions in Hausaland adopted the local language and other aspects of local culture, and social, political, and economic organization to a much greater extent than the Fulbe in Futa Jallon and Adamawa, where it was rather the non-Fulbe local populations that adopted the Fulbe lan-guage, culture, and social organization patterns.

3. In Hausaland, unlike Futa Jallon and Adamawa, the bulk of the non-Fulbe local population, the Hausa, were considered Muslim by the Fulbe. They could, therefore, participate in the Muslim community that the new centers claimed to represent. The community of Islam in Hausaland did not correspond closely to the community of the Fulbe ethnic group as was the case in Futa Jallon and Adamawa.

4. As a result of the above factors, the Hausa had a greater degree of participation in the center formed by the Fulbe and they felt a higher degree of commitment to, and identification

with, that center than did any other non-Fulbe group in Futa
Jallon, Adamawa, and Sokoto.

It is interesting that because of the impact of the Hausa presence in Sokoto (absent in both Adamawa and Futa Jallon) the
position of the Fulbe compared to non-Fulbe in Adamawa
showed greater resemblance to that prevailing in Futa Jallon located at the other end of West Africa with which Adamawa had
no contact than to that in Sokoto whose vassal state it was, from
which it had copied its basic political organization, and to
which it was bound by numerous political, economic, and cultural ties.

Another difference between the three societies, whose effect
on Fulbe adjustment to change is less apparent, concerns the
numerical proportions of Fulbe and non-Fulbe populations in
the three areas. If we can rely on rough colonial estimates,[2] it
seems that Futa Jallon was differentiated from Sokoto and
Adamawa in that the Fulbe there formed a slight majority of the
population, while in Sokoto and Adamawa they formed a small
minority. We do not know what direct effect this difference had
on the Fulbe's adjustment to change in the three territories, but
it does draw attention to the important fact that there was a
much greater proportion of sedentary Fulbe commoners in Futa
Jallon than in Adamawa and Sokoto. Therefore, the differentiation, and at times conflict, between aristocratic and commoner
elements within the Fulbe ethnic group was much more salient
in Futa Jallon than in the other two territories in all periods.

The study of the colonial period focused on the impact of
colonial innovations in the Fulbe-inhabited areas and on the
Fulbe's response to them. We saw that, while undergoing
change and adopting many colonial innovations, especially in
the economic sphere, the Fulbe also continued to maintain control over most resources that provided wealth, power, and prestige. In dealing with this matter, we addressed ourselves to two
basic questions: (a) what new resources were introduced into
Fulbe-inhabited areas as part of the overall colonial innovations
and what modifications occurred in the value and uses of old
resources; and (b) what changes occurred in the distribution of
those resources among different groups of people in Futa Jallon,
Northern Nigeria, and North Cameroon? For the Fulbe the introduction of new resources, or modification of old ones, pre-

sented the threat that some other groups, by acquiring them, could challenge their dominant position. In order to check such a challenge the Fulbe had either to prevent the introduction of those innovations into their territory or themselves engage in the new activities and try to control the new resources. In the educational and cultural fields, the Fulbe tried, and to some extent succeeded, in limiting the introduction of new activities that could upset their traditional dominance. A clear illustration of this was their opposition to missionary activities in their territories and their general resistance to western education. However, generally speaking, the Fulbe could do very little to prevent the introduction of colonial innovations into their territory, especially in the more instrumental political and economic spheres, because these innovations were strongly encouraged, sometimes even imposed, by the colonial administration. Therefore, the Fulbe's main hope of retaining their dominant position lay in trying to adopt innovations, engage in new activities, and acquire new resources.

We have seen that the Fulbe were quite successful in transferring old resources that they already controlled to new uses that increased their value and provided them with more power, wealth, or prestige, thereby displaying a rather successful adjustment to change. For instance, their control of land enabled them to be the principal beneficiaries of income generated by extensive cash-crop production. Their control of land and of political positions enabled them to control indirectly their former slaves (whose land they owned and whose chiefs they were), turning them into free or cheap labor and thus reducing the prospective loss that could have followed the legal emancipation of slaves. In trade, whose value as wealth resource rose rapidly in the colonial period, the Fulbe achieved a dominant position in Futa Jallon and North Cameroon but not in Northern Nigeria where the Hausa control of commerce was well established already in the precolonial period. Besides that, the Fulbe also continued to control old resources which were not affected much by colonial innovations, such as the Muslim religion and the Fulbe identity and way of life. Finally, in Northern Nigeria but not in Futa Jallon and North Cameroon, the expansion of the activities of the local political authorities (the so-called native authorities) into the "western sector"—opening western schools, hospitals, directing agricultural experiments, financing building projects, and engaging in various economic activities—gave the Fulbe an opportunity to use their traditional control of local political and administrative positions to extend their control over the local population in those western sectors too, thus increasing their power over those populations and receiving from them income in the form of fees, dues, and unofficial presents.

Another question closely related to the Fulbe adjustment to change in the colonial period was the extent to which the Fulbe could maintain a separate collective identity that was seen as distinctive and superior to that of other people. One effect of the rapid Islamization process was an increasing challenge to the distinctive Fulbe identity of the settled Fulbe commoners. We have seen that in North Cameroon and Futa Jallon many non-Fulbe pagan populations adopted Islam in an attempt to be more like Fulbe, and after their Islamization many of them also became Fulbeized, speaking the Fulbe language, acting like Fulbe, and even calling themselves Fulbe. This effort at Fulbe-ization through Islamization, while increasing the prestige related to Islam and the Fulbe identity, began to blur the distinction between genuine Fulbe and people who claimed to be Fulbe. The ruling aristocratic Fulbe families could easily distinguish themselves from non-Fulbe by the fact that they alone held ruling positions. However, for the settled Fulbe commoners, it became increasingly difficult to keep a distinction between themselves and the Muslimized and Fulbeized non-Fulbe. In Northern Nigeria, a different phenomenon had the same result: Because the Hausa were considered Muslim and because the settled Fulbe adopted the Hausa language and social organization, it became increasingly difficult to distinguish between settled Fulbe commoners and the Hausa. Only the Fulbe ruling aristocracy could be easily distinguished from the Hausa, because they monopolized most ruling positions.

Another important aspect of Fulbe adjustment to change was the extent of their participation in the new colonial center. In this respect, we have seen that general indigenous participation remained relatively limited until World War II. Continuing Fulbe dominance in their own region was related to their central position in their own precolonial center and not to the newly built colonial center. However, in the limited participation at the colonial center that did occur (and all adoption of innovations could, in a sense, be considered as participation in the colonial center), the Fulbe of Futa Jallon were differentiated from those of North Cameroon and Northern Nigeria when comparing their participation in the colonial center with that of other populations *outside* their own regions. The Fulbe of Futa Jallon participated much more in the colonial center compared to other Guinean populations than did the Fulbe of Northern Nigeria and North Cameroon compared to other Nigerian and Cameroonian populations.

This brings us to a more general comparison of Fulbe adjustment to change in the three areas. On reviewing our findings from a comparative perspective, we note that, except for the differences caused by the economic and cultural presence of the Hausa in Northern Nigeria, until 1945 the Fulbe of the three territories were strikingly similar in their reaction to colonial change. At first they all tried to resist colonial penetration, this culminating in a military clash in which they were easily defeated. Immediately after that, they started to collaborate closely with the colonial forces, with very few cases of insubordination or attempts at revolt. Their readiness to cooperate closely with the colonial power enabled them to keep their local ruling position, to assume the role of local government agents of the colonial administration, and to maintain the liaison between the colonial administration and the local indigenous population. The precolonial centers that they had formed were allowed to survive within the colonial periphery, performing local government functions and ensuring cultural and religious continuity at a time of great change. By occupying the central positions within their old precolonial center, the Fulbe continued to control most of the old resources, and they transformed them into new resources or used them for new purposes, thereby maintaining their overall dominance within their own society. Generally speaking the passage from the precolonial to the colonial period, despite the great innovations that it introduced, was not crucial in any of the three societies in terms of Fulbe dominance over other local populations. In contrast, the passage from the colonial to the postcolonial period as a result of the opening of the colonial center to indigenous political participation, and later control, had a crucial effect on the dominance of the Fulbe in their respective societies and also, in this respect, important differences were detected between the Fulbe in the three societies.

The similarities and differences observed in the different aspects of Fulbe adjustment to colonial change in the three societies could not be attributed so much to their own activities or capabilities as they were to external "situational" factors over which they had very little control. The overall similarity that existed in their reaction showed that when external factors or stimuli were similar, they tended to react in a similar fashion and occupy a similar position in the colonial period. The difference between Futa Jallon, North Cameroon, and Northern Nigeria with respect to the political autonomy accorded to Fulbe chiefs arose from the different policies of the colonial powers (French in Futa Jallon, British in Northern Nigeria, German and French in North Cameroon). The greater crystallization of the native authority system, its financial strength, and its entrance into so-called western activities in Northern Nigeria were again a direct result of British indirect rule which, if conducted in North Cameroon and Futa Jallon, probably would have led to the same results.

Some differences in Fulbe reaction to colonial changes were also related to general geographical factors. For example, the greater Fulbe participation in the Guinean colonial center compared to other Guinean populations was partly due to the geographical proximity of Futa Jallon to the capital city of Conakry and to the coastal zone where most of the colonial innovations were introduced. Northern Nigeria and North Cameroon, on the other hand, were very distant and somewhat isolated from the south of their respective colonial territory where most colonial innovations were concentrated, and this partly explained their relative lack of participation in the colonial center compared to other Nigerian or Cameroonian populations. Topographic factors could perhaps also explain the nondevelopment of export agriculture in Futa Jallon in contrast with its development in Northern Nigeria and North Cameroon. The only major difference between the three societies in Fulbe adjustment to social change which could be attributed to a factor internal to the three societies and which existed already in the precolonial period was again the one emanating from the Hausa presence in Northern Nigeria. However, even this difference was not due to a factor that could be controlled or prevented by the Fulbe; it was a situational factor that existed in Northern Nigeria, but not in the other two areas, already before colonial change, but it was external to the Fulbe group's readiness or capability to adjust to change.

Decolonization was a process of gradual takeover of political positions in the colonial center by indigenous groups struggling with each other for their share of control. The outcome of the struggle determined what indigenous groups occupied central positions when those positions entitled them to rule the whole country and introduce changes that could affect the position of any social group within its own region. The process of decolonization was a turning point in the general transformations that occurred in colonial territories. The precolonial aristocracies were faced with a new situation to which they had to adjust, and on this point (unlike their adjustment to colonial changes) great differences were found between the Fulbe aristocracies of the three territories. In Guinea, the Fulbe were evicted from political positions at the colonial center just before independence. In Cameroon and Nigeria, in contrast, independence was achieved with political forces representing the Fulbe aristocracy (though not formed exclusively by aristocrats) holding most important political positions at the center. This, in turn, explained the fact that the Fulbe aristocracy lost a great deal of its dominance within Futa Jallon during the last years of the colonial period, while in North Cameroon and Northern Nigeria they continued to maintain their dominant position.

What were the reasons for this differential outcome? One important factor which contributed to the success of the Fulbe aristocracy was their ability to mobilize support not only among Fulbe commoners bound to them by ethnic ties, but also among non-Fulbe populations living in Fulbe-inhabited regions by forming with them a common front on the basis of Islam and/or regional solidarity against other regions. We have seen that in both Nigeria and Cameroon, when the Fulbe entered into the struggle for the control of the colonial center, they entered as a northern bloc including other Muslims and even some non-Muslim northerners. In both places, the formation of such a northern Muslim bloc was made possible mainly by the fact that the northern provinces were ethnically, culturally, and religiously very different and remained very isolated and separated from the more developed south throughout the colonial period. A very clear dividing line existed between north and south in both Nigeria and Cameroon. This mobilized most northerners to support a united north (even if led by the Fulbe, whom they might have disliked) against a threatening south, whose representatives were the southerners who migrated to the north and competed for jobs with the local populations and whom the non-Fulbe northerners disliked much more than they disliked the Fulbe. For the Muslim northerners the confrontation was basically one between Muslim and non-Muslim people, and they naturally sided with the Islamic community of the north. For the non-Muslim northerners who had contact with the outside world, the issue was that of competition between local people and more advanced southerners who threatened to dominate them and limit their economic and professional opportunities.

In contrast with Cameroon and Nigeria, in Guinea a clear north-south dividing line did not exist. The populations who lived outside Futa Jallon were not culturally, religiously, or ethnically very different from those who lived in Futa Jallon. During the colonial period Futa Jallon was not isolated from other regions as North Cameroon and Northern Nigeria were from the southern provinces. Therefore, no united regional front transcending narrow ethnic boundaries could be formed. Nor could an Islamic front be created in Futa Jallon against other regions, since the great majority of the populations living outside Futa Jallon were also Muslims. Therefore, the non-Fulbe elements of Futa Jallon did not rise to the support of their Fulbe leaders on the basis of regional loyalty to the same extent that non-Fulbe elements did in Northern Nigeria and North Cameroon. Consequently, most of the non-Fulbe populations living in Futa Jallon remained independent of Fulbe influence, and in 1956–57 they turned against them, contributing to their eviction from the political center.

The outcome of the struggle for political control at the colonial center did not depend only on the reaction of the populations within the Fulbe-inhabited regions; it depended also on the reaction of other groups outside Futa Jallon, Northern Nigeria, and North Cameroon. After all, in Guinea the decline of the Fulbe position in the political center did not result from what the Fulbe did or did not do, but rather from what their opponents, based mainly outside Futa Jallon and organized in the PDG, did in the last years of decolonization. The decline of the Fulbe presence in the colonial center in Guinea was the result of the emergence of the PDG, which carried out a very successful campaign against the French administration in the process of which it established a united front of all major non-Fulbe groups and won elections in every region except the areas of highest Fulbe concentration. In the later stages of its development (after 1955), the PDG penetrated Futa Jallon too, mainly in the areas where most non-Fulbe people were concentrated. There, it associated its anticolonial struggle with a struggle against the traditional elite and succeeded in arousing most non-Fulbe people and quite a few Fulbe commoners against the Fulbe aristocrats.

In Cameroon and Nigeria there was no political organization comparable to the PDG which could successfully unite all the regions outside those inhabited by the Fulbe, wage a strong anticolonial campaign against the colonial administration, and come to political predominance in the colonial center without needing the support of the Fulbe-inhabited area. In both Cameroon and Nigeria, the major political parties of the south—the NCNC and the AG in Nigeria; the UPC, the MANC, and the Democrats in Cameroon—were deeply divided among themselves. They fought each other rather than forming a united front against the north. While such a southern front would have become dominant in the Cameroonian center, in Nigeria it would have needed some support from the north in any case, since the northern region, because of its size, was allocated absolute majority in central political positions.

The Southern Nigerian and South Cameroonian parties were much less successful than the PDG in penetrating the Fulbe-inhabited areas. The geographical separation of the north from the south and the great cultural differences between the two regions made it very difficult for southern groups and political parties to penetrate the north and establish political bases there. To that was added the complication of the federal structure in Nigeria (different electoral laws, separate elections for regional legislative assemblies, legal discrimination against southerners' political activities in the north). The NCNC's alliance with the radical opponents of the traditional elite in Hausaland did not provide significant electoral support. The AG's effort to mobilize the support of some non-Muslim Middle Belters against the Fulbe-led northern front was somewhat more successful, but it was not sufficient to challenge the overall supremacy of the Fulbe-led NPC. In Cameroon the UPC tried to penetrate the north in the years 1948–50, shortly after it was formed, but it met with little success in the face of strong opposition by the traditional elite. Perhaps it could have been more successful toward 1955–57, when there were more anticolonial elements among northerners and the franchise was extended to peripheral populations more prone to be mobilized against the Fulbe and other traditional elites, but by then the UPC had been outlawed and had gone underground. Consequently, the Fulbe aristocracy and other Muslim chiefs were never faced with a real opponent political force which could eventually organize non-Fulbe non-Muslim elements or dissident Fulbe elements against them. If the PDG in Guinea had been outlawed like the UPG, it would probably have been equally ineffective, and the Fulbe aristocrats would have preserved their dominant position in the country.

This brings us to the extent of support that the Fulbe received from the European colonial administration in their bid for political domination at the center. Interestingly, this factor had contradictory effects in Guinea, on the one hand, and in Nigeria and Cameroon, on the other. In Guinea the French administration for a long time supported the Fulbe-dominated parties in their struggle with their opponents in the PDG, but this seems to have hurt the Fulbe by portraying them as collaborators of the colonial regime. In Nigeria, and especially in Cameroon, on the other hand, the support given by the colonial administration to the Fulbe was instrumental in bringing them to a position of power within the colonial center. In Cameroon, Ahmadou Ahidjo's becoming Prime Minister in 1958, which brought the Fulbe to political dominance at the center, was instigated and fully supported by the French administration. In Nigeria, the British were more favorable to the NPC than to its opponents in the north. Moreover, the successive constitutions promulgated between 1946 and 1954 always favored the north more than the south. The federal constitution of 1954 was especially instrumental in enabling the Fulbe to extend their control over the federal center by virtue of their domination of the northern region.

Generally speaking, then, we can conclude that the Fulbe had little control over the factors which enabled their being on the winning side in the struggle for central positions vacated by the European power. The fate of the Fulbe in Futa Jallon showed, in fact, that one aspect of adjustment to change over which they did have some control, namely, the degree of their general receptivity to westernization and early participation in the colonial center, was not an important factor in determining the extent to which they could maintain their supremacy, because it was not a crucial factor in determining the final outcome of the struggle for political control of the center. A certain degree of westernization was very important, since it was a necessary condition for entering the struggle but it was not a sufficient condition for winning it. On the contrary, too much westernization could even have been a serious handicap, if it was regarded as evidence of too close collaboration with the colonial administration.

It is also possible that the early entrance of a certain group to the political arena for the control of central political positions raised its salience as a rival and threat to other groups and hence contributed to the strengthening of opposition to it or even to the formation of a common front against it, thereby reducing its chances of coming to a dominant position at the political center at the end of decolonization. In our cases, it is possible that the early predominance of the Fulbe-led political party in the Guinean political center crystallized against it the opposition of all those who feared Fulbe dominance and contributed to the final failure of the Fulbe's bid for a controlling position at the center at the end of decolonization, while the relative absence of the Fulbe (and of the north as a whole) in the early stages of political struggle in Nigeria and especially in Cameroon may have contributed to the deepening of divisions within the south instead of forming a united southern front to fight the northern threat, and this may have contributed to the north's reaching a dominant position at the political center at the later stages of decolonization.

Granted that the Fulbe had little control over the factors which determined their differential success in the struggle for the political control of the center, can we generalize from the Fulbe case and say that for all the populations involved, external situational factors and not internal adjustment capabilities were the principal determinants of being on the winning side? In other words, can we also claim that the extent of success of other groups with whom the Fulbe competed for control of the center (such as the Ibo or Yoruba in Nigeria; the Bamiléké, Bassa, or Ewondo in Cameroon; the Malinké or Soussou in Guinea) was also determined by external factors and not by their own internal adjustment capabilities? One might put forward the counterclaim that the result obtained by the Fulbe was the outcome not of their own adjustment capabilities but of those of their competitors. If this was the case, it would certainly be an external factor for the Fulbe, but it would show that adjustment capabilities did play a role in determining the winning side. Since we did not study closely the performance of the competitors of the Fulbe, we cannot give a definite answer as to whether their performance was affected mostly by external factors or by their own adjustment capabilities. However, if we consider early westernization and greater responsiveness to western economic, educational, and cultural innovations as a sign of greater adjustment capability, then we do have some evidence against the relationship between that kind of adjustment capability and final victory in the struggle for the political control of the center. Many competitors of the Fulbe, such as the Yoruba in Nigeria, the Bamiléké in Cameroon, and the Soussou in Guinea who were among the earliest people to adopt various colonial innovations were also among the ones who were relatively less successful in occupying central political positions at the end of the colonial period. So, not only in the case of the Fulbe, but also in those of some of their competitors we see that early or greater westernization was not related to greater political control of the center at the end of the colonial period. This might hint that in their case, as in the case of the Fulbe, differential success in controlling the political center depended more on external factors than on any internal adjustment capability.

The position that various indigenous groups occupied in the postcolonial center in the first years after independence reflected the outcome of the struggle that was waged during decolonization. The people who were in ruling position when independence was attained used the sovereign political power accorded to the center to weaken their opponents and strengthen their own position at the center. However, struggle for the political control of the center continued, and in the case of Nigeria it led to military interventions which changed the composition of the ruling group in the country. So, to the factors determining the winners in the struggle for political control, we should now add another factor, the differential success of military coups or other insurrectional attempts after independence and whether those actions were directed by or against the Fulbe.

Comparing the position occupied by the Fulbe in the postcolonial centers of Guinea, Cameroon, and Nigeria, we have seen that in Guinea the Fulbe were completely eliminated from the political center except for a token number of representatives kept in central positions for symbolic purposes. In Cameroon, on the other hand, the consolidation of the postcolonial center brought with it a strengthening of Fulbe political predominance as the leading representative of a united Muslim-northern front, and their predominance at the center was seen as the general predominance of the north over the south. However, the Fulbe predominant at the center were western-educated new elements, most of them of commoner origins. Their rising power was accompanied by a decline of aristocratic elements' influence on them. Unlike the early stages of decolonization, now the traditional elite depended on them more than vice-versa. So, the Fulbe dominance in the Cameroonian political center was that of an ethnic group but not that of a traditional ruling class. In Nigeria, which until 1966 seemed to have a multiplicity of postcolonial centers because of its loose federal structure, the Fulbe were predominant both within the federal center and within the northern regional center. At the federal level they acted, like their Cameroonian counterparts, as leading representatives of a united northern front. In Nigeria, too, power started to shift from the traditional elite to its representatives at the northern regional and federal center. However, here, since most of the new officeholders, mainly at the regional centers, were also Fulbe of aristocratic origin, the trend did not incur a loss to the Fulbe qua aristocracy. Until 1966 the Fulbe remained predominant, not only as an ethnic group, but also as a traditional ruling class, whether occupying positions in the native authority or in the federal or regional center. In any case, Fulbe political predominance came to an end with the military takeover of 1966. In the decade of military rule that followed and which included two other military coups, one attempted coup, and a civil war, dominance changed hands frequently but never returned to the Fulbe, either as an ethnic group or as a traditional aristocracy.

These developments at the center had a strong effect on the position that the Fulbe occupied within their own region. With the decline of "duality" between the national center and precolonial traditional centers in the periphery, the latter were more directly affected by developments that occurred in the former. Comparing the Fulbe's position in their own regions after independence on the basis of main resources for power, wealth, and prestige, we found the following:

In Futa Jallon, the Fulbe in general, and the traditional aristocracy in particular, incurred great losses in their control of political and administrative offices, native judicial positions, taxes and other incomes related to administrative offices, land and its products, cheap or free labor, trade benefits, cattle, and western education and professional positions. In some of those resources, such as trade, cattle, and land, although they incurred important losses compared to the colonial period, they still held more control than non-Fulbe people in Futa Jallon. In most other resources, on the other hand, as in local political offices, judicial positions, and availability of cheap labor, their loss eliminated the gap that existed between them and the local non-Fulbe populations and might have even created a reverse gap, putting the non-Fulbe in a superior position over the Fulbe. The resource in which the Fulbe incurred least loss was related to Islamic knowledge and piety. It was fought, without much success, by the regime, which saw in it a source of conservatism. Its preservation and the prestige benefits that the Fulbe received from it were basically a result of the disjunction that existed between the center and the periphery. Generally speaking, with passage from the colonial to the postcolonial period, in addition to being evicted from the central political positions, the Fulbe lost all their power and most of their wealth in their own region but were able to keep some prestige related to their traditional proximity to Islam.

In great contrast to their kinsmen of Futa Jallon, the Fulbe of North Cameroon kept control of almost all the resources that they controlled in the colonial period, namely, political-administrative positions, income related to them, native judicial positions, Islamic knowledge and piety, cattle, trade, land

and its products, and cheap or free labor (replacing slaves). The only loss that they incurred was in control over the local police force and prisons (except in Rey Bouba) and, as in the colonial period, they did not hold a prominent position among the western-educated northerners, although through political patronage they were well represented in "western" professions occupied by northerners, especially in the civil service and other politically important positions. In great contrast with Futa Jallon, the Fulbe ethnic group kept intact its domination over power, wealth, and prestige resources in North Cameroon, and this corresponded to its predominance in the Cameroonian postcolonial political center. However, within the Fulbe group, the differences between the aristocratic and commoner elements started to decline in wealth and especially local power as a result of the commoners' predominance in the new central and regional administration.

In Northern Nigeria, until the military coup of 1966 the Fulbe continued to have greater control than local non-Fulbe people over all the resources that they had controlled already in the colonial period, namely, political and administrative offices, incomes related to them, the local police force, native judicial positions, Islamic knowledge and piety, cattle, land and its products, and a cheap or free labor force. The only two sets of resources that they did not control, those related to trade and to western education, were controlled by non-Fulbe people already in the colonial and, in the case of trade, even in the precolonial period. So, as in the colonial period, the Fulbe kept much more power and prestige than other local populations but lost some ground to the Hausa in wealth because of the great development of the latter's income from commercial activities. However, the situation changed after the military coups of 1966. The decline of Fulbe presence in the Nigerian political center was accompanied by important changes in their position within the north too. They incurred great losses in the control of political and administrative offices, the local police force, and the judicial apparatus, as well as income related to administrative positions. These changes reduced the gap between the Fulbe and other populations in controlling power resources, and this was added to a reduction of the wealth gap which had started with the development of commerce in the colonial period. However, no change occurred in the supremacy of the

Fulbe in prestige related to their proximity to Islam and to the precolonial center of Sokoto.

We have seen, therefore, that some important differences existed in the extent of Fulbe dominance in Futa Jallon, Northern Nigeria, and North Cameroon after independence, especially when compared with the general similarity that existed between them in the precolonial period. Although starting from a very similar point, the Fulbe ended up in very different positions relative to other populations in the three societies. We have seen that the main factors of this differential adjustment to change were external to the Fulbe and had very little to do with their internal adjustment capabilities. The reaction of the Fulbe to external factors of change was very similar in the three societies, but since the external factors themselves were different, the outcome was different adjustment to change.

At this stage, it might be interesting to broaden our focus of analysis and look at the general African scene from a comparative perspective. Taking into consideration other major examples of sub-Saharan African aristocracies (such as the ruling aristocratic groups among the Mossi in Upper Volta, the Lozi in Zambia, the Tutsi in Rwanda, the Baganda in Uganda, and many other examples[3]), we can see that some of our findings on the Fulbe adjustment to change might have broader applications.

Our study showed first of all that in social change occurring in the colonial context, we deal with far-reaching transformations introduced and even imposed from outside without any real possibility of resistance on the part of the receiving side. As resistance to the change itself was futile, the best strategy for the receiving side (in this case, the native population and more particularly a certain group within it) was to achieve control of the locus where change was initiated (i.e., of the new center whose formation had brought all the changes into the area) in order to model the changes according to the receiver's own interests. However, was the receiving side (the native population) free to try to control the locus of change? The answer to that question appears in the great difference between the situation in the colonial period proper, on the one hand, and that in the period of decolonization and after independence, on the other. In the colonial period it was impossible for any indigenous group to achieve control of the new center where changes were determined and initiated, since the colonial center was monopolized by alien European elements who restricted indigenous participation in it, especially in the political sphere. However, starting with decolonization and after independence, as the center was opened to indigenous political participation and later control, it became possible for indigenous elements to try and control the locus of change in order to shape the changes according to their own advantage. This, in turn, changed completely the patterns of adjustment to change and the factors involved in it.

In the colonial period proper, patterns of change depended mainly on the policy of the European colonial administration to which the native population generally could not object but could accommodate itself in various ways without controlling the force of change. Precolonial ruling groups who continued the struggle to the bitter end or with whom the colonial power (for any reason) did not want to come to an understanding (such as Samori in Guinea and the Toucouleurs in Mali) were utterly destroyed and ceased to exist. More cooperative aspirants were always found to replace uncooperative indigenous elites. As Crowder and Ikime well point out,[4] there were important differences between French and British (and certainly also other European powers') colonial policies regarding the preservation of precolonial political systems, and this had serious consequences on the degree of political autonomy left to traditional rulers, the degree of preservation of precolonial territorial units, and freedom in deciding on succession to political office. The difference between Futa Jallon and Northern Nigeria illustrated the consequences of differences between French and British policies. Important differences were found also between different territories of the same colonial power. The traditional elite among the Mossi in Upper Volta and the Fulbe in North Cameroon held much more autonomous power than its counterpart in Guinea and Mali. The same was true of the rulers of Buganda compared to those of Ashanti. However, beyond these differences and if we exclude areas of large-scale white settlement where the attitudes and activities of the settlers, as opposed to the colonial administration, introduced other complications, we also find important points of resemblance and standard patterns in the colonial powers' policies. Generally speaking, each colonial power tried to accord its innovative functions (in-

troducing large-scale changes into the territories) with a more
basic regulative function, the need to preserve basic social order
and administration in a time of rapid transformation. For this
regulative function the colonial powers needed the assistance of
traditional structures and traditional leadership to which they
left important functions in local political and especially cultural
fields. This led to what we called the colonial duality, the
coexistence of a traditional sector around precolonial indigenous centers next to a western sector around the newly formed
alien colonial center. To the extent that such precolonial centers
existed and were willing to cooperate with the colonial center,
the precolonial aristocratic groups preserved their position in
that center, and that enabled them to maintain their dominance
over local populations in terms of control of power, wealth, and
prestige resources, despite the many innovations that were introduced in the colonial period. They were able to translate
their old resources into new uses in order to maintain overall
dominance in a rapidly changing situation, that is, they were
able to adjust successfully to change in the colonial period. In
this respect we found no great difference between our three
societies and, generally speaking, no great difference is expected between other aristocratic groups' adjustment to change.
Factors affecting the establishment of colonial duality, on the
other hand, include both factors internal to the precolonial systems themselves, such as their ability to develop elaborate political structures or their ability to exert widespread cultural or
religious influence on other populations, and situational factors
beyond their direct control, such as their geographical position
within the new colonial boundaries, the extent of white settlement in their area, etc.

With the opening of the new center to indigenous participation and control in the period of decolonization and after independence, the maintenance of a dominant position within
the group's own area became closely dependent on the given
group's ability to dominate, or at least be influential at, the central positions whose control passed to indigenous elements. In
this regard, comparing the major examples of African traditional
aristocracies, we can detect the following patterns.

If the traditional aristocracy was identified with the losing
side in the struggle between indigenous groups for the control
of central positions, its position obviously declined sharply, not

only in the center, but also in its own region in the periphery. The classic example of that was Futa Jallon, but other examples were also found in the case of the Lozi aristocracy in Zambia, the Tutsi in Rwanda, and to some extent the Ashanti under Nkrumah's regime in Ghana. If, on the other hand, the traditional elite was on the winning side, its position depended on the patterns of association formed with other populations in the winning front and especially the identity of its associates. With the possible exception of Swaziland, I can think of no case in which the political center vacated by the colonial powers was handed over to the traditional aristocracy without association with some other indigenous group. The traditional aristocracy could be in alliance with: (*a*) westernized elements within its own ranks, (*b*) westernized elements of the same region and ethnic origin but not of aristocratic origin, (*c*) elements of the same region or religion but not of the same ethnic group, and (*d*) populations from other regions of the colonial territory. Obviously, the last of these associations, illustrated in the NCNC-NPC coalition in Nigeria and in the Obote-Kabaka alliance in Uganda, was the most fragile one. The coalition tended to break apart soon after independence, struggle resumed between the coalition partners, and if the traditional elite lost the renewed struggle, its fate was not much different from those who lost the struggle in the first place. The decline of the traditional rulers was quite rapid in this case, as could be seen in the Buganda King's demise under Obote's rule in Uganda.

In the other three cases mentioned above, the alliances had firmer bases since they were formed with groups who had some common ties with the ruling aristocracy in question—whether class, ethnic, or religious ties—or at least common hostility to people from other regions; hence one could expect a longer cooperation between their component parts. In these cases (illustrated in Northern Nigeria and North Cameroon, but possibly also in Botswana, among the Mossi in Upper Volta, and the Ashanti under the first military regime and Busia's civilian regime in Ghana), the traditional elite again lost its predominance to its westernized partners who occupied the new central positions. This was true (though perhaps to a lesser extent) even when the new central positions were occupied by westernized elements belonging to the aristocracy itself (as in Botswana and as was the case in Nigeria during the civilian regime). This phenomenon could again be explained by the decline of duality, which is inseparable from the effort to Africanize the new center and consolidate its supremacy. On the whole, the new elites, claiming to be the only true representatives of the African population (this justified their replacement of the colonial authority which did not represent the native population), tended to be less tolerant of continuing autonomous loci of power in the periphery. So, in any case, the takeover of the colonial center by indigenous groups and the formation of a new postcolonial center on the basis of the older center entailed some decline of power for the traditional aristocracy, though the extent of this loss varied greatly according to the type of relationship between the traditional elite and the new holders of the national political center.

It remains to be seen what factors affected the outcome of the struggle for the control of the center, which had such a crucial effect on the traditional aristocracies within their own region. Here again, factors which explained the differential outcome of the struggle in the three areas studied in this book might be found to have wider applications. Among the factors determining the outcome of the struggle we could count the following:

(a) *The size of the population in the region inhabited by the group in question, compared to other regions of the country.* The more populous the region, the greater were the given group's chances of achieving a controlling position at the center. We have seen how much the Fulbe's dominance in Nigeria depended on the disproportionate size of the northern region compared to the south. In Swaziland, the indigenous population was almost wholly composed of Swazi who took for granted the traditional elite's authority; hence, the latter had no difficulty in dominating the postcolonial center as well. In contrast, the relatively small proportion of Lozi in the overall Zambian population reduced their traditional aristocracy's influence on the Zambian center and compelled them to think more in terms of secession than of conquering the Zambian center.

(b) *The extent to which the group in question found allies outside its own region and especially among other populations living within its own region.* We have already seen that alliances with people of other regions were fragile coalitions and were easily replaceable. The formation of regional fronts, on the other hand, was of utmost importance in the struggle for the control of the center. Their existence in Northern Nigeria and North Cameroon was essential to the Fulbe success in coming to dominant positions in the center as independence was achieved. In contrast, the decline of the Mossi traditional rulers' position during the civilian regime in Upper Volta was closely related to a lack of regional-ethnic unity due to a rift between Mossi of aristocratic and commoner origins. Regional solidarity based on ethnic unity could also explain the strength of the Buganda king at the later stages of decolonization but could not explain his demise shortly after independence. Obviously other factors, such as the control of military power and the unity of other regions fearing Buganda domination, weighed more heavily than the ethnic-regional unity of Buganda.

(c) *The degree of unity among populations living outside the region inhabited by the group in question.* When such unity existed, the chances of preventing the given group's political domination at the center were greater. Such unity also improved the likelihood of movements based in other regions penetrating into the group's own region, mobilizing there certain elements against the given group, and thus preventing the formation of an ethnic or regional front. Obviously, this factor was also closely related to that of size. When the group in question did not control a large region, it was relatively easier for other regions, if united, to reach power without needing the support of the region in question, as occurred to some extent in Guinea regarding Futa Jallon, in Zambia regarding Barotseland, but could not occur in Nigeria regarding the north or in Upper Volta regarding Mossiland. When the region was relatively large, outside forces had to try to mobilize some support in that region in order to succeed in the struggle; southern Nigerians attempted this without much success in the north, but Nkrumah was more successful in Ashanti. A certain size and resourcefulness, by giving salience to a region, could also be a factor in uniting all the other regions against it and preventing its dominance, as occurred against the Baganda after Uganda achieved independence. In any case, when the people living outside the region in question were divided among themselves, as were the Ibo and Yoruba in Southern Nigeria and the various southern groups in Cameroon, the chances of the group in question coming to dominant positions were greatly enhanced, as happened in those two countries.

(*d*) Very closely related to the preceding two factors are the *geographical, cultural, and constitutional barriers and distance that existed between the regions inhabited by the group in case and other areas of the colonial territory.* The existence of such distance helped the group's domination at the center by facilitating the formation of a regional front and by reducing the penetration into its area of movements based outside, as was the case in Northern Nigeria, North Cameroon, and to some extent also in Barotseland and Buganda. The special constitutional arrangements that existed between Barotseland and the rest of Northern Rhodesia and between Buganda and the rest of Uganda helped maintain the respective ruling aristocracies as especially powerful groups to contend with, though this did not prevent their eventual demise.

(*e*) *The extent to which the colonial administration favored the given group against other groups.* This factor was found to have contradictory effects. Colonial favor certainly did help the Fulbe in North Cameroon and Northern Nigeria as well as in Niger. However, it could also be a liability by portraying the group in question as a collaborator with colonialists and making it a target of anticolonial movements and aspirations. This happened to the Fulbe in Futa Jallon as well as to the Lozi aristocracy in Barotseland and contributed in both cases to the downfall of the aristocracy and the elimination of traditional chiefdom.

(*f*) Finally, an important factor which should not be overlooked is *the differential success of military coups or other insurrectional attempts after independence and whether those actions were directed by forces supporting or opposing the group in question.* In many cases the position reached by a group at the end of decolonization was radically changed by political developments that occurred after independence. Many traditional elites who were on the losing side at the end of decolonization had their position improved by military coups which toppled the first generation of postcolonial rulers. This was the case in Ghana following the fall of Nkrumah. The military coup of 1966 in Upper Volta also improved the position of the Mossi traditional rulers following a steady decline during the civilian regime of

Yaméogo. In Uganda, on the other hand, the Kabaka of
Buganda, who seemed so powerful at the center as independence was achieved, was forced into exile and the kingship
abolished after a few years. In Burundi where, in contrast with
neighboring Rwanda, the precolonial monarchy seemed dominant as independence was achieved, the kingship was abolished
and the ruling Ganwa aristocracy lost all power following the
military coup which brought to power the Tutsi elements
in the army.

The factors enumerated above are obviously very closely
interrelated, and it is quite difficult to separate them for analytical purposes as we have tried to do here. In any case, they
show us again the rather narrow margin of manipulation that
the struggling groups had on the outcome of their struggle. Of
the six factors discussed above, only factor (b) and possibly also
(f) could be said to be controllable by the group in question, and
even factor (b) was closely dependent on other factors which
were beyond the group's control. During the colonial period,
the indigenous population's lack of control over forces of
change was due to inaccessibility to the locus of change, the
new center formed by the colonial enterprise. However, even
after the center was opened to the indigenous population, the
various competing groups in it lacked control over the factors
determining which of them would accede to that locus of
change in order to model the changes according to their own
advantage.

The findings of this work raise some serious doubts about the
tendency to concentrate on systems' internal adjustment
capabilities in analyzing adjustment to change, at least as far as
it concerns traditional aristocratic groups' effort to maintain
their dominance in changing situations. We are certainly not
the only ones to raise doubts about this tendency. Historians
have for a long time criticized sociologists and political scientists for their neglect of external, "historical" factors in their
analysis of social change. There have been also some
sociologists who stressed the necessity of paying greater attention to external situational factors in the analysis of social
change. Bendix proposed that studies of modernization be
more interested in the external factors that affect change.[5] Nisbet thoroughly criticized the tendency, which he attributed to a

"social systems" approach, to concentrate on internal systemic attributes of societies in explaining social change.[6] We should point out, however, that the main thrust of Nisbet's argument regarding social change is somewhat different from ours. Nisbet states that although social change originates from the exterior, adjustment or reaction to change might be determined by the internal properties of the society or group in question.[7] We wanted to determine precisely to what extent those internal properties determined traditional aristocracies' adjustment to colonial and postcolonial change, and we came to the conclusion that they were less important than factors which were unrelated to the aristocracies' internal properties.

However, the big problem with external, historical factors is that because those factors can be unlimited and can vary widely from case to case, it becomes very difficult, if not impossible, to derive high-level generalizations that would be valid beyond the immediate cases that are compared. Historians might not be very concerned about this difficulty since, in essence, they stress much more the particularity of events in the unique context of time and space. Sociologists, on the other hand, need generalizations; they try to get rid of particularities and want to arrive at social laws, patterns, regularities that give some order to social phenomena. If no generalizations are possible, what is the use of comparative study, they might ask, and how can one move beyond the mere collecting or reporting of data? This problem is by no means close to being resolved. One possible solution could be to use comparative study simply to increase one's understanding of his own subject matter by showing similarities and differences with other cases or phenomena. A person who studies case a may perhaps understand it and explain it (i.e., communicate his understanding to others) better if he is aware of the way in which case a is similar to or different from case b or c or d, even if he cannot generate statements at a higher level of abstraction that would show some kind of generalized relationship between all these cases and possibly others. However, one can also use the knowledge gathered by the comparative study of cases a, b, c, and d to develop some general propositions that could be set as hypotheses to be tested in further case studies. This is what we tried to do when we developed, out of our study of the three cases of Fulbe adjustment to

change, some general ideas on the factors determining traditional aristocratic groups' differential adjustment to colonial
and postcolonial change.

Beyond its comparative purpose, this book has tried to shed
light on the mechanisms by which dominant, privileged
groups, or those who have most to lose from change, try to
maintain their position in a radically changing, potentially
more hostile environment. In addition, the study tried to look at
social change from the "receiving" side in the periphery and
suggested that perhaps the most effective reaction of the periphery in response to change imposed by the center is to try to
conquer that center and model it to its own advantage. We have
seen that the differential success of the Fulbe in doing just that
was the most crucial determinant of the extent to which they
could maintain their dominant position at the outcome of social
change.

Notes

Introduction

1. The "Sokoto Caliphate" refers to the whole empire of Sokoto formed by Usman dan Fodio and not simply to the province of Sokoto, which was only one of the many emirates of the Sokoto empire. Even though Adamawa was also part of the Sokoto empire, its discussion is separated from that of Sokoto because most of Adamawa became part of the German and then French Cameroon territory, while the rest of the Sokoto empire became part of British Northern Nigeria. Adamawa encountered the major social change that interests us here under very different conditions from the rest of Sokoto, and this warrants its separate treatment.

2. The word *Fulbe* denotes the people whom English speakers mostly call *Fulani*, using the Hausa word for it. Because we deal with the population living also outside the Hausa linguistic zone, I preferred to use the terms by which they are called in their own language, i.e., *Pullo* in the singular (as in "a rich Pullo") and *Fulbe* in the plural or to denote the totality of the collectivity (as in "many Fulbe came" or "the Fulbe fought"). I also used the term Fulbe in "the Fulbe identity," "the Fulbe state," etc., meaning the identity or the state of the Fulbe.

3. There might be some basic goals or desires that cannot easily be included in acquisition of power, wealth, and prestige. One such desire is the desire for security. However, unlike power, wealth and prestige, which are directly related to a desire for dominance, desire for security does not necessarily lead to dominance. On the contrary, it often motivates people to give up some dominance, relinquish some power, wealth, or prestige. For this reason the desire for security is not taken into consideration here and does not disturb our triplet of desiderata leading to dominance.

4. Max Weber, "Class, Status and Party," in *Class, Status and Power,* ed. Reinhard Bendix and Seymour M. Lipset (New York: Free Press, 1966), pp. 21–28.

5. Shmuel N. Eisenstadt, *Social Differentiation and Stratification* (Glenview, Ill.: Scott, Foresman, 1971), p. 9.

6. Lenski's "power," "privilege," and "prestige" provide a similar triad to power, wealth, and prestige used here. On the possible interrelationships between power, privilege, and prestige, see G. E. Lenski, *Power and Privilege* (New York: McGraw-Hill, 1966), passim.

7. Eisenstadt, *Social Differentiation and Stratification*, p. 49.

8. As the mere distribution of resources does not specify the different "strata" in society and the distinctions between them, I prefer to state that the distribution of resources merely points to the structure of inequality in the society and not to the social stratification system. Whether and how this inequality crystallizes into a hierarchical structure of distinct strata is a separate problem into which we shall not enter at this stage.

9. Edward A. Shils, "Center and Periphery," in *Center and Periphery: Essays in Macrosociology* (Chicago: University of Chicago Press, 1970), p. 3.

10. I owe these four point to discussions that I had with Professor Shmuel Eisenstadt at the Hebrew University, Jerusalem, Israel in the years 1968–70.

11. See Shmuel N. Eisenstadt, "Modernization and Conditions of Sustained Growth," *World Politics* 16 (July 1961): 576–94; W. H. Friedland, "A Sociologial Approach to Modernization," in *Modernization by Design*, ed. Chandler Morse (Ithaca, N.Y.: Cornell University Press, 1969), pp. 36–37; D. E. Apter, "The Role of Traditionalism in the Political Modernization of Ghana and Uganda," *World Politics* 13 (October 1960): 45–68; Marion J. Levy, "Contrasting Factors in the Modernization of China and Japan," *Economic Development and Cultural Change* 2 (October 1953): 161–98.

Part One

1. For a somewhat outdated approximation of the distribution of the Fulbe in Africa, see Derrick J. Stenning, *Savannah Nomads* (London: Oxford University Press, 1959), p. 1. The estimate of the Fulbe in Senegambia excludes the large number of Toucouleurs who are Fulfuldé (the Fulbe language) speakers and who have close ethnic affinity to the Fulbe. The relationship between the Fulbe and the Toucouleurs is an interesting subject which needs separate treatment.

2. For details on Pulaaku, see Derrick J. Stenning, "The Pastoral Fulani of Northern Nigeria," in *Peoples of Africa*, ed. J. L. Gibbs (New York: Holt, Rinehart & Winston, 1960), pp. 368–70; F. W. de St. Croix, *The Fulani of Northern Nigeria* (Lagos: Government Printer, 1945), p. 9.

3. See Marguerite Dupire, *Peuls Nomades* (Paris: Institut d'Ethnologie, 1962), p. 53; S. Baldé, "L'Elevage au Fouta Djallon," *Bulletin de l'IFAN* 1 (1939): 630–43; St. Croix, *The Fulani of Northern Nigeria*, pp. 8–9.

4. The affiliation to one of the four Yettoré gained some importance during the colonial period with the spread of usage of family name. In Western Sudan (Futa Jallon, Futa Toro, Massina), the Fulbe adopted their Yettoré as family name, as a result of which all the Fulbe in Mali, Guinea, Senegal today have as second name Ba, Bari, Diallo, Sow, or some derivative of them, such as *Dya, Baldé, Dikko,* while in Central Sudan (Nigeria, Niger, Cameroon) Yettoré were so insignificant that

instead of them fathers' names were used as second name, e.g., Muhamadu Aliu, Hamidu Usmanu, Abdulahi Umaru, etc.

5. Ousmane Diallo and Oumar Ba, interviews at the Institut Fondamental d'Afrique Noire, Dakar, May 1972; Eldridge Mohamadou, interview at the Centre Fédéral Culturel et Linguistique, Yaoundé, Cameroon, March 1972. In his study of Futa Jallon, William Derman stresses the division into maximal, major, and minimal patrilineages, the first being a geographically dispersed group based on common ancestry and providing an important basis of identity for the Fulbe; see William Derman, *Serfs, Peasants and Socialists* (Berkeley: University of California Press, 1973), pp. 15–18, 21–22.

6. See Louis Tauxier, *Moeurs et Histoire des Peuls* (Paris: Payot, 1937), pp. 45–77; Pierre F. Lacroix, "Matériaux pour servir à l'Histoire des Peuls de l'Adamawa," *Etudes Camerounaises* 5, nos. 37–38 (Septembre–Decembre 1952): 5–11.

7. E. W. Bovill, *The Golden Trade of the Moors* (London: Oxford University Press, 1958), p. 238.

8. This was true even when the rulers were themselves Fulbe, as in Massina and Futa Toro.

9. H. C. F. Smith, "The Islamic Revolutions of the 19th Century," *Journal of the Historical Society of Nigeria* 2 (December 1961): 169–86; J. S. Trimingham, *History of Islam in West Africa* (London: Oxford University Press, 1962).

10. On the relationship between Fulbe and non-Fulbe before the Jihads, see Michael Crowder, *The Story of Nigeria* (London: Faber & Faber, 1962), pp. 90–95; Lacroix, "Histoire des Peuls," pp. 18–20; Thierno Diallo, "Les Institutions Politiques du Fouta Djalon au 19e Siècle" (doctoral diss., Université de Paris, Sorbonne, 1970 [?], pp. 21–29.

11. See Paul Marty, *L'Islam en Guinée, Fouta Djalon* (Paris: Leroux, 1921), pp. 1–4; Diallo, "Fouta Djalon," pp. 33–40.

12. For details on the Jihad, see Marty, *Islam en Guinée,* pp. 2–7; Diallo, "Fouta Djalon," pp. 40–41; Derman, *Serfs, Peasants and Socialists,* pp. 12–14.

13. To avert any confusion between Adamawa as a whole and the Adamawa highlands (or plateau), we should point out that the Adamawa plateau formed only part of the whole country called Adamawa. The other parts were located mainly in the Benue valley, the plain of Diamaré, and the Mandara mountains. Confusion arises mainly from the fact that in Cameroon today the word Adamawa is used only for the Adamawa plateau. However, in precolonial times it denoted the whole country ruled by Adama and his subordinate chiefs.

14. For details on the Jihad in Adamawa, see Lacroix, "Histoire des Peuls," pp. 20–31; A. H. M. Kirk-Greene, *Adamawa, Past and Present* (London: Oxford University Press, 1958), pp. 126–35; C. O. Migeod,

"Yola Province" (1927), in *Gazetteers of the Northern Provinces of Nigeria*
ed. A. H. M. Kirk-Greene (London: Cass, 1972), 2:10–15.

15. Thomas Hodgkin, *Nigerian Perspectives* (London: Oxford University Press, 1960), p. 89.

16. Michael Smith, *The Economy of Hausa Communities of Zaria* (London: Colonial Office, 1955), p. 66; see also St. Croix, *The Fulani of Northern Nigeria*, p. 7.

17. For details on the Jihad, see Crowder, *The Story of Nigeria*, pp. 93–106; M. R. Waldman, "The Fulani Jihad: A Reassessment," *Journal of African History* 6 (1965): 340–54.

18. See V. N. Low, *Three Nigerian Emirates* (Evanston, Ill.: Northwestern University Press, 1972), p. 30; C. G. Ames, "The Highland Chieftancies (Plateau Province)" (1934) in Kirk-Greene, ed., *Gazetteers of Northern Nigeria*, 4:33.

19. See the very interesting correspondence on this question between the ruler of Bornu, Al Kanemi, and the ruler of Sokoto, Mohamadu Bello, quoted in Hodgkin, *Nigerian Perspectives*, p. 198.

20. Yet there must have remained some feelings of hostility to the Fulbe on the part of the Hausa. This can be seen perhaps in the very negative light in which Fulbe from Sokoto are depicted in many Hausa folktales; see *Hausa Tales and Traditions*, ed. N. Skinner (London: Cass, 1969), 1:176–80, 190–93.

21. Pierre F. Lacroix, "L'Islam Peul de l'Adamawa," in *Islam in Tropical Africa*, ed. I. M. Lewis (London: Oxford University Press, 1966), p. 402; A. Arcin, *Histoire de la Guinée Française* (Paris: Chalamel, 1911), pp. 519–20; Derman, *Serfs, Peasants and Socialists*, p. 42.

22. J. Vossart, "Histoire du Sultanat du Mandara," *Etudes Camerounaises* 4, nos. 35–36 (1953): 43–46; Y. Urvoy, "Histoire de l'Empire du Bornou," *Mémoires de l'IFAN*, no. 7 (1949), pp. 98–101; Michael G. Smith, "A Hausa Kingdom: Maradi," in *West African Kingdoms*, ed. Daryll Forde and Phyllis Kaberry (London: Oxford University Press, 1967), pp. 93–99; E. Y. Arnett, "Sokoto Province" (1920), in Kirk-Greene, ed., *Gazetteers of Northern Nigeria* 1:9.

23. Such as the Moundang, the Toupouri, the Matakam in Adamawa, the Tiv, the Jukun, some populations inhabiting the Jos plateau in Sokoto, and the Coniagui in Futa Jallon. For details, see Ames, "Highland Chieftancies," pp. 30–32; F. H. Ruxton, "Notes on the Tribes of the Muri Province," *African Affairs* 1 (1907–1908): 370–83; Bertrand Lembezat, *Les Populations Païennes du Nord-Cameroun et de l'Adamaoua* (Paris: Presses Universitaires de France, 1961), pp. 12–15, 67–70, 138–40; Gilbert Vieillard, "Notes sur les Peuls du Fouta Djallon," *Bulletin de l'IFAN* 2 (1940): 106.

24. Such as the Laka, Dourou, Fali, Bata in Adamawa; most of the Jallonké, Bassari, Badyaranké in Futa Jallon; and a multitude of different groups living in southern Zaria, Bauchi, Borgu, and Kontagora in Sokoto. See Lembezat, *Populations Païennes*, pp. 162–64, 212–13, 227–29; Vieillard, "Peuls du Fouta Djalon," pp. 102–6; G. Mollien, *Travels*

in the Interior of Africa, ed. reissue (London: Cass, 1967), p. 314; Ames, "Highland Chieftancies," pp. 33–35; R. K. Udo, *Geographical Regions of Nigeria* (Berkeley: University of California Press, 1970), pp. 116, 159.

25. This was the case of the Dama, the Mboum in Adamawa, various pagan groups in Bauchi and around the central highlands in Sokoto, many Jallonkés, Soussous, and various coastal populations (Baga, Nalou, Landouma) in Futa Jallon; see Ames, "Highland Chieftancies," pp. 33–35; Lembezat, *Populations Païennes,* pp. 193–97; Arcin, *Histoire de la Guinée Française,* p. 520; Mollien, *Travels in Africa,* p. 314; J. Champaud, "L'Immigration Foula en Basse Guinée," unpublished paper (Conakry, Guinea: Service Hydraulique de l'AOF, 1957), pp. 7–8.

26. See Diallo, "Fouta Djalon," pp. 41–51, 190–91; Marty, *Islam en Guinée,* pp. 9–13.

27. See S. Hogben and A. H. M. Kirk-Greene, *The Emirates of Northern Nigeria* (London: Oxford University Press, 1966), pp. 116–23, 376–408; Trimingham, *History of Islam in West Africa,* pp. 200–206; Murray Last, *The Sokoto Caliphate* (New York: Humanities Press, 1967), pp. 46–102.

28. Adamawa being outside the Hausa linguistic zone, the Fulbe word *Lamido* was used for chief instead of the Hausa work *Sarki* or the Arabic word *Emir.* However, for other titles of state officials the Hausa words were adopted.

29. Kirk-Greene, *Adamawa, Past and Present,* pp. 130–44.

30. Diallo, "Fouta Djalon," pp. 153–54; 164–65; 251–60.

31. See Last, *The Sokoto Caliphate,* pp. 49–59, 89–93, 178–80; J. C. Froelich, "Le Commandement et l'Organisation Sociale chez les Foulbé de l'Adamaoua," *Etudes Camerounaises,* no. 45–46 (Septembre–Decembre 1954), p. 34.

32. For details on the provincial and local government structure in Futa Jallon, see Diallo, "Fouta Djalon," pp. 204–11, 238–40; Derman, *Serfs, Peasants and Socialists,* pp. 14–17, 22–23; A. Demougeot, "Notes sur l'Organisation Politique et Administrative de Labé," *Mémoires de l'IFAN,* no. 6 (1944), p. 16; *Fonds Gilbert Vieillard, Serie Fouta Djalon,* Cahier 30, Institut Fondamental d'Afrique Noire, Dakar, Senegal.

33. Low, *Three Nigerian Emirates,* pp. 15–17; Last, *The Sokoto Caliphate,* pp. 158–60; M. G. Smith, *Government in Zazzau* (London: Oxford University Press, 1960), pp. 73–75, 89–91; E. R. Yeld, "Islam and Social Stratification in Northern Nigeria," *British Journal of Sociology* 11, no. 2 (1960): 120.

34. Jean Hurault, "Antagonisme de l'Agriculture et de l'Elevage sur les Hauts Plateaux de l'Adamaoua," *Etudes Rurales,* no. 15 (Octobre–Decembre 1964), pp. 29–31; Froelich, "Commandement Foulbé," p. 6.

35. The only major exception was the emirate of Bauchi in Sokoto whose ruling dynasty was not Fulbe.

36. Diallo, "Fouta Djalon," p. 60.

37. J. Lestringeant, *Les Pays de Guider au Cameroun* (Versailles: n.p., 1964), p. 115.

38. Diallo, "Fouta Djalon," p. 164.

39. See M. G. Smith, *Government in Zazzau*, pp. 100, 127, 344–47; Michael G. Smith, "The Hausa System of Social Status," *Africa* 29 (July 1959): 242.

40. Yeld, "Social Stratification," p. 120.

41. Eldridge Mohamadou, interview at the Centre Federal Culturel et Linguistique, Yaoundé, Cameroon, March 1972.

42. Stenning, *Savannah Nomads*, pp. 1–7.

43. For more details on precolonial slavery, see Derman, *Serfs, Peasants and Socialists*, pp. 27–41; H. Fréchou, "Les Régimes Fonciers dans la Region des Timbi (Fouta Djalon)," in *Etudes de Droit Africain et de Droit Malgache*, ed. Jean Poirier (Paris: Editions Cujas, 1965), pp. 460–61; Mollien, *Travels in Africa*, pp. 299–300; Michael G. Smith, "Slavery and Emancipation in Two Societies (Jamaica and Zaria)," *Social and Economic Studies* 3, no. 4 (1954): 264–66; Skinner, *Hausa Tales and Traditions*, p. 193; Lacroix, "Histoire des Peuls," pp. 32–34; Froelich, "Commandement Foulbé," pp. 19–25.

44. M.G. Smith, "Slavery," p. 266.

45. Jean-Jacques Richard-Molard, "Notes Démographiques sur la Région de Labé," in *Hommage à Jean-Jacques Richard-Molard* (Paris: Présence Africaine, 1956 [?]), p. 86; Derman, *Serfs, Peasants and Socialists*, pp. 8–9; M. G. Smith, "Slavery," p. 241.

46. Quoted in Hodgkin, *Nigerian Perspectives*, p. 265.

47. Froelich, "Commandement Foulbé," p. 35; Yeld, "Social Stratification," p. 116. Derman, on the other hand, claims that in Futa Jallon children of Fulbe's concubines remained servile and were not considered Fulbe. Only offspring of Fulbe's *marriage* with slave girls were considered free Fulbe; see *Serfs, Peasants and Socialists*, p. 41.

48. In this study we are interested mainly in the sedentary Fulbe. For details on the differentiation between sedentary and pastoral Fulbe, see Derrick J. Stenning, "Transhumance, Migratory Drift, Migration," in *Cultures and Societies in Africa*, ed. Simon Ottenberg and Phoebe Ottenberg (New York: Random House, 1960), p. 155; Eldridge Mohamadou, *Les Traditions Historiques des Peuls de l'Adamawa* (Niamey, Niger: Centre Régional des Traditions Orales, 1970), p. 152.

49. Interviews in North Cameroon and Dakar, Senegal, February–June 1972; see also Derman, *Serfs, Peasants and Socialists*, pp. 27–28.

50. Low, *Three Nigerian Emirates*, p. 35; M. G. Smith, "Slavery," pp. 244–45; 250; Marguerite Dupire, *Organisation Sociale des Peul* (Paris: Plon, 1970), p. 430.

51. Dupire, *Peuls Nomades*, p. 23. In some areas new groups developed out of the mixture of Fulbe and local populations among whom they settled, such as the Wassulonké in today's Upper Guinea and southern Mali and the Khassonké in today's western Mali; see Sten-

ning, *Savannah Nomads,* pp. 8–9; G, Brasseur, "Les Etablissements Humains au Mali," *Mémoires de l'IFAN,* no. 83 (1968), p. 249.

52. Demougeot, "Labé," p. 14; Derman, *Serfs, Peasants and Socialists,* pp. 25–27.

53. F. H. Ruxton, *Maliki Law* (London, 1916), p. 78.

54. For details on the land tenure system in the three societies, see Diallo, "Fouta Djallon," pp. 104–105; M. G. Smith, *Economy of Zaria,* p. 105; M. G. Smith, *Government in Zazzau,* pp. 81, 145; "Taxation in Northern Nigeria," *Journal of the African Society,* no. 19 (April 1906), p. 315; Low, *Three Nigerian Emirates,* pp. 30–31; H. A. Oluwasanmi, *Agriculture and Nigerian Economic Development* (Ibadan, Nigeria: Oxford University Press, 1966), pp. 31–32; Froelich, "Commandement Foulbé," pp. 28–29, 77–80. Additional information was collected also from Ousmane Diallo in an interview at the Institut Fondamental d'Afrique Noire, Dakar, Senegal, May 1972 and in various interviews in North Cameroon between February and April 1972.

55. See in this matter Oluwasanmi, *Agriculture,* pp. 23–32; D. F. H. MacBride, "Land Survey in the Kano Emirate, Northern Provinces, Nigeria," *African Affairs* 37 (January 1938): 77–80; Polly Hill, *Rural Hausa* (Cambridge: Cambridge University Press, 1972), pp. 21, 240–41; J. Binet, "Droit Foncier Coutumier au Cameroun," *Monde Non Chrétien,* no. 18 (1951), pp. 12–13; G. Roland, "Etude sur les Règles Coutumières dans la Circonscription de Ngaoundéré" (1932–33), *Documentation ORSTOM, Dossier Adamaoua,* No. 1-10-a, Yaoundé, Cameroon, pp. 3, 6–7, 15–17; Derman, *Serfs, Peasants and Socialists;* Fréchou, "Régimes Fonciers," pp. 411–13; Dupire, *Organisation Sociale des Peul,* p. 280.

56. R. M. Prothero, "Land Use, Land Holdings and Land Tenure at Sobo, Zaria Province, Northern Nigeria," *Bulletin de l'IFAN* 19, nos. 3–4 (July–October 1957): 558; H. A. Luning, "The Impact of Socio-Economic Factors on the Land Tenure Patterns in Northern Nigeria," *Journal of Local Administration Overseas* 4 (July 1965): 175; *Fonds Vieillard, Série Fouta Djalon* (Cahiers 82–83); interviews in North Cameroon, February–April 1972.

57. At this point, the analysis has moved to a broader comparison of the sedentary Fulbe as a whole with the non-Fulbe populations. We should emphasize that here, as well as throughout the book, we intermittently shift between a more narrow examination of the Fulbe as a ruling group (compared with all commoners, Fulbe and non-Fulbe alike) and the equally important study of the sedentary Fulbe as a separate ethnic group compared with other non-Fulbe ethnic groups. It is quite tedious to repeat at every point what levels of comparison are intended, and it would, hopefully, be apparent in the context it is used, but the reader should nevertheless be alert to the distinction between: (*a*) the Fulbe chiefs as actual rulers; (*b*) the Fulbe as an aristocratic ruling class, and (*c*) the Fulbe as an ethnic group holding, as a whole, superior positions to non-Fulbe populations.

58. A. L. Mabogunje, *Urbanization in Africa* (London: University of London Press, 1968), pp. 60–62; E. P. Skinner, "West African Economic Systems," in *Economic Transition in Africa*, ed. Melville J. Herskovits and Mitchell Harwitz (Evanston, Ill.: Northwestern University Press, 1964), pp. 89–92.

59. Lestringeant, *Guider*, pp. 130–32; Capitaine Meyer, "Rapport sur la Tournée dans le Boubandjida" (1918), *Documentation ORSTOM, Dossier Benoué*, no. III-242, Yaoundé, Cameroon, p. 20.

60. On precolonial commerce in Futa Jallon, see Yves Person, "The Atlantic Coast and the Southern Savannahs, 1800–1880," in *The History of West Africa* ed. J. F. A. Ajayi and M. Crowder (London: Longman, 1974), 2:262–67; Diallo, "Fouta Djalon," pp. 119–22; Vieillard, "Peuls du Fouta Djalon," pp. 121, 195; Derman, *Serfs, Peasants and Socialists*, p. 26.

61. Yeld, "Social Stratification," p. 117; Dupire, *Organisation Sociale des Peul*, pp. 432–36, 445; Claude Rivière, "Système et Dynamique des Castes dans les Sociétés Peules et Mandingues," *Culture et Developement* 2, no. 2 (1969–70): 334–35, 344–45; interviews in North Cameroon, February–April 1972.

62. Claude Rivière, "Guinée: La Difficile Emergence d'un Artisanat Casté," *Cahiers d'Etudes Africaines* 9, no. 4 (1969): 609; Diallo, "Fouta Djalon," pp. 115–18; Derman, *Serfs, Peasants and Socialists*, pp. 37–39.

63. Michael J. Campbell, *Law and Practice of Local Government in Northern Nigeria* (Lagos: African University Press, 1963), p. 2; Last, *The Sokoto Caliphate*, pp. 104–06; Diallo, "Fouta Djalon," p. 168; Genin, "Etude des Redevances Coraniques et Coutumières Perçues par les Chefs Musulmans du Nord Cameroun" (1937), *Documentation ORSTOM, Dossier Benoué*, no. III-799, Yaoundé, Cameroon, pp. 1–3.

64. M. G. Smith, *Economy of Zaria*, pp. 11, 14, 91.

65. See, for example, Michael G. Smith, "Historical and Cultural Conditions of Political Corruption among the Hausa," *Comparative Studies in Society and History* 6, no. 2 (January 1964): 174.

66. Froelich, "Commandement Foulbé," pp. 43, 51; Diallo, "Fouta Djalon," pp. 176–80; C. W. J. Orr, *The Making of Northern Nigeria* (London: Macmillan, 1911), p. 158.

67. In 1900 the British estimated that there were 20,000 koranic schools in Northern Nigeria with no less thatn 250,000 pupils in them. D. H. Williams, *A Short Survey of Education in Northern Nigeria* (Kaduna, Nigeria: Government Printer, Northern Region, 1960), p. 6.

68. Thierno Diallo, in interview at the University of Dakar, Senegal, May 1972; interviews in North Cameroon, February–April, 1972; see also Derman, *Serfs, Peasants and Socialists*, p. 24.

69. Although the bulk of the Hausa were Muslims and were so considered by the Fulbe, not all Hausa were Muslims. There was a sizeable group of Hausa-speaking people called *Maguzawa* who were (and some still are) pagan. As there are no clear ethnic boundaries by which the Hausa people could be delimited, and as we call Hausa all the non-

Fulbe autochthonous people of Sokoto who spoke the Hausa language at the time of the Jihad, the Maguzawa should also be considered Hausa. Here, for the sake of simplicity, we chose not to deal with the Maguzawa, but their existence should not be ignored. For details on the Maguzawa, see J. Greenberg, *The Influence of Islam on a Sudanese Religion*, 2d printing (Seattle: University of Washington Press, 1966).

70. If we compare our findings regarding the interconvertibility between power, wealth, and prestige with Lenski's thesis of relationship between privilege and prestige we find some interesting similarities (G. E. Lenski, *Power and Privilege* [New York: McGraw-Hill, 1966], pp. 44–46). We see in Lenski's diagram on p. 46 that power is directly convertible to privilege, while privilege has to pass through prestige in order to be reconverted to power. This is very similar to our finding that power is directly convertible to wealth (which is a narrower version of Lenski's privilege), while wealth has to pass through prestige in order to purchase power. Our finding of close and direct interconvertibility between power and prestige supports Lenski, even though in his diagram the conversion of power into prestige is stressed more heavily than vice-versa while in our case no such difference is found. Finally, regarding the relationship between prestige and wealth, our finding that prestige is not readily covertible to wealth unless it passes through the intermediary of power suits his diagram and provides support to his argument that power is the key causal and explanatory variable in the triad. However, his diagram shows that privilege is directly convertible to prestige, while we found that, although the conversion of wealth into prestige is easier than vice-versa, it still needs the intermediary power in order to reach the highest levels of prestige.

71. See M. G. Smith, *Economy of Zaria*, pp. 16, 92–93; Williams, *Education in Northern Nigeria*, p. 19; Marty, *Islam en Guinée*, pp. 441–45, 454; J. C. Froelich, "Ngaoundéré, La Vie Economique d'une Cité Peule," *Etudes Camerounaises*, no. 43 (Juin–Juillet 1954), p. 8.

Part Two

1. On the establishment of French colonial rule in Futa Jallon, see J. E. Harris, "Les Précurseurs de la Domination Coloniale au Fouta Djalon," *Présence Africaine* 60 (1966): 54–66; J. D. Hargreaves, *Prelude to the Partition of West Africa* (London: Macmillan, 1964), pp. 269–70; Thierno Diallo, "Les Institutions Politiques du Fouta Djalon au 19ᵉ Siècle" (doctoral diss., Université de Paris, Sorbonne, 1970 [?]), pp. 78–79; Jean Suret-Canale, "La Fin de la Chefferie en Guinée," *Journal of African History* 7, no. 3 (1966): 466, 486.

2. A. Demougeot, "Notes sur l'Organisation Politique et Administrative de Labé," *Mémoires de l'IFAN*, no. 6 (1944), pp. 38, 61–81; William Derman, *Serfs, Peasants and Socialists* (Berkeley: University of California Press, 1973), pp. 44–46; Jean Suret-Canale, "La Guinée dans le Système Colonial," *Présence Africaine*, no. 29 (1959–60), pp. 15–19.

3. Demougeot, "Labé," pp. 42–53.

4. See Pierre F. Lacroix, "Matériaux pour Servir à l'Histoire des Peuls de l'Adamawa," *Etudes Camerounaises* 5, nos. 37–38 (Septembre–Decembre 1952): pp. 40–41; R. A. Adeleye, *Power and Diplomacy in Northern Nigeria* (London: Longmans, 1971), pp. 146–59; H. R. Rudin, *Germans in the Cameroons* (New Haven, Conn.: Yale University Press, 1958), pp. 17–55; A. H. M. Kirk-Greene, *Adamawa, Past and Present* (London: Oxford University Press), pp. 26–34, 47–56.

5. Eldridge Mohamadou, *L'Histoire du Tibati* (Yaoundé: Editions Abbia, 1965), pp. 64–66; E. Mohamadou, *Les Traditions Historiques des Peuls de l'Adamawa* (Niamey, Niger: Centre Régional des Traditions Orales, 1970), pp. 229–34, 402–4; Kirk-Greene, *Adamawa, Past and Present,* pp. 47–49, 56–65; Adeleye, *Power and Diplomacy,* pp. 200–203, 232–33.

6. A "mahdi" is a person proclaiming to have been divinely guided to restore Islamic faith and order.

7. Ahmadou Bassoro, in interview in Garoua, North Cameroon, March 1972; Pierre F. Lacroix, "L'Islam Peul de l'Adamawa," in *Islam in Tropical Africa,* ed. I. M. Lewis (London: Oxford University Press, 1966), pp. 404–6; Mohamadou, *Traditions Historiques,* pp. 216–29, 408–9.

8. Lacroix, "Histoire des Peuls," pp. 45–50.

9. Ibid., p. 49; J. Lestringeant, *Les Pays de Guider au Cameroun* (Versailles, 1964), p. 297; Mohamadou, *Traditions Historiques,* pp. 257–63.

10. Adeleye, *Power and Diplomacy,* pp. 165–92; Michael Crowder, *The Story of Nigeria* (London: Faber & Faber, 1962), pp. 185–90, 219; S. Hogben and A. H. M. Kirk-Greene, *The Emirates of Northern Nigeria* (London: Oxford University Press, 1966), pp. 275–76, 299–302.

11. C. W. J. Orr, *The Making of Northern Nigeria,* (London: Macmillan, 1911), pp. 26–27, 38–39; Crowder, *The Story of Nigeria,* pp. 223–26; Adeleye, *Power and Diplomacy,* pp. 250–92.

12. Crowder, *The Story of Nigeria,* p. 226.

13. See details in ibid., chap. 14.

14. Ibid., pp. 228–30

15. In our discussion of the colonial and postcolonial periods we shall generally use the terms "Northern Nigeria" and "North Cameroon" instead of "Sokoto" and "Adamawa," even though they include areas that were not under Fulbe rule in the precolonial period (such as Bornu and Tivland in Northern Nigeria and the Lake Chad region in North Cameroon). The reason is that since the colonial period the terms "Sokoto" and "Adamawa" have come to denote only a specific part of the precolonial states. "Sokoto" has been used only for the province (or emirate) of Sokoto, as separate from Kano, Zaria, Katsina, etc., all parts of the precolonial Sokoto empire. "Adamawa" has been used only for the Adamawa highlands (chiefdoms of Ngaoundéré Tignère, Tibati, Banyo) as separated from the Benue valley or the plain of Diamaré which were also part of the precolonial state of Adamawa. The most relevant administrative territorial units for the entire area for-

merly ruled by the Fulbe states are, therefore, Northern Nigeria and North Cameroon. In Guinea, on the other hand, Futa Jallon continues to be used to denote the region ruled by the precolonial Fulbe state; hence, we continue to use the same term in our discussion of the colonial and postcolonial periods.

16. Suret-Canale, "Fin de la Chefferie," pp. 463–68; Derman, *Serfs, Peasants and Socialists,* pp. 45–46. The French officials who appointed the chiefs took care to choose them from among chiefly lineages, but they often selected them from collateral lines of former chiefs and not from their direct descendants. Many chiefs were people who had legitimate claim to office but who under ordinary circumstances had little chance of actually acceding to that office, thereby owing their selection to French favor. In this way a compromise was found between traditional legitimacy and personal loyalty to the French; see Derman, p. 46.

17. On the German colonial administration, see Rudin, *Germans in the Cameroons,* pp. 186–90; Lacroix, "Histoire des Peuls," p. 43.

18. On the French colonial administration, see Victor T. LeVine, *The Cameroons: From Mandate to Independence* (Berkeley: University of California Press, 1964), pp. 91–98. Cameroon stood apart from most other African colonial territories (including Guinea and Nigeria) because of its special international status as mandate and then trusteeship territory. But the international supervision that these statuses enabled had only minimal influence on the way the territory was administered. For details on the international status of Cameroon, see D. E. Gardinier, *Cameroon: United Nations Challenge to French Policy* (London: Oxford University Press, 1963), pp. 3–10.

19. See A. H. M. Kirk-Greene, ed., *The Principles of Native Administration in Nigeria: Selected Documents, 1900–1947* (London: Oxford University Press, 1965).

20. Ibid., pp. 9–10; Lord W. M. Hailey, *Native Administration in the British African Territories,* 5 vols., (London: His Majesty's Stationery Office, 1950–53), vol. 3, chap. 7, pp. 70–71.

21. The duality that is mentioned here should be distinguished from the idea of "dual economy" set forth by people like Furnivall (1939) and Boeke (1953), which conceptualized a society where two economies, a westernized monetary economy and a traditional subsistence economy, existed side by side with minimal interaction. In contrast to those ideas of dual economy, I argue that the economic sphere, compared to other spheres, was the one in which least duality existed between the "western" and "traditional" sectors. The economic sphere was the one in which colonial innovations made the deepest inroads into the so-called traditional periphery. For a criticism of the idea of the dual economy, see P. Bohannan and G. Dalton, *Markets in Africa* (Evanston, Ill.: Northwestern University Press, 1962), p. 25.

22. General name give by the Fulbe to all pagan populations inhabiting the northwestern fringes of Futa Jallon and composed mainly of the Coniagui, the Bassari, and the Badyaranké.

23. See Kirk-Greene, *Principles of Native Administration*, pp. 26, 195; James O'Connell, "Political Integration: The Nigerian Case," in *African Integration and Disintegration*, ed. Arthur Hazelwood (London: Oxford University Press, 1967), p. 135; R. Heussler, *The British in Northern Nigeria* (London: Oxford University Press, 1968), p. 31; C. D. Ames, "The Highland Chieftancies (Plateau Province)," in *Gazetteers of the Northern Provinces of Nigeria*, ed. A. H. M. Kirk-Greene (London: Cass, 1972), 4:279–80.

24. Lestringeant, *Guider*, pp. 297–306, 339; Bertrand Lembezat, *Les Populations Païennes du Nord-Cameroun et de l'Adamaoua* (Paris: Presses Universitaires de France, 1961), pp. 2–3.

25. Capitaine Ripert, "Situation Politique de la Region de Ngaoundéré" (1918), *Documentation ORSTOM, Dossier Adamaoua*, no. III-384, Yaoundé, Cameroon,

26. "Kirdi" is the word used to denote all populations of North Cameroon who were pagan at the time of the Fulbe Jihad. It comprises all the non-Fulbe populations of North Cameroon with the exception of the Mandara, the Kanuri, the Hausa, the Kotoko, and the Shuwa Arabs. It seems that the word was brought to North Cameroon by French officers coming from Chad where they heard it used to describe pagans in the Baguirmi language; see Lestringeant, *Guider*, p. 422.

27. Lacroix, "Histoire des Peuls," pp. 55–57.

28. Ibid., pp. 57–58; see also various reports of colonial officials recommending such a course of action in *Documentation ORSTOM, Dossiers Adamaoua, Benoué, Margui-Wandala*, Yaoundé, Cameroon.

29. "Situation Politique dans l'Adamaoua" (1934), *Documentation ORSTOM, Dossier Adamaoua*, no. III-385, Yaoundé, Cameroon, pp. 6–8; G. Lavergne "Rapport sur l'Etude du Groupement Kapsiki-Visite du Poste de Mubi" (1942), *Documentation ORSTOM, Dosier Margui-Wandala*, no. III-369, Yaoundé, Cameroon, pp. 12–14.

30. Lestringeant, *Guider*, pp. 325–33, 345–47; "Etude sur le Commandement Indigène de Garoua" (1934), *Documentation ORSTOM, Dossier Benoué*, no. III-979, Yaoundé, Cameroon, pp. 1–5; Lavergne, "Groupement Kapsiki," pp. 15–17.

31. J. Guillard, *Golonpui: Nord Cameroun* (The Hague: Mouton, 1965), pp. 144–45; various reports of colonial officials in *Documentation ORSTOM, Dossiers Adamaoua, Benoué, Margui-Wandala*, Yaoundé, Cameroon.

32. Lestringeant, *Guider*, p. 328.

33. T. N. Tamuno, *The Police in Modern Nigeria, 1861–1965* (Ibadan, Nigeria: Ibadan University Press, 1970), pp. 52, 174; interviews in North Cameroon, March 1972.

34. Alhaji Sir Ahmadu Bello, *My Life* (Cambridge: Cambridge University Press, 1962), p. 23.

35. J. H. Vaughan, "Culture, History and Grass-Roots Politics in a Northern Cameroons Kingdom," *American Anthropologist* 66 (October 1964): 1087.

36. Tamuno, *Police in Nigeria*, pp. 55, 90–95, 98–101; A. C. Burns, *History of Nigeria* (London: Allen & Unwin, 1955), p. 170.

37. Interviews in Maroua, Garoua, and Rey Bouba, North Cameroon, March–April 1972.

38. Richard L. Sklar, *Nigerian Political Parties* (Princeton, N.J.: Princeton University Press, 1963), p. 355; Tamuno, *Police in Nigeria*, p. 60.

39. Hailey, *Native Administration*, p. 70; G. O. Orewa, *Local Government Finance ·in Nigeria* (Ibadan, Nigeria: Oxford University Press, 1966), p. 94.

40. Camara I. Nbady, "La Guinée avant l'Independence et l'Heritage Français," unpublished paper (Paris: CHEAM, 1960), p. 43.

41. Rudin, *Germans in the Cameroons*, pp. 186–90, 198–207; R. Cagan, "Contribution à l'Histoire de la Justice au Cameroun," *Penant*, no. 639, pp. 6–8; E. Y. Arnett, "The French Mandate in Cameroons," *African Affairs* 37 (April 1938): 193–94.

42. Kirk-Greene, *Principles of Native Administration*, pp. 136–38; Hailey, *Native Administration*, pp. 80–84; Burns, *History of Nigeria*, p. 269.

43. C. S. Whitaker, Jr., *The Politics of Tradition: Community and Change in Northern Nigeria* (Princeton, N.J.: Princeton University Press, 1970), p. 221.

44. Michael J. Campbell, *Law and Practice of Local Government in Northern Nigeria* (Lagos: African University Press, 1963), pp. 2–3; Polly Hill, *Rural Hausa* (Cambridge: Cambridge University Press, 1972), pp. 291, 312–13, 323–25; B. Dudley, *Parties and Politics in Northern Nigeria* (London: Cass, 1968), p. 15; Genin, "Redevances Coraniques," pp. 1–6; interviews in North Cameroon, March–April 1972; Thierno Diallo, in interview at the University of Dakar, Senegal, May 1972.

45. Derman, *Serfs, Peasants and Socialists*, pp. 50–51; interviews in North Cameroon, March–April 1972.

46. J. C. Sciortino, "Nassarawa Province" (1920), in Kirk-Greene, ed., *Gazetteers of Northern Nigeria*, 3:30, E. Y. Arnett, "Zaria Province" (1920), in Kirk-Greene, ed., *Gazetteers of Northern Nigeria*, 1:21, F. B. Gall, "Bauchi Province" (1920), in Kirk-Greene, ed., *Gazetteers of Northern Nigeria*, 1:22–25, E. Y. Arnett, "Sokoto Province" (1920), in Kirk-Greene, ed., *Gazetteers of Northern Nigeria*, 1:69; Orewa, *Local Government Finance*, pp. 6, 76; Dudley, *Parties and Politics*, p. 15.

47. J. C. Froelich, "Le Commandement et l'Organisation Sociale chez les Foulbé de l'Adamaoua," *Etudes Camerounaises*, no. 45–46 (Septembre–Decembre 1954), p. 50; Genin, "Redevances Coraniques," pp. 1–3.

48. B. C. Smith, "The Evolution of Local Government in Northern Nigeria," *Journal of Administration Overseas* 6 (January 1967): 34–35. For another striking illustration of such native authority activities, see the Kano Native Authority Revenues and Expenditure for 1938–39 in A. W. Pim, "Public Finance," in *Mining, Commerce and Finance*, ed. M.

Perham (London: Faber & Faber, 1947), pp. 272–79. For more details on native authorities' expenditure growth, see also Orewa, *Local Government Finance*, pp. 84–91.

49. Hailey, *Native Administration*, p. 97.

50. Froelich, "Commandement Foulbé," p. 15.

51. Interviews in North Cameroon, February–April 1972; also, the French closed their eyes to continuing slavery in Rey Bouba. See André M. Podlewski, "Le Dynamique des Principales Populations du Nord du Cameroun (2è partie)," *Cahiers d'ORSTOM, Serie Sciences Humaines* 8, 3 (1971): 24–25.

52. Michael G. Smith, *Government in Zazzau* (London: Oxford University Press, 1960), p. 214; Hill, *Rural Hausa*, p. 320.

53. Quoted in Derman, *Serfs, Peasants and Socialists*, p. 49.

54. Jean Suret-Canale, *La République de Guinée* (Paris: Editions Sociales, 1970), p. 136; Derman, *Serfs, Peasants and Socialists*, p. 49.

55. Gilbert Vieillard, "Notes sur les Peuls du Fouta Djallon," *Bulletin de l'IFAN* 2 (1940): 155, 173; Suret-Canale, *La République de Guinée*, pp. 88–89; M. G. Smith, *Government in Zazzau*, pp. 223, 257–58; Jean Hurault, "Antagonisme de l'Agriculture et de l'Elevage sur les Hauts Plateaux de l'Adamaoua," *Etudes Rurales*, no. 15 (Octobre–Decembre 1964), pp. 34–38; interviews in North Cameroon and Senegal, March–May 1972. Reporting on Futa Jallon, Derman claims, on the other hand, that as slaves were forced to pay their own taxes to the French and did not pay through their masters as before, they had to work more for their own production and spent less time working for their masters' (*Serfs, Peasants and Socialists*, pp. 51–52). My reading of the evidence, however, is that the increased pressure on slaves as a result of French taxation did not come at the expense of their service to their masters but simply as an addition to it. It did not reduce significantly their work for their masters, it just forced them to work even harder than before (Suret-Canale, *La République de Guinée*, p. 89; interviews with Guinean intellectuals in Senegal, May 1972). Therefore, French taxation did not lead to a gradual decline of serfdom, as Derman claims, it just made its conditions even more difficult than before.

56. H. Fréchou, "Les Régimes Fonciers dans la Région des Timbi (Fouta Djalon)," in *Etudes de Droit Africain et de Droit Malgache*, ed. Jean Poirier (Paris: Editions Cujas, 1965), p. 462; Derman, *Serfs, Peasants and Socialists*, p. 56.

57. These conclusions on the relations between the Fulbe and their former slaves in the colonial period differ in some important respects from those of Derman in *Serfs, Peasants and Socialists*. My analysis emphasizes much more the preservation of inequality and differentiation between the Fulbe and their former slaves (or serfs) and also between the aristocracy and the commoners among the Fulbe. For this reason I object to Derman's attempt to characterize all the populations of colonial Futa Jallon by the common term "peasant." Whether his use of the term fits the most accepted definitions of peasantry or not (see his

discussion of this point in pp. 57–65 of his book), calling peasant all the populations of Futa Jallon blurs the very real and important differences that still existed in the colonial period between the Fulbe aristocrats, the free Fulbe commoners, and the non-Fulbe slaves (or serfs). Derman himself acknowledged the continuing basic inequality between the Fulbe and the serfs, due to the exclusive land ownership by the former. Regarding the relations between Fulbe aristocrats and commoners, on the other hand, he might be right in stressing the declining inequality as a result of political and economic innovations. However, those innovations certainly did not eliminate completely the precolonial inequality and separate existence of the two strata. Therefore, I see no use in uniting the two categories in a single term "peasant" (see Derman, *Serfs, Peasants and Socialists*, pp. 4, 48, 237, and Part Two, passim). For the reasons mentioned above I cannot agree either with Polly Hill's attempt to ignore strata differences in Hausaland and incorporate the whole sedentary Muslim population into a single category, the Hausa. I am not even sure that strata differences did not exist in the village that she studied (she does acknowledge that at least one family, that of the District Head, who incidentally was Fulbe, had a much higher status than others). But even if her assertion is correct in that particular village, it certainly is misleading for Hausaland as a whole. Different strata did exist in Hausaland, and families of the ruling elite, one example of whom is found in Hill's village, together formed a ruling aristocracy, predominantly Fulbe, and easily distinguishable (conceptually and empirically) from the other sedentary Muslim commoners, most of whom were Hausa, though including also some commoners of Fulbe origin who were assimilated among the Hausa (see Hill, *Rural Hausa*, pp. 9, 16, 175–79, 265–66).

58. On land tenure in colonial Northern Nigeria, see Hailey, *Native Administration*, pp. 90–93; H. A. Oluwasanmi, *Agriculture and Nigerian Development* (Ibadan, Nigeria: Oxford University Press, 1966), pp. 33–36; Hill, *Rural Hausa*, p. 240; D. F. H. MacBride, "Land Survey in the Kano Emirate, Northern Provinces, Nigeria," *African Affairs* 37 (January 1938): pp. 77–78; H. A. Luning, "The Impact of Socio-Economic Factors on the Land Tenure Patterns in Northern Nigeria," *Journal of Local Administration Overseas* 4 (July 1965): 174, 178, 181; K. D. Baldwin, "Land Tenure Problems in Relation to Agricultural Development in the Northern Region of Nigeria," in *African Agrarian Systems*, ed. D. Biebuyck (London: Oxford University Press, 1963), p. 76.

59. Froelich, "Commandement Foulbé," pp. 29–31; "Rapport sur le Problème de la Reconnaissance des Droits Fonciers Autochtones" (1949), *Documentation ORSTOM, Dossier Adamaoua*, no. III-1209, Yaoundé, Cameroon, pp. 1–8; Fréchou, "Régimes Fonciers," pp. 411, 456–57; Vieillard, "Peuls du Fouta Djalon," p. 84; Ousmane Diallo Poréko, "Evolution Sociale Chez les Peuls du Fouta Djalon," *Recherches Africaines* 4 (Octobre–Decembre 1961), p. 80. Whether legally alienable or not, Derman's claim that land was not sold much in colonial Futa Jallon is definitely contradicted by most other sources; see Derman, *Serfs, Peasants and Socialists*, p. 4.

60. Oluwasanmi, *Agriculture*, pp. 53–54; Baldwin, "Land Problems," pp. 67–69.

61. See Fréchou, "Régimes Fonciers," p. 492; Derman, *Serfs, Peasants and Socialists*, p. 4; Lestringeant, *Guider*, p. 408; R. M. Prothero, "Land Use, Land Holdings and Land Tenure at Sobo, Zaria Province, Northern Nigeria," *Bulletin de l'IFAN* 19 (July–October 1957): 562; Bello, *My Life*, p. 3.

62. See J. S. Coleman, *Nigeria: Background to Nationalism* (Los Angeles: University of California Press, 1958), p. 56; K. Buchanan and J. C. Pugh, *Land and People in Nigeria* (London: University of London Press, 1955), pp. 135–41, 143–48; G. K. Helleiner, *Peasant Agriculture, Government and Economic Growth in Nigeria* (Homewood, Ill.: Irwin, 1966), pp. 107–15, 126–31; J. S. Hogendron, "The Origins of the Groundnut Trade in Northern Nigeria," in *Growth and Development of the Nigerian Economy*, ed. C. K. Eicher and C. Liedholm (East Lansing: Michigan State University Press, 1970), pp. 30–47.

63. D. A. Wells and W. A. Warmington, *Studies in Industrialization: Nigeria and the Cameroons* (London: Oxford University Press, 1962), pp. 79–82; Helleiner, *Peasant Agriculture*, pp. 129–30.

64. *Handbook of Commerce and Industry in Nigeria* (Lagos, Nigeria: Federal Department of Commerce and Industry, 1967), pp. 104–6; Oluwasanmi, *Agriculture*, pp. 160–61; Hill, *Rural Hausa*, p. 289.

65. Daryll C. Forde and Richenda Scott, *The Native Economies of Nigeria* (London: Faber & Faber, 1946), p. 120.

66. Ibid., p. 245; J. Mars, "Extra-Territorial Enterprises," in Perham, ed., *Mining, Commerce and Finance*, p. 120; M. G. Smith, "Corruption among the Hausa," pp. 188–91.

67. Lacroix, "Histoire des Peuls," pp. 44–45.

68. See Guillard, *Golonpoui*, pp. 269–71; Igor de Garine, *Les Massa du Cameroun* (Paris: Presses Universitaires de France, 1966), p. 68; Guy Pontié, *Les Guiziga du Cameroun Septentrional* (Paris: ORSTOM, 1970), pp. 171–78.

69. M. Lavit, "Le Coton dans le Nord Cameroun," unpublished paper (Yaoundé: Université du Cameroun, n.d.), pp. 1–2; Guillard, *Golonpoui*, pp. 269–72.

70. *L'Industrie Africaine en 1969* (Paris: Ediafric, 1969), 1:42, 64.

71. See table of cotton cultivated areas in North Cameroon in Philippe Couty, "Notes sur la Production et le Commerce du Mil dans le Departement du Diamaré," *Cahiers d'ORSTOM, Série Sciences Humaines* 2, no. 4 (1965): 76. See also Antoinette Hallaire, "Les Monts du Mandara au Nord de Mokolo et la Plaine de Mora," unpublished paper (Yaoundé, Cameroon: ORSTOM, 1965), pp. 24, 69.

72. Jean Boulet, in interview in the ORSTOM center in Yaoundé, Cameroon, April 1972.

73. According to Guinean refugees interviewed in Senegal (in May 1972), fruits and vegetables were cultivated by women of both free and

servile status in yards around their huts. Derman, on the other hand claims that women's gardens were rather important sources of subsistence goods, while other gardens, cultivated mostly by male serfs, produced fruits and vegetables for commercial purposes (Derman, *Serfs, Peasants and Socialists,* pp. 122–24, 144).

74. Suret-Canale, *La République de Guinée,* p. 104. According to Derman most of the workers in this enterprise were former serfs; Derman, *Serfs, Peasants and Socialists,* p. 155.

75. Coleman, *Nigeria,* pp. 56–58; Suret-Canale, *La République de Guinée,* pp. 92–94; Derman, *Serfs, Peasants and Socialists,* p. 3.

76. Bello, *My Life,* p. 43.

77. On the development of communication and transportation facilities in the colonial period, see V. Thompson and R. Adloff, *French West Africa* (London: Allen & Unwin, 1958), p. 293; E. Mveng, *Histoire du Cameroun* (Paris: Présence Africaine, 1963), pp. 382–84; Buchanan and Pugh, *Land and People in Nigeria,* pp. 208–11.

78. Mars, "Extra-Territorial Enterprises," in Perham, ed., *Mining, Commerce and Finance,* pp. 58–61; Claude Rivière, "Les Bénéficiaires du Commerce dans la Guinée Précoloniale et Coloniale," *Bulletin de l'IFAN* 23 (Avril 1971): 268–83; J. Willbois, *Le Cameroun* (Paris: Payot, 1934), pp. 106–12; personal observation and interviews, Cameroon, January–May 1972.

79. It must be clear that when we deal with "indigenous commerce," we mean not only the sale of surplus products for the satisfaction of consumption needs but also the buying of goods for the purpose of reselling them at a profit. The first type of commercial activity was undertaken by everyone who had a surplus, both Muslim and non-Muslim, but the second type of commercial activity, the buying of goods in order to resell them with profit, was undertaken almost exclusively by Muslims.

80. As we have done several times throughout this book, here we have moved into a comparison of the Fulbe as a whole with non-Fulbe populations; hence, we do not differentiate at this point between the Fulbe aristocracy and the Fulbe commoners. We, unfortunately, do not know exactly whether the Fulbe who entered commercial activities were of aristocratic or commoner origin. In North Cameroon, where the great majority of the sedentary Fulbe were of aristocratic origin, it is most probable that some of them engaged in commerce. On the other hand, in Futa Jallon, where a large number of sedentary Fulbe were commoners, they might have been the ones who undertook most commercial activities.

81. On the Fulbe entrance into commercial activities in colonial Guinea, see Derman, *Serfs, Peasants and Socialists,* pp. 53–55; J. Binet, "Marchés en Pays Soussou," *Cahiers d'Etudes Africaines* 3, 9 (1963): 104, 111.

82. Michael G. Smith, "Exchange and Marketing among the Hausa," in Bohannan and Dalton, eds., *Markets in Africa,* pp. 313–16; Forde and Scott, *Native Economies,* p. 245.

83. In Northern Nigeria, for example, Buchanan and Pugh estimated that 95 percent of the cattle were owned by pastoral Fulbe. (*Land and People in Nigeria*, p. 121).

84. Interviews in Ngaoundéré, North Cameroon, March 1972; H. Fréchou, "L'Elevage et le Commerce du Bétail dans le Nord du Cameroun," *Cahiers d'ORSTOM, Série Sciences Humaines* 3, no. 2 (1966): 87–88; P. F. Lacroix, "Matériaux pour Servir à l'Histoire des Peuls de l'Adamawa (Suite)," *Etudes Camerounaises*, no. 39–40 (Mars–Juillet 1953): 34; Hurault, "Antagonisme," p. 42.

85. Poréko, "Evolution chez les Peuls," p. 82.

86. Abner Cohen, "The Social Organization of Credit in a West African Cattle Market," *Africa* 35 (January 1965): 8–19; G. I. Jones, "The Beef Cattle Trade in Nigeria," *Africa* 16 (January 1946): 29–37.

87. Interviews in North Cameroon, February–April 1972; Forde and Scott, *Native Economies*, p. 165; Derman, *Serfs, Peasants and Socialists*, pp. 146–47.

88. Thierno Diallo, interview at the University of Dakar, Senegal, May 1972; interviews in North Cameroon, February–April 1972; Forde and Scott, *Native Economies*, p. 246; M. G. Smith, "Exchange among the Hausa," p. 315. On trade as a channel to wealth for energetic young farmers, see also Hill, *Rural Hausa*, pp. 153–55, 186–87.

89. M. G. Smith, *Economy of Zaria*, p. 92.

90. Ibid., pp. 92, 101.

91. Ibid., p. 100; Claude Rivière, *Mutations Sociales en Guinée* (Paris: Rivière, 1971), p. 319; Lacroix, "Histoire des Peuls (Suite)," p. 28; interviews in North Cameroon, February–April 1972.

92. Forde and Scott, *Native Economies*, pp. 288–89; Buchanan and Pugh, *Land and People in Nigeria*, pp. 117–18, 125–27; A. Sokolski, *The Establishment of Manufacturing in Nigeria* (New York: Praeger, 1965), App., pp. 287–343; *Handbook of Commerce and Industry*, pp. 44–45.

93. On the Bassari, see Monique de Lestrange, *Les Coniagui et les Bassari* (Paris: Presses Universitaires de France, 1955), p. 2.

94. See, e.g., Stanthrope White, "The Agricultural Economy of the Hill Pagans of the Dikwa Emirate, Cameroons," *Empire Journal of Experimental Agriculture* 9, no. 33 (1941): 65–73.

95. I used the word "Muslim" here because in this category are included also the Hausa and Kanuri in Northern Nigeria and the Mandara in the hill region of North Cameroon. In North Cameroon, most of the Muslims were Fulbe; in Northern Nigeria most of them were Hausa.

96. Jean Boutrais, "Une Enquête Agricole sur un Perimètre de Colonisation," unpublished paper (Yaoundé, Cameroon: ORSTOM, 1971), pp. 3–8; Jean Boutrais, "Aspects Géographiques de l'Installation des Montagnards en Plaine au Nord du Cameroun," unpublished paper (Yaoundé, Cameroon: ORSTOM, 1969); Jean Y. Martin, *Les Matakam du Cameroun* (Paris: ORSTOM, 1970), p. 43.

97. See P. Lesselingue, "Aspects Psycho-Sociaux du Phenomène de Desserrement des Montagnards au Nord-Cameroun," unpublished paper (Yaoundé, Cameroon, ORSTOM, 1968), p. 88; André M. Podlewski, "Enquêtes sur l'Emigration des Mafa hors du Pays Matakam," *Recherches et Etudes Camerounaises*, no. 5 (1961–62), pp. 79–85, 93; R. M. Netting, *Hill Farmers of Nigeria: Cultural Ecology of the Kofyar of the Jos Plateau* (Seattle: University of Washington Press, 1968), pp. 203–11.

98. Only 73 percent of those migrants originated in Sokoto province, 17 percent came from French territories and 10 percent from other areas of Northern Nigeria (reported in R. M. Prothero, "Migratory Labour from Northwestern Nigeria," *Africa* 27 [1957]: 254–55).

99. Interviews with Guinean refugees living in Senegal, May 1972.

100. J. Champaud, "L'Immigration Foula en Basse Guinée," unpublished paper (Conakry, Guinea: Service Hydraulique de l'AOF, 1957), pp. 10–43, esp. pp. 16–18, 23–26.

101. On the biggest cities of Northern Nigeria, North Cameroon and Futa Jallon, see A. L. Mabogunje, *Urbanization in Nigeria* (London: University of London Press, 1968), p. 64; Coleman, *Nigeria*, p. 74; Renaud Santerre, "L'Ecole Coranique de la Savane Camerounaise" (doctoral diss., Université de Paris, 1968), p. 85; Rivière, *Mutations Sociales en Guinée*, p. 47.

102. Santerre, "Ecole Coranique," pp. 90–91.

103. For numbers of expatriates who lived in Northern Nigeria, see Buchanan and Pugh, *Land and People in Nigeria*, pp. 97–99.

104. John N. Paden, "Communal Competition, Conflict and Violence in Kano," in *Nigeria: Modernization and the Politics of Communalism*, ed. Robert Melson and Howard Wolpe (East Lansing: Michigan State University Press, 1971), pp. 119–33; M. G. Smith, *Economy of Zaria*, pp. 143, 153–54.

105. An illustration of that was the fact that the few people who adopted Christianity in the Muslim-dominated areas saw in it a means to detach themselves from the Muslim political center. Colonial officials and missionaries had difficulty in making them understand that a change in religion did not necessarily lead to a change in government; see Arnett, "Zaria Province," p. 34.

106. André M. Podlewski, "La Dynamique des Principales Populations du Nord du Cameroun," *Cahiers d'ORSTOM, Série Sciences Humaines* 4 (1966): 183.

107. J. B. Grimley, "Church Growth in Central Nigeria," in *Church Growth in Central and Southern Nigeria*, ed. J. B. Grimley and G. E. Robinson (Grand Rapids, Mich.: Eerdmans, 1966), pp. 54–57; Williams, *Education in Northern Nigeria*, p. 2; interviews in Cameroon, Senegal, and France, January–June 1972.

108. Ames, "Highland Chieftancies," p. 309; interviews in North Cameroon, February–April 1972; Derman, *Serfs, Peasants and Socialists*, pp. 223, 246.

109. Interviews in North Cameroon, February–April 1972; inter-

views with Guinean refugees in Senegal, May 1972; Lacroix, "Histoire des Peuls (Suite)," p. 31.

110. In Northern Nigeria Hausa was chosen, together with English, as the official language of the region and, written in Roman script, it was used as the basic language of instruction in Western schools. The language was learned by many of the Europeans stationed in the area. John N. Paden, "Language Problems of National Integration in Nigeria: The Special Position of Hausa," in *Language Problems of Developing Nations*, ed. J. A. Fishman et al. (New York: Wiley, 1968), pp. 202–3.

111. Forde and Scott, *Native Economies*, pp. 6–9. See also John N. Paden, "Urban Pluralism Integration and Adaptation of Communal Identity in Kano, Nigeria," in *From Tribe to Nation in Africa*, ed. R. Cohen and J. Middleton (San Francisco: Chandler, 1970), p. 253; W. F. Gowers, "Kano Province" (1921), in Kirk-Greene, ed., *Gazetteers of Northern Nigeria*, 1:43.

112. Kirk-Greene, *Adamawa, Past and Present*, pp. 182–83; Rupert M. East, *Stories of Old Adamawa* (Lagos: West Africa Publicity, 1935), pp. 6–9.

113. Williams, *Education in Northern Nigeria*, p. 6.

114. Santerre, "Ecole Coranique," pp. 62, 70.

115. Renaud Santerre, "Linguistique et Politique au Cameroun," *Journal of African Languages* 8, no. 3 (1969): 155; Coleman, *Nigeria*, p. 135.

116. Rivière, *Mutations Sociales en Guinée*, p. 315; Suret-Canale, "Système Coloniale," p. 42.

117. Rivière, *Mutations Sociales en Guinée*, p. 199; Suret-Canale, "Système Coloniale," p. 42; N'bady, "Guinée avant l'Indépendence," pp. 32–38.

118. Vieillard, "Peuls du Fouta Djalon," pp. 160–63; Lestrange, *Coniagui et Bassari*, p. 74.

119. The importance of missionary activities in western education at that time was illustrated by the fact that in 1913 there were only nine government schools with less that 1,000 students in Cameroon, compared to 600 schools with about 40,000 students run by missionary organizations with some financial help from the colonial government. This policy was not changed after the advent of the French. In 1937, 85,000 students attended mission schools compared to 10,000 students attending secular schools. In Nigeria in 1942, 99 percent of the western schools were controlled by missions, and in them studied 97 percent of the total student population. See Bertrand Lembezat, *Le Cameroun* (Paris: Editions Maritimes et Coloniales, 1954), pp. 117–18; Coleman, *Nigeria*, p. 113. For more details and statistical data on the development of western education in North Cameroon and Northern Nigeria, see Jean Y. Martin, *L'Ecole et les Sociétés Traditionelles au Cameroun Septentrional* (Yaoundé, Cameroon: ORSTOM, 1970), pp. 13–59; Santerre, "Ecole Coranique," pp. 45–63; Williams, *Education in Northern Nigeria*; Coleman, *Nigeria*, pp. 113–40.

120. In 1937, it was transferred to the northern capital, Kaduna.

121. Williams, *Education in Northern Nigeria*, p. 42.

122. Martin, *Ecole*, pp. 54–57; Santerre, "Ecole Coranique," pp. 61–62.

123. Coleman, *Nigeria*, p. 134. See also David B. Abernethy, "Education and Integration," in Melson and Wolpe, eds., *Nigeria: Modernization and the Politics of Communalism*, p. 412.

124. Willard R. Johnson, *The Cameroon Federation* (Princeton, N.J.: Princeton University Press, 1970), p. 61. For 1958 Martin gives the somewhat different figures of 11 percent enrollment in North Cameroon, compared to more than 90 percent in South Cameroon; see Martin, *Ecole*, p. 59; see also Santerre, "Ecole Coranique," pp. 62–63.

125. Quoted in G. O. Gbadamosi, "The Establishment of Western Education among Muslims in Nigeria, 1896–1926," *Journal of the Historical Society of Nigeria* 4 (1967): 100.

126. Whitaker, *Politics of Tradition*, p. 137. Similar cases were reported also on North Cameroon and Futa Jallon; see Martin, *Ecole*, p. 46; Suret-Canale, *La République de Guinée*, p. 157; interviews in Senegal and North Cameroon, February–May 1972.

127. The non-Fulbe pagan populations of northwestern Futa Jallon, namely, the Coniagui and Bassari, were heavily represented among army veterans and soldiers in Guinea; see Monique Gessain, *Les Migrations des Coniaguis et Bassaris* (Paris: Société des Africanistes, 1957), p. 65.

128. N. J. Miners, *The Nigerian Army, 1956–1966* (London: Methuen, 1971), pp. 25, 38–51, 119.

Part Three

1. On pre-World War II indigenous political activities in Southern Nigeria see Lord W. M. Hailey, *Native Administration in the British African Territories,* 5 vols. (London: His Majesty's Stationery Office, 1950–53) 3:3; R. L. Sklar and C. S. Whitaker, Jr., "The Federal Republic of Nigeria," in *National Unity and Regionalism in Eight African States,* ed. Gwendolen M. Carter (Ithaca, N.Y.: Cornell University Press, 1966), pp. 33–36.

2. The club was named after a French official who had made extensive studies of the Fulbe society and who died in World War II. On the AGV, see Ruth S. Morgenthau, *Political Parties in French-Speaking West Africa* (Oxford: Clarendon, 1964), pp. 19, 221.

3. The Malinké, for example, were represented in the *Union du Mandé;* the tribes living in the forest zone established their own regional association, the *Union Forestière;* the populations of the coastal region were represented by two associations, the *Foyer de la Basse Guinée,* and the *Union de la Basse Guinée,* etc.; see Morgenthau, *Political Parties,* p. 224.

4. It is possible that the opposition to Diawadou Barry was also motivated by the old rivalry between the Alfaya and Soriya lineages.

Diawadou was the son of the chief of Dabola, head of the Soriya branch, while the chief backer of Yacine Diallo was the chief of Mamou, who headed the Alfaya branch and who did not want to see an heir of the Soriya head become the Fulbe's top representative in the new political institutions. On the chief of Mamou's support of Yacine Diallo, see R. W. Johnson, "The 'Parti Démocratique de Guinée' and the Mamou 'Deviation,' " in *African Perspectives*, ed. C. Allen and R. W. Johnson (Cambridge: Cambridge University Press, 1970), pp. 349–50.

5. Morgenthau, *Political Parties*, pp. 219–26.

6. Jean Suret-Canale, *La République de Guinée* (Paris: Editions Sociales, 1970), pp. 145–46; Morgenthau, *Political Parties*, pp. 225–28; Johnson, "Mamou Deviation," pp. 350–51.

7. Suret-Canale, *La République de Guinée*, pp. 144–45.

8. See issues of *Phare de Guinée* between September 1948 and June 1949 and *Coup de Bambou* between April and May 1950.

9. For details on the CGTG and other trade unions, see Elliot J. Berg, "French West Africa," in *Labor and Economic Development*, ed. Walter Galenson (New York: Wiley, 1954), pp. 217–18. For details on Sékou Touré, see Bernard Charles, *Guinée* (Lausanne: Editions Rencontre, 1963), pp. 190–92.

10. Morgenthau, *Political Parties*, pp. 144, 229.

11. Ibid., pp. 396–97.

12. Ibid., pp. 229–49.

13. J. Beaujeu-Garnier, "Essai sur la Géographie Electorale Guinéenne," *Les Cahiers d'Outre-Mer* 11, no. 44 (1958): 331.

14. Morgenthau, *Political Parties*, p. 233; Suret-Canale, *La République de Guinée*, p. 163.

15. Morgenthau, *Political Parties*, p. 246; Johnson, "Mamou Deviation," p. 347; L. G. Cowan, "Guinea," in *African One-Party States*, ed. Gwendolen M. Carter (Ithaca, N.Y.: Cornell University Press, 1962), p. 162.

16. See L. G. Cowan, *Local Government in West Africa* (New York: Columbia University Press, 1958), pp. 247–50.

17. The disappointment of the Fulbe at finding themselves evicted from the political center after having dominated it for so long was apparent in the following comments attributed to Diawadou Barry: "Le Fouta Djallon est le groupement ethnique le plus important de Guinée. Va-t-il se laisser exploiter par les etrangers? Va-t-il tolérer plus longtemps de ne pas être representé au sein du conseil du gouvernement?" (*La Guinée Nouvelle* [May 8, 1958], p. 2).

18. See the 1956–58 issues of the following Guinean newspapers: *Voix du Peuple, Populaire de Guinée, La Guinée Nouvelle*.

19. Beaujeu-Garnier, "Géographie Electorale," pp. 317, 327–28.

20. See Aristide R. Zolberg, *Creating Political Order* (Chicago: Rand-McNally, 1966), p. 30.

21. Ousmane Diallo, Thierno Diallo, Idrissa Barry, Jumaa Barry, interviews in Dakar, Senegal, May 1972.

22. On the PDG grass-roots organization and campaign tactics, see Morgenthau, *Political Parties*, pp. 228–46. For the relationship between the PDG's strength in the countryside and its antichief activities, see Johnson, "Mamou Deviation," pp. 348, 352. At the same time that the party structure was also being tightened, the central institutions asserted their control over the branches. However, this generally forced moderation on the uprising against the chiefs. Indeed, there were cases in which the central leadership reached agreements with some traditional chiefs, to the discontent of the local branch of the party or the local population involved. On this subject, see Johnson, "Mamou Deviation," pp. 355–63.

23. Suret-Canale, "Fin de la Chefferie," pp. 487–90.

24. Ibid., pp. 486–91.

25. Ibid., p. 488; Johnson, "Mamou Deviation," p. 356.

26. Suret-Canale, "Fin de la Chefferie," p. 488.

27. Territoire de la Guinée Française, *Conférence des Commandants de Cercle, Conakry, 25, 26, 27 Juillet 1957* (Conakry, Guinea: 1957), pp. 7–43.

28. Lucien David, "La Formation des Cadres Administratifs en Guinée," unpublished paper (Paris: CHEAM, 1961), pp. 1–3; Suret-Canale, *La République de Guinée*, p. 166.

29. David, "Cadres Administratifs," pp. 1–3; Cowan, "Guinea," p. 208.

30. Morgenthau, *Political Parties*, p. 253.

31. Ibid., pp. 71–74.

32. This decision was not taken easily by the PDG, and it was possibly pushed toward it by the opposition's advocacy of immediate independence. After having come to power in 1957, the PDG clearly enjoyed its "constructive collaboration" with the French and did not stress too much the wish for immediate independence. On the equivocal stand of the PDG on independence, see Johnson, "Mamou Deviation," pp. 347–48, 359–60.

33. See Sékou Touré, *L'Expérience Guinéenne et l'Unité Africaine* (Paris: Présence Africaine, 1959), p. 190.

34. Interviews with Guinean refugees in Senegal, May 1972.

35. W. R. Johnson, *The Cameroon Federation,* (Princeton, N.J.: Princeton University Press, 1970), pp. 159–60.

36. D. E. Gardinier, *Cameroon: United Nations Challenge to French Policy* (London: Oxford University Press, 1963), pp. 35–47; Victor T. LeVine, *The Cameroons from Mandate to Independence* (Berkeley: University of California Press, 1964), pp. 147–50; Johnson, *The Cameroon Federation,* pp. 50–51; Georges Chaffard, *Les Carnets Secrets de la Décolonisation,* 2 vols. (Paris: Calmann-Levy, 1965; 1967), 2:349–54.

37. Gardinier, *Cameroon,* pp. 46–52, 66–69; Chaffard, *Carnets Secrets,* 2:352–57, 363–80.

38. Gardinier, *Cameroon*, pp. 78–79; Victor LeVine, "Cameroun," in *Five African States*, ed. Gwendolen M. Carter (Ithaca, N.Y.: Cornell University Press, 1963), pp. 276–77.

39. For details on Ahidjo, see *Ahmadou Ahidjo par Lui-Même* (Monaco: Paul Bory, 1968).

40. Other voluntary associations that were formed in the north shortly afterwards included the following: ASPEN (Association Progressive Sociale Evolutionnaire du Nord) formed in Ngaoundéré; ASMD (Association des Musulmans du Diamaré) formed in Maroua; APRO-NORD (Association du Progrès du Nord-Cameroun) formed in Mokolo; see ibid., pp. 8–11.

41. Perhaps his opponents in the north thought that the formation of a parliamentary bloc, unlike the formation of a united political party within the north, would be directed only against the south without changing the balance of power within the north, and for this reason they agreed to the formation of a parliamentary bloc while refusing to set up a united political party of the north.

42. One notable exception was the chief of Maroua, who despised Ahidjo because of his commoner origins and considered him too radical. Because of his opposition to Ahidjo, Maroua always remained the weak spot of the northern alliance under Ahidjo's leadership.

43. For details on the Loi Cadre reforms in Cameroon, see P. M. Gaudemet, "L'Autonomie Camerounaise," *Revue Française de Sciences Politiques* 8 (Mars, 1958): 42–72.

44. Victor T. LeVine, "Cameroun," in *Political Parties and National Integration in Tropical Africa*, ed. James S. Coleman and Carl G. Rosberg (Berkeley: University of California Press, 1964), pp. 143–44.

45. See Chaffard, *Carnets Secrets*, 1:302–8.

46. "Cameroons under French Administration," unpublished paper, 2 pts. (Yaoundé, n.d.), 2:4; Philippe Antoine, "L'Essor des Partis Politiques au Cameroun," *Latitudes*, no. 3 (1er semestre 1958), p. 53.

47. Chaffard, *Carnets Secrets*, 1:313–28.

48. *Ahidjo par Lui-Même*, p. 15; G. Millet, "L'Union Camerounaise," unpublished paper (Paris: CHEAM, n.d.), pp. 3–4.

49. Personal observation and interviews in Cameroon, January–April 1972.

50. In this study we have not dealt at all with British Cameroons. For the political development there, see LeVine, "Cameroun," in Carter, ed., *Five African States*, pp. 278–81.

51. Gardinier, *Cameroon*, pp. 85–88; "Cameroons under French Administration," 2:15; Chaffard, *Carnets Secrets*, 2:386–87; LeVine, *Cameroons*, pp. 171–88.

52. The identification of Catholicism with colonialism hurt the Catholic Church in the late 1950s and apparently induced Abbé Zoa, who later became Archbishop of Cameroon, to ask Catholics not to oppose every nationalist movement as being UPC inspired in order not to help

the enemies of the Church in portraying Catholicism as closely associated with colonialism; see Jean Zoa, *Pour un Nationalism Chrétien au Cameroun* (Yaoundé, Cameroon: Imprimerie St. Paul, 1957).

53. Johnson, *The Cameroon Federation,* p. 160; LeVine, "Cameroun," in Coleman and Rosberg, eds., *Parties and Integration,* p. 153.

54. Michael Crowder, *The Story of Nigeria,* (London: Faber & Faber, 1962), pp. 273–76; Hailey, *Native Administration,* pp. 3–6.

55. Crowder, *The Story of Nigeria,* pp. 280–88.

56. Sklar and Whitaker, "The Federal Republic of Nigeria," in Carter, ed., *National Unity and Regionalism,* p. 51.

57. Richard L. Sklar, *Nigerian Political Parties* (Princeton, N.J.: Princeton University Press, 1963), pp. 52–54, 66–70, 101–7; J. S. Coleman, *Nigeria: Background to Nationalism* (Los Angeles: University of California Press, 1958), pp. 324–25.

58. Such as the *General Improvement Union* at Bauchi, the *Youth Social Circle* at Sokoto, and the *Friendly Society of Zaria;* see B. Dudley, *Parties and Politics in Northern Nigeria* (London: Cass, 1968), pp. 78–79.

59. The NPC was created in 1949 as a cultural organization to which many of the NEPU members belonged. But in 1951, as it transformed itself into a political party, the NPC proscribed dual membership and expelled the NEPU members from its ranks. See Dudley, *Parties and Politics,* pp. 79–83; R. L. Sklar and C. S. Whitaker, Jr., "Nigeria," in Coleman and Rosberg, eds., *Parties and Integration,* pp. 607–8.

60. On Ahmadu Bello and Abubakar Tafawa Balewa, see C. S. Whitaker, Jr., "Three Perspectives on Hierarchy: Political Thought and Leadership in Northern Nigeria," *Journal of Commonwealth Political Studies* 2 (March 1965): 2–6.

61. Sklar and Whitaker, "Nigeria," in Coleman and Rosberg, eds., *Parties and Integration,* p. 617; Sklar and Whitaker, "The Federal Republic of Nigeria," in Carter, ed., *National Unity and Regionalism,* p. 78.

62. Sklar, *Nigerian Political Parties,* p. 443.

63. Sklar and Whitaker, "The Federal Republic of Nigeria," in Carter, ed., *National Unity and Regionalism,* p. 42.

64. In Hausaland it is very difficult to detect a separate category of sedentary Fulbe commoners, because the Fulbe commoners who settled permanently were soon absorbed within the Hausa population, adopting their language and culture, intermarrying with them, and becoming virtually indistinguishable from the other Hausa-speaking Muslims.

65. Sklar and Whitaker, "The Federal Republic of Nigeria," in Carter, ed., *National Unity and Regionalism,* p. 82; Dudley, *Parties and Politics,* p. 177.

66. On Middle Belt parties, see Sklar, *Nigerian Political Parties,* pp. 344–45.

67. Ibid., p. 328.

68. On the development of interparty and interregional struggles in the 1950s and on the progress toward independence, see Crowder, *The Story of Nigeria*, pp. 280–84; Sklar and Whitaker, "The Federal Republic of Nigeria," in Carter, ed., *National Unity and Regionalism*, pp. 47–48, 52–56.

69. Sklar, *Nigerian Political Parties*, pp. 131–32.

70. C. S. Whitaker, Jr., *The Politics of Tradition: Community and Change in Northern Nigeria* (Princeton, N.J.: Princeton University Press, 1970), p. 31.

71. See Ahmadu Bello's own explanations of that in Alhaji Sir Ahmadu Bello, *My Life* (Cambridge: Cambridge University Press, 1962), p. 99.

72. Taylor Cole, "Bureaucracy in Transition: Independent Nigeria," *Public Administration* 38 (Winter 1960): 333–34; Sklar and Whitaker, "The Federal Republic of Nigeria," in Carter, ed., *National Unity and Regionalism*, pp. 99–100.

73. Quoted in Cole, "Bureaucracy," p. 334.

74. Dudley, *Parties and Politics*, p. 221.

75. On the Institute of Administration, see J. Bennion and A. H. M. Kirk-Greene, "The Institute of Administration, Zaria," *Journal of Local Administration Overseas* 2 (January 1963): 40–45.

76. G. K. Helleiner, *Peasant Agriculture, Government and Economic Growth in Nigeria* (Homewood, Ill.: Irwin, 1966), pp. 245–53; *Handbook of Commerce and Industry in Nigeria* (Lagos, Nigeria: Federal Department of Commerce and Industry, 1967), pp. 34–35, 104–6.

77. Dudley, *Parties and Politics*, p. 142; Whitaker, *Politics of Tradition*, pp. 388–89.

78. Sklar, *Nigerian Political Parties*, p. 327; Whitaker, *Politics of Tradition*, pp. 332–33, 337–39; Dudley, *Parties and Politics*, p. 151.

79. B. J. Dudley, "Traditionalism and Politics: A Case Study of Nigeria," *Government and Opposition* 2 (July–October 1967): 518; Dudley, *Parties and Politics*, p. 210.

80. See B. J. Dudley, "The Nomination of Parliamentary Candidates in Northern Nigeria," *Journal of Commonwealth Political Studies* 2 (November 1963): 52–55; Sklar, *Nigerian Political Parties*, pp. 386–88; Sklar and Whitaker, "Nigeria," in Coleman and Rosberg, eds., *Parties and Integration*, p. 628.

81. Whitaker, *Politics of Tradition*, pp. 259–86; Sklar and Whitaker, "Nigeria," in Coleman and Rosberg, eds., *Parties and Integration*, p. 619; Dudley, "Nomination of Candidates," p. 52.

82. Cowan, *Local Government in West Africa*, p. 80; Michael J. Campbell, *Law and Practice of Local Government in Northern Nigeria* (Lagos: African University Press, 1963), pp. 66–68, 120.

83. Campbell, *Local Government*, p. 150; A. H. M. Kirk-Greene, "A Redefinition of Provincial Administration: The Northern Nigerian Approach," *Journal of Local Administration Overseas* 4 (January 1965): 9–11.

84. See Cowan, "Guinea," p. 171.

85. Henri de Decker, *Nation et Dévéloppement Communautaire en Guinée et au Senegal* (The Hague: Mouton, 1967), p. 134; William Derman, *Serfs, Peasants and Socialists* (Berkeley: University of California Press, 1973), pp. 5, 173–78; *Africa Research Bulletin* (Political, Social and Cultural Series) 12 (1975): 3756.

86. Claude Rivière, *Mutations Sociales en Guinée* (Paris: Rivière, 1971), pp. 171–79; *Africa Research Bulletin* (Political) 6–8, 12 (1969–71, 1975): 1353, 1442, 1678, 1935, 2229, 3623.

87. For the general economic situation and policies in Guinea, see Suret-Canale, *La République de Guinée*, pp. 180–84, 202–4; Claude Rivière, "Les Conséquences de la Réorganisation des Circuits Commerciaux de Guinée," *Revue Française d'Etudes Politiques Africaines*, no. 66 (Juin 1971): 79–94; Michael O'Connor, "Guinea and the Ivory Coast: Contrasts in Economic Development," *Journal of Modern African Studies* 10 (1972): 412, 416–17; *Africa Reasearch Bulletin* (Economic, Financial and Technical Series) 9, 12 (1972, 1975): 2492, 3553, 3587, 3646.

88. On bauxite extraction in Guinea, see Suret-Canale, *La République de Guinée*, pp. 121–29, 288–98; O'Connor, "Guinea and Ivory Coast," pp. 412–13; *Africa Reasearch Bulletin* (Economic) 9–12 (1972–75), passim. In the 1970s the Guinean government, now confident of its bauxite wealth, started to take a tougher stand toward foreign companies. In 1973 the Fria enterprise's name was changed to Friguia with greater Guinean control. The number of expatriate workers was reduced from 300 to 30. Similar arrangements were made with other foreign enterprises. In 1975 a special tax was put on bauxite exports in order to increase the government's earnings and also to encourage refining of the bauxite inside Guinea.

89. Victor Dubois, "The Rise of an Opposition to Sékou Touré," *American Universities Field Staff Reports, West Africa Series*, IX, nos. 1–3, 7 (1966); *Africa Research Bulletin* (Political) 5–13 (1968–76), passim.

90. Ousmane Diallo, interview at the Institut Fondamental d'Afrique Noire, Dakar, Senegal, May 1972.

91. Touré, *Expérience Guinéenne*, pp. 432–36; *Africa Research Bulletin* (Political) 5 (1968): 1210.

92. Bernard Charles has a very different estimate of the ethnic distribution of the population, but I disregard his estimate because it differs greatly from every other estimate and from official census figures; see Rivière, *Mutations Sociales en Guinée*, p. 67. For the official census figures of 1955, see ibid., p. 30; see also Cowan, "Guinea," pp. 175–76.

93. Quoted in Rivière, *Mutations Sociales in Guinée*, pp. 69–71.

94. Interviews with Guinean refugees in Senegal, May 1972; see also Rivière, *Mutations Sociales en Guinée*, p. 74.

95. Reporting on the 1961 incidents, *Africa Report* worte that "The Guinean system has a vast built-in opposition, the Foulah [Fulbe] na-

tion, far more powerful than the handful of ineffectual schoolteachers who went to prison after the 1961 plot." ("Guinea after Five Years," *Africa Report* 9 [June 1964]: 4).

96. *Africa Research Bulletin* (Political) 5–6, 8 (1968–69, 1971): 952, 1410, 1990.

97. Rivière, *Mutations Sociales en Guinée,* pp. 63–64, and private interview with Claude Rivière, Paris, June 1972.

98. Diallo Telli served as Minister of Justice between 1972 and 1976 before he was arrested in May 1976 on charges of plotting to assassinate Sékou Touré. Many other people were arrested following this incident, most of whom were Fulbe, *Africa Research Bulletin* (Political) 13 (1976): 4089, 4123.

99. Interview with Guinean refugees in Dakar, Senegal, May 1972.

100. *Africa Research Bulletin* (Political) 9–10 (1972–3): 2437, 3073.

101. Interview with Senegalese and Guinean researchers at the University of Dakar and the Institut Fondamental d'Afrique Noire, Dakar, Senegal, May 1972. According to DuBois, the total number of Guinean refugees living in all neighboring countries and in France in 1972 was 600–700,000. If we assume that the total population of Guinea is about 4 million, the refugee figures amount to about 15 percent of the total population of the country; see DuBois, "Opposition to Sékou Touré," *American Field Staff Reports* 9, no. 7 (1966): 22; Suret-Canale, *La République de Guinée,* p. 385.

102. For details, see Chaffard, *Carnets Secrets,* 2:397–410.

103. Gardinier, *Cameroon,* pp. 103–4; *Africa Research Bulletin* (Political) 1 (1964): 176.

104. For general information on the economic development of Cameroon after independence, see P. Platon, "Le Marché Camerounais, 1971," *Marchés Tropicaux et Mediterannéens,* 12, no. 1325 (Avril 1971).

105. Johnson, *The Cameroon Federation,* pp. 158, 240–48; Gardinier, *Cameroon,* pp. 103–8; J. F. Bayart, "L'Union Nationale Camerounaise," *Revue Française de Sciences Politiques* 20 (Août 1970): 689–90.

106. Johnson, *The Cameroon Federation,* pp. 246–50; Gardinier, *Cameroon,* pp. 107, 122.

107. It is interesting to note that in their common manifesto the four opposition leaders argued that the authoritarian tendencies of the UC and its wish to form a dictatorship had its roots in the Muslim background of its leaders. For more details on the events of 1962, see Gardinier, *Cameroon,* pp. 125–26; Johnson, *The Cameroon Federation,* pp. 251–55.

108. Bayart, "L'Union Nationale Camerounaise," pp. 692, 695; Johnson, *The Cameroon Federation,* pp. 253–54, 378–79.

109. For details on West Cameroon's reunification with East Cameroon, see E. Ardener, "The Nature of the Reunification of Cameroon," in *African Integration and Disintegration,* ed. Arthur Hazelwood (London: Oxford University Press, 1967), pp. 285–337.

110. *Africa Research Bulletin* (Political) 5–9 (1968–72): 1146, 1183, 1527, 1988, 2039, 2533.

111. Only six of the twenty-four ministers in the 1972 cabinet and only five of the twenty-four ministers in the 1975 cabinet were northerners. Johnson, *The Cameroon Federation*, p. 231; *Africa Research Bulletin* (Political) 9, 12 (1972, 1975): 2531–32, 3649–50.

112. Personal observations and interviews in Cameroon, January–April 1972; *Africa Research Bulletin* (Political), 10 (1972), 2601. On prominent political leaders, see also République du Cameroun, *Annuaire Nationale*, 1971 (Yaoundé, Cameroon: 1971); Victor T. LeVine, *The Cameroon Federal Republic* (Ithaca, N.Y.: Cornell University Press, 1971), pp. 133–34; Willard R. Johnson, *The Cameroon Federation*, pp. 229–32.

113. Interviews in Cameroon, February–April 1972; Johnson, *The Cameroon Federation*, p. 160.

114. J. Binet, "Les Cadres au Cameroun," *Civilisations*, 9 (1961): 23.

115. *Les Cinq Cents Premières Sociétés d'Afrique Noire* (Paris: Ediafric, 1970).

116. Based on the list in *Annuaire Nationale*, 1971, pp. 46–50.

117. *Africa Research Bulletin* (Economic) 11 (1974): 3371.

118. Personal observations and interviews in Cameroon, February–April 1972; see also Bayart, "L'Union Nationale Camerounaise," p. 703; *Africa Research Bulletin* (Political) 10, 12–13 (1973, 1975–76): 2861, 2890, 2924, 3701, 4095; *Jeune Afrique*, no. 652 (7 July 1973), p. 10.

119. B. J. Dudley, "Federalism and the Balance of Political Power in Nigeria," *Journal of Commonwelath Political Studies* 4 (March 1966): 22–24.

120. With this decision the NPC also shrewdly exploited the existing rifts between different southern groups, since the NCNC of the east expected to seize control of the new region and hence did not oppose its creation.

121. See Crowder, *The Story of Nigeria*, pp. 317–19; Sklar and Whitaker, "The Federal Republic of Nigeria," in Carter, ed., *National Unity and Regionalism*, pp. 116–22.

122. Walter Schwarz, *Nigeria* (London: Pall Mall, 1968), p. 163; Dudley, "Federalism," p. 21.

123. Schwarz, *Nigeria*, pp. 165–75; Dudley, *Parties and Politics*, pp. 264–67, 282–83; Sklar and Whitaker, "The Federal Republic of Nigeria," in Carter, ed. *National Unity and Regionalism*, p. 126.

124. N. J. Miners, *The Nigerian Army, 1956–1966* (London: Methuen, 1971), pp. 116, 132; M. J. Dent, "The Military and Politics: A Study of the Relation between the Army and the Political Process in Nigeria," in *Nigeria: Modernization and the Politics of Communalism*, ed. Robert Melson and Howard Wolpe (East Lansing: Michigan State University Press, 1971), pp. 371–72.

125. John N. Paden, "Communal Competition, Conflict and Violence in Kano," in Melson and Wolpe, eds., *Nigeria: Modernization and the Politics of Communalism,* p. 130; Leonard Plotnicov, *Strangers to the City: Urban Man in Jos, Nigeria* (Pittsburgh: University of Pittsburgh Press, 1967), pp. 38, 58.

126. See Morris E. Zukerman, "Nigerian Crisis: Economic Impact on the North," *Journal of Modern African Studies* 8 (1970): 39.

127. For details on the military coups since 1966 and on the civil war, see A. H. M. Kirk-Greene, *Crisis and Conflict in Nigeria,* 2 vols. (London: Oxford University Press, 1971); S. K. Panter-Brick, ed., *Nigerian Politics and Military Rule: Prelude to the Civil War* (London: Athlone Press, University of London, 1970); *Africa Research Bulletin* (Political) 3–8 (1966–76), passim.

128. Dent, "Military and Politics," p. 374; Miners, *Nigerian Army,* pp. 168, 170; see also Alexander R. Luckham, "The Nigerian Military" (Ph.D. diss., University of Chicago, December 1969), p. 163.

129. Dent, "Military and Politics," p. 382; Schwarz, *Nigeria,* p. 205; Luckham, "The Nigerian Military," pp. 188, 213.

130. Miners, *Nigerian Army,* p. 208.

131. Paden, "Communal Conflict," pp. 137–39; Miners, *Nigerian Army,* pp. 215–17; Luckham, "The Nigerian Military," p. 233. Ironically, most of the actual conspirators of the January coup were not harmed because they were detained in the eastern region. Those who died had nothing to do with the conspiracy. They were killed for no other reason than for being Ibo.

132. Schwarz, *Nigeria,* pp. 215–19; Dudley, *Parties and Politics,* pp. xii–xiii; James O'Connell, "Authority and Community in Nigeria," in Melson and Wolpe, eds. *Nigeria: Modernization and the Politics of Communalism,* p. 650; Richard L. Sklar, "Nigerian Politics in Perspective," *Government and Opposition* 2 (July–October 1969): 534.

133. It seems that originally the instigators of the second coup were Muslims from the Far North, possibly Fulbe, but that later Middle Belters who did not play a prominent part in the coup itself emerged to power; see Luckham, "The Nigerian Military," p. 429; Sklar, "Politics in Perspective," pp. 535–36; M. J. Dent, "The Military and Politicians," in Panter-Brick, ed., *Nigerian Military Rule,* p. 86.

134. M. J. Dent, "Tarka and the Tiv: A Perspective on Nigerian Federation," in Melson and Wolpe, eds., *Nigeria: Modernization and the Politics of Communalism,* p. 458; S. K. Panter-Brick, "From Military Coup to Civil War," in Panter-Brick, ed., *Nigerian Military Rule,* p. 30.

135. On the July 1975 coup, see *Africa Research Bulletin* (Political) 12 (1975): 3696–97; *Africa Diary* 15 (1975): 7586–87, 7593.

136. On the contrary, five military officers who took part in Nigeria's first military coup of January 1966 against the north-dominated civilian regime were released under Murtala's orders. On the other hand, it might be significant to note that the Christian governors of the two Middle Belt states (Kwarra and Benue-Plateau) were replaced by Mus-

lim governors. After the creation of more states in February 1976, two of the three Middle Belt states were governed by Muslim military governors. After Obasanjo came to power in the place of the assassinated Murtala Muhammed, military governors were changed again, this time two of the three governors of the Middle Belt states being Christian. However, these data in themselves do not allow us to draw any conclusions on the changing balance between Christian and Muslim elements in the Middle Belt. See *Africa Research Bulletin* (Political) 12–13 (1975–76): 3729, 3924, 3957; *Africa Report*, 20 (September–October 1975), p. 13.

137. On the creation of the nineteen-state federation and on the corruption charges brought against former governors and other public servants, see *Africa Research Bulletin* (Political) 12–13 (1975–76): 3727–29, 3827, 3832, 3923–25; *Africa Diary* 16 (1976): 7742–43, 7826–27, 7834, 7866, 7926; *West Africa* (15 September 1975), p. 1074, (22 September 1975), p. 1130, (1 December 1975), p. 1463.

138. Many of the executed officers originated from Middle Belt states, while Yorubas seemed to be prominent in top political positions after the attempted coup, but again we do not know whether this was coincidental or meant a regional or ethnic shift of power. For details on the February 1976 coup attempt and its aftermath, see *Africa Research Bulletin* (Political) 13 (1976): 3932–34, 3965–67, 3989, 3998, 4027; *Africa Diary* 16 (1976): 7896.

139. See *Nigeria Yearbook* (1969), pp. 287–96, (1971), pp. 40–60; *Africa Research Bulletin* (Political) 11–13 (1974–76): 3328, 3371, 3697, 3789, 3924, 3957–58, 3989; *Africa Diary* 15 (1975): 7223, 7586–87, 7593; *Africa Report* 20 (September-October 1975), pp. 12–13; *West Africa* (4 August 1975), p. 912; *Jeune Afrique*, no. 770, (10 Octobre 1975), pp. 24–25.

140. *Africa Research Bulletin* (Political) 13, (1976): 4120, 4255; *West Africa*, (16 August 1975), p. 923, (15 September 1975), p. 1075.

141. *Africa Research Bulletin* (Political) 11 (1974): 3298, 3394; *Africa Research Bulletin* (Economic) 11 (1974): 3104, 3107; *Africa Report* 20 (September-October 1975): 13.

142. For more details on the draft constitution, see *Africa Research Bulletin* (Political) 13 (1976): 4184–88, 4222; on federal revenue allocations, see *Africa Research Bulletin* (Economic) 11–13 (1974–76): 3107, 3459, 3846; *Africa Diary* 15–16 (1975–76): 7507, 7935.

143. Jean Suret-Canale, "La Fin de la Chefferie en Guinée," *Journal of African History* 7, no. 3 (1966): 490–92; Derman, *Serfs, Peasants and Socialists*, pp. 173–77.

144. LeVine, *Cameroons*, pp. 9–14; *Tableau de la Population du Cameroun*, (Yaoundé, Cameroon: ORSTOM, 1971), p. 82.

145. See Renaud Santerre, "L'Ecole Coranique de la Savane Camerounaise" (doctoral diss., Université du Paris, 1968), p. 37.

146. The most striking exception was the case of Rey Bouba. As in the colonial period, the chief of Rey Bouba was left with great autonomy in local government. The Sub-Prefect of Rey Bouba (who, sig-

nificantly, was seated not in the chief's capital city but in a small town about twenty miles away) had practially no power compared to the chief. He symbolized the central government's presence in the area but had very little to say on local administration (personal observation and interviews in North Cameroon, March–April 1972).

147. Dudley, *Parties and Politics,* pp. 212–15, 304–10; Kirk-Greene, "Redefinition of Provincial Administration," p. 12; J. D. Chick, "Some Reflections on the Political and Administrative Functions of Provincial Authorities in Northern Nigeria," *Journal of Local Administration Overseas* 5 (April 1966): 90–95.

148. Whitaker, *Politics of Tradition,* pp. 279–81; Dudley, *Parties and Politics,* pp. 214–17.

149. Whitaker, *Politics of Tradition,* p. 351.

150. G. V. Summercharges, "The Changing Relations between the Native Authorities and the New Northern States," *Administration* 3 (April 1969): 213; S. K. Panter-Brick and C. K. Dawson, "The Creation of New States in the North," in Panter-Brick, ed., *Nigerian Military Rule,* pp. 133–34. The removal of the native courts from native authority control was implemented only one year later under the second military regime.

151. For details on reforms in each state, see Panter-Brick and Dawson, "Creation of New States," in Panter-Brick, ed., *Nigerian Military Rule,* p. 130; Summercharges, "Native Authorities," pp. 213, 218; M. J. Balogun, "The Development of Kwarra State," *Administration* 3 (July 1969): 326–27; P. C. Daudu, "Administrative Stocktaking: The Cases of North Central, North Western and Kano States," *Administration* 3 (July 1969): 307–11; D. J. Murray, "Kwarra State and Its Administration," *Administration* 2 (April 1968): 130–40; J. Smith, "Benue-Plateau State: First Year," *Administration* 3 (July 1969): 315; *Northern States Local Government Yearbook* (1968), p. 4, (1970), pp. 1–6, 21.

152. *Africa Research Bulletin* (Political) 13 (1976): 4120, 4255.

153. Johnson, *The Cameroon Federation,* p. 160; personal observations in North Cameroon in February–April 1972. The chiefdom of Rey Bouba was again the only exception to this general pattern. There the Ahidjo government allowed the chief to keep a well-armed, well-trained military force of Dogari, who, besides their regular police duties, assisted in the collection of taxes, guided visitors, and were the principal agents of liaison between the subprefect and the chief. Another interesting task given to them was to make sure that all registered children attended western school every day. In case of absence, the teachers were supposed to inform the Dogari assigned to the school, and they went to find out whether the absentees had legitimate excuses, otherwise inflicting heavy penalties on their parents. We see here an interesting illustration of how traditional forces were put to so-called modern uses to enforce response to "western" innovations.

154. Luckham, "The Nigerian Military," p. 300; see also T. N. Tamuno, *The Police in Modern Nigeria, 1861–1965* (Ibadan, Nigeria: Ibadan University Press, 1970), p. 162.

155. Summercharges, "Native Authorities," p. 213; Panter-Brick and Dawson, "Creation of New States," in Panter-Brick, ed., *Nigerian Military Rule*, p. 133; Tamuno, *Police in Nigeria*, pp. 159–67.

156. Rivière, *Mutations Sociales en Guinée*, pp. 130–34; Derman, *Serfs, Peasants and Socialists*, pp. 244, 247.

157. For an illustrative case, see Derman, *Serfs, Peasants and Socialists*, pp. 190–91.

158. A. Marticou-Riou, "L'Organisation Judicaire du Cameroun," *Penant*, no. 7.23 (Mars 1969): 43–53.

159. Whitaker, *Politics of Tradition*, pp. 225–28; Sklar and Whitaker, "The Federal Republic of Nigeria," pp. 108–9.

160. Whitaker, *Politics of Tradition*, pp. 221, 405.

161. Panter-Brick and Dawson, "Creation of New States," in Panter-Brick, ed., *Nigerian Military Rule*, pp. 133–34; Summercharges, "Native Authorities," p. 213; *Northern States Yearbook* (1968), pp. 106–10.

162. Interviews in North Cameroon, March–April 1972; see also Willard R. Johnson, *The Cameroon Federation*, p. 160.

163. M. W. Norris, "Some Aspects of Local Government Recurrent Revenue and their Relationship to State and Local Government Functions in the Northern States," *Administration* 3 (April 1969): 229; G. O. Orewa, *Local Government Finance in Nigeria* (Ibadan, Nigeria: Oxford University Press, 1966), pp. 49–50, 53–54; Polly Hill, *Rural Hausa*, (Cambridge: Cambridge University Press, 1972), pp. 265, 272.

164. Whitaker, *Politics of Tradition*, p. 211; B. C. Smith, "The Evolution of Local Government in Northern Nigeria," *Journal of Administration Overseas* 6 (January 1967): 37–40; G. W. Fairholm, "Local Government and Community Development in the Emirates of Northern Nigeria," *Journal of Local Administration Overseas*, 3 (July 1964): 158–63.

165. Helleiner, *Peasant Agriculture*, pp. 177, 268–69; Whitaker, *Politics of Tradition*, pp. 388–90.

166. Miners, *Nigerian Army*, p. 201; Alexander R. Luckham, *The Nigerian Military* (Cambridge: Cambridge University Press, 1971), p. 264; C. R. Nixon, "The Role of the Marketing Boards in the Political Evolution of Nigeria," *Growth and Development of the Nigerian Economy*, ed. C. K. Eicher and C. Liedholm (East Lansing: Michigan State University Press, 1970), p. 158; Zukerman, "Nigerian Crisis," p. 49; *Africa Research Bulletin* (Economic) 10 (1973): 2652–53.

167. See Daudu, "North Central, North Western and Kano States," pp. 308–9; Murray, "Kwarra State," p. 138; Norris, "Local Government Revenue," p. 228; Panter-Brick and Dawson, "Creation of New States," in Panter-Brick, ed., *Nigerian Military Rule*, p. 136; *Northern States Yearbook* (1970), pp. 2, 46; *Africa Diary* 16 (1976): 7459; *Nigerian News Bulletin* (Washington, D.C., Embassy of Nigeria) 1, no. 2 (May 1966).

168. Suret-Canale, *La République de Guinée*, p. 375.

169. See Derman, *Serfs, Peasants and Socialists,* pp. 79–80, 124–25, 159–60, 239–40.

170. Rivière, *Mutations Sociales en Guinée,* p. 79; interviews with Guinean refugees in Senegal, May 1972. We should emphasize that until then the descendants of former slaves, although speaking the Fulbe language and trying to act very much like Fulbe, were not considered so by the real Fulbe. That was the big difference between Fulbe commoners and non-Fulbe of servile origin who inhabited Futa Jallon. The Fulbe commoners, even if economically and politically not much better off than former slaves, still had much higher status deriving from their recognized Fulbe identity. The Fulbe of 28 September were only the non-Fulbe who came to ruling positions as a result of the PDG victory; the term did not apply to the genuine Fulbe, whether commoner or aristocrat, who achieved high positions by supporting the PDG.

171. Suret-Canale, *La République de Guinée,* p. 374; Derman, *Serfs, Peasants and Socialists,* pp. 120, 242–43, 248–49; interviews with Guinean refugees in Senegal, May 1972.

172. Hill, *Rural Hausa,* pp. 16–17, 207, 330; interviews in North Cameroon, February–April 1972.

173. Suret-Canale, *La République de Guinée,* pp. 184–86.

174. On this point, see Derman, *Serfs, Peasants and Socialists,* pp. 133, 238–40.

175. For differences in the amount of land owned by aristocrats and commoners in Northern Nigeria, see Hill, *Rural Hausa,* pp. 93–94, 257. Also, in Northern Nigeria native authority heads still enjoyed the control of farms attached to their office; see Hill, *Rural Hausa,* p. 286.

176. Michel Bachelet, *Systèmes Fonciers et Réformes Agraires en Afrique Noire* (Paris: Pichon et Durand Auzias, 1968), pp. 341–43; *République Unie du Cameroun, Ordonance No. 74-1 du 6 Juillet 1974 Fixant le Régime Foncier* (Yaoundé, Cameroon: Imprimerie Nationale, 1974), art. 17, p. 9.

177. Campbell, *Local Government,* p. 154.

178. Ibid., pp. 154–56; *The Industrial Potentialities of Northern Nigeria* (Kaduna, Northern Nigeria: Ministry of Trade and Industry, 1963), p. 195; Hill, *Rural Hausa,* pp. 229–30 (for other details of land tenure, see also Hill, pp. 84–85, 241).

179. Hill, *Rural Hausa,* pp. 77, 196, 208. For the widespread practice of hired labor in Northern Nigeria, see ibid., pp. 105, 122, 280.

180. H. M. A. Onitri, "Nigeria's External Trade Balance of Payments and Capital Movements, 1959–63," in *Reconstruction and Development in Nigeria,* ed. A. A. Ayida and H. M. A. Onitri (Ibadan, Nigeria: Oxford University Press, 1971), p. 240; *Africa Research Bulletin* (Economic) 9–11 (1972–75): 2416, 2914, 2976, 3015, 3689.

181. Onitri, "Nigeria's External Trade," p. 241; W. A. Lewis, *Reflections on Nigeria's Economic Growth* (Paris: Development Centre for the Organization for Economic Cooperation and Development, 1967),

pp. 17–21; *Africa Research Bulletin* (Economic) 9–12 (1972–75): 2702, 2724, 2976, 3657, 3751.

182. P. Platon, "Le Marché Camerounais, 1971" *Marchés Tropicaux et Mediterranéens* 27 (Avril 1971): pp. 862, 868–69; *Mémento de l'Economie Africaine* (Paris: Ediafric, 1968), pp. 29–31; *Africa Research Bulletin* (Economic) 10–13 (1973–76): 2989, 3237, 3633, 3689, 3775.

183. Suret-Canale, *La République de Guinée*, pp. 202–4; Derman, *Serfs, Peasants and Socialists*, pp. 162–71; *Africa Research Bulletin* (Economic), 12 (1975): 3427, 3587.

184. Suret-Canale, *La République de Guinée*, p. 249; interviews with Guinean refugees in Senegal, May 1972, and with Claude Rivière in Paris, June 1972. In spite of this situation, the development of livestock remains a low-priority item in Guinean economic plans, being surpassed by the development of infrastructure, health, education, agriculture, water, and forests; see *Africa Research Bulletin* (Economic) 11 (1974): 3100.

185. *L'Industrie Africaine en 1969*, (Paris: Ediafric, 1969), 1:21; *Africa Research Bulletin* (Economic) 7, 12 (1970, 1975): 1595, 3751.

186. H. Fréchou, "L'Elevage et le Commerce du Bétail dans le Nord du Cameroun," *Cahiers d'ORSTOM, Série Sciences Humaines* 3, no. 2 (1966): p. 56.

187. Ibid., pp. 92–95; *L'Industrie Africaine en 1969*, 1:21–22; *Industrial Potentialities*, p. 157; *Le Marché du Nigeria* (Paris: Centre National du Commerce Exterieur, 1962), pp. 39–41; *Africa Research Bulletin* (Economic) 12 (1975): 3672–73, 3751.

188. Interviews and personal observation in North Cameroon, February–April 1972; H. Fréchou, "L'Arrondissement de Kaélé: Etude Géographique Régionale," unpublished paper (Yaoundé, Cameroon: ORSTOM, 1966) pp. 78–87; Antoinette Hallaire and Henri Barral, *Atlas Régional Mandara-Logone* (Yaoundé, Cameroon: ORSTOM, 1967), p. 28; Hill, *Rural Hausa*, pp. 132–33, 153, 310–11.

189. Suret-Canale, *La République de Guinée*, pp. 262–63.

190. Quoted in *Africa Research Bulletin* (Economic) 7 (1970): 1880–81. See also Suret-Canale, *La République de Guinée*, pp. 224, 316–17; O'Connor, "Guinea and Ivory Coast," p. 414.

191. For details on industrial developments in North Cameroon, see Platon, "Marché Camerounais," pp. 862, 868–69; *L'Industrie Africaine en 1969*, 1:7, 43, 54, 64–65, 78; *Mémento de l'Economic Africaine*, p. 39; *Africa Research Bulletin* (Economic) 10–11, 13 (1973–74, 1976): 2660, 3237, 3775, 3817.

192. Helleiner, *Peasant Agriculture*, p. 241; *Africa Research Bulletin* (Economic) 9 (1972): 2436.

193. See details in A. Sokolski, *The Establishment of Manufacturing in Nigeria* (New York: Praeger, 1965) app., pp. 287–343; *Africa Research Bulletin* (Economic) 4–13 (1967–76), passim.

194. Rivière, *Mutations Sociales en Guinée*, p. 47.

195. Interviews with Guinean refugees in Senegal, May 1972.

196. On the descent of hill tribes to the plains, see Jean Boutrais, "Aspects Géographiques de l'Installation des Montagnards en Plaine au Nord du Cameroun," unpublished paper (Yaoundé, Cameroon: ORSTOM, 1969), pp. 28–29, André M. Podlewski, "Enquêtes sur l'Emigration des Mafa hors du Pays Matakam," *Recherches et Etudes Camerounaises*, no. 5 (1961–62), pp. 73–97; P. Lesselingue, "Aspects Psycho-Sociaux du Phenomène de Desserrement des Montagnards au Nord-Cameroun," unpublished paper (Yaoundé, Cameroon: ORSTOM, 1968); Jean Boulet, "Etude des Zones d'Accueil dans Six Cantons au Nord de Mokolo," unpublished paper (Yaoundé, Cameroon: ORSTOM, 1967); R. M. Netting, *Hill Farmers of Nigeria: Cultural Ecology of the Kofyar of the Jos Plateau* (Seattle: University of Washington Press, 1968); R. K. Udo, *Geographical Regions of Nigeria* (Berkeley: University of California Press, 1970), pp. 131, 144.

197. Interviews in North Cameroon, March–April 1972; Lesselingue, "Desserrement des Montagnards," p. 104; Boutrais, "Montagnards en Plaine," pp. 12–19.

198. Podlewski, "Emigration Mafa," p. 87.

199. See Schwarz, *Nigeria*, p. 235; Paden, "Communal Conflict," in Melson and Wolpe, eds. *Nigeria: Modernization and the Politics of Communalism* pp. 123–27. For details on the economic impact of the Ibo exodus from Northern Nigeria, see Zukerman, "Nigerian Crisis."

200. Stanley Meissler, "The Nigeria which Is Not at War," *Africa Report* 15 (January 1970): 16–17.

201. Murray, "Kwarra State," p. 135; Panter-Brick and Dawson, "Creation of New States," in Panter-Brick, ed., *Nigerian Military Rule*, p. 137.

202. See Derman, *Serfs, Peasants and Socialists*, pp. 193, 235, 242–49.

203. Thierno Diallo, interview at the University of Dakar, Senegal, May 1972; Rivière, *Mutations Sociales en Guinée*, p. 332. On Hajj from Nigeria, see Hill, *Rural Hausa*, p. 264.

204. Podlewski, "Emigration Mafa," p. 93.

205. Whitaker, *Politics of Tradition*, p. 349; Schwarz, *Nigeria*, pp. 238, 249.

206. Dudley, *Parties and Politics*, p. 185; interviews in Cameroon, January–April 1972. Many of my young non-Muslim informants from North Cameroon indicated to me their obligation sooner or later to become Muslim if they wanted to advance in life. They pointed to the broken dreams of the few who had tried to resist Islamization. The foremost example in everyone's mind was Dakolé Daissala, the bright Toupouri who, after a brilliant beginning in administration (becoming Secretary General of the North Cameroon Provincial Government), was sacked when he refused to embrace Islam and emphasized in public his non-Fulbe Toupouri identity.

207. Letter from Wouter Van Beek, 28 November 1972.

208. John N. Paden, "Language Problems of National Integration in Nigeria: The Special Position of the Hausa," in *Language Problems of Developing Nations*, ed. J. A. Fishman et al. (New York: Wiley, 1968), p. 206; Santerre, "Ecole Coranique," p. 42.

209. Santerre, "Ecole Coranique," pp. 207–8, 235; Martin, *Ecole*, p. 206.

210. Ousmane Diallo, interview in Dakar, Senegal, May 1972. Also see Rivière, *Mutations Sociales en Guinée*, pp. 329–33.

211. For details on the conflict between the Guinean government and the Christian missionary establishments, see Rivière, *Mutations Sociales en Guinée*, pp. 357–62; Charles, *Guinée*, pp. 103–8; 183.

212. Orewa, *Local Government Finance*, p. 103; C. S. Whitaker, Jr., "A Dysrhythmic Process of Political Change," *World Politics* 19 (January 1967): 215.

213. N. Okafor, *The Development of Universities in Nigeria* (London: Longmans, 1971), p. 201.

214. Helleiner, *Peasant Agriculture*, p. 310; Dudley, *Parties and Politics*, p. 281. Lately the Nigerian government started a great effort to reach universal primary education throughout the country, though we doubt that this goal could be reached, mainly because of a lack of teaching staff.

215. Martin, *Ecole*, p. 234.

216. Platon, "Marché Camerounais," p. 841; Santerre, "Ecole Coranique," p. 64; *Tableau de Population*, p. 82. For later figures on the development of education in Cameroon, see *Africa Research Bulletin* (Political) 11, 13 (1974, 1976): 3155, 4041.

217. Interviews with Guinean refugees in Senegal, May 1972. See also Rivière, *Mutations Sociales en Guinée*, p. 199; O'Connor, "Guinea and Ivory Coast," p. 417.

218. Claude Rivière, "Les Investissements Educatifs en République de Guinée," *Cahiers d'Etudes Africaines* 5 (1965): 618–34.

219. Dudley, *Parties and Politics*, p. 275.

220. Podlewski, "Populations du Nord Cameroun (première partie)," pp. 14–15.

221. Podlewski, "Populations du Nord Cameroun (deuxième partie)," p. 104.

222. Martin, *Ecole*, p. 78.

223. For details on Franco-Arabic schools, see Santerre, "Ecole Coranique," pp. 236–72.

224. Dudley, *Parties and Politics*, p. 224.

225. Plotnicov, *Strangers to the City*, p. 58; Campbell, *Local Government*, pp. 157–58; Paden, "Communal Conflict," p. 130.

226. Paden, "Communal Conflict," p. 131.

227. For more details on the impact of the Ibo exodus on the northern economy, see Zukerman, "Nigerian Crisis," pp. 45–51.

Conclusion

1. On this point the focus of this book is markedly different from books dealing with the status of chiefs in Africa, such as M. Crowder and O. Ikime's *West African Chiefs* (Ile-Ife, Nigeria: University of Ife Press, 1970). This might also explain some of the differences between the conclusions reached in that book compared to this one.

2. Unfortunately, on this question we stand on rather shaky ground and only vague estimates and approximations can be advanced. All the information that we have on the number of Fulbe and other populations in Futa Jallon, Sokoto, and Adamawa were collected in the colonial and postcolonial periods, when an important trend of Islamization (and in Futa Jallon and Adamawa "Fulbeization") was under way. The colonial census and other estimates also classified populations according to colonial administrative boundaries that did not correspond to the precolonial boundaries of Sokoto, Adamawa, and Futa Jallon. See Jean-Jacques Richard-Molard, *Afrique Occidentale Française* (Paris: Berger-Levrault, 1956), p. 124; Gilbert Vieillard, "Notes sur les Peuls du Fouta Djallon," *Bulletin de l'IFAN* 2 (1940) p. 89; Claude Rivière, *Mutations Sociales en Guinée* (Paris: Rivière, 1971), p. 30; Victor T. LeVine, *The Cameroons: From Mandate to Independence* (Berkeley: University of California Press, 1964), pp. 9–14; "Inventaire Ethnique et Linguistique du Cameroun sous Mandat Français," *Journal de la Société des Africanistes* 4, no. 2 (1934): 203–8; James S. Coleman, *Nigeria: Background to Nationalism* (Los Angeles: University of California Press, 1958), p. 15.

3. The Ethiopian aristocracy, on the other hand, would not fit our case since changes were not introduced there in a "colonial" context. Similarly excluded are areas such as South Africa and Rhodesia which are still under white rule. For details on some African traditional aristocracies taken into consideration here, see E. P. Skinner, "The Changing Status of the 'Emperor of the Mossi' under Colonial Rule and since Independence," in *West African Chiefs*, ed. Michael Crowder and O. Ikime (Ile-Ife, Nigeria: University of Ife Press, 1970), pp. 98–124; L. A. Fallers, ed., *The King's Men: Leadership and Status in Buganda on the Eve of Independence* (London: Oxford University Press, 1964); G. L. Caplan, *The Elites of Barotseland* (London: Hurst, 1970); M. D'Hertefelt, "The Rwanda of Rwanda," in *Peoples of Africa*, ed. J. L. Gibbs (New York: Holt, Rinehart & Winston, 1960), pp. 422–37; R. Lemarchand, "Social Change and Political Modernization in Burundi," *Journal of Modern African Studies* 4, no. 4 (1966): 401–33.

4. M. Crowder and O. Ikime, "Introduction," in *West African Chiefs*, pp. vii–xxix.

5. Reinhard Bendix, "Tradition and Modernity Reconsidered," *Comparitive Studies in Society and History* 9 (July 1967): 249–346.

6. Robert A. Nisbet, *The Social Bond* (New York: Knopf, 1970), p. xi.

7. Ibid., p. 340.

Selected Bibliography

Books

Adeleye, R. A., *Power and Diplomacy in Northern Nigeria, 1804–1906.* London: Longmans, 1971.

Ahmadou Ahidjo par Lui-Même. Monaco: Bory, 1968.

Arcin, A. *Histoire de la Guinée Française.* Paris: Chalamel, 1911.

Barth, Henry. *Travels and Discoveries in North and Central Africa.* London: Ward, Lock, 1890.

Bello, Alhaji Sir Ahmadu. *My Life.* Cambridge: Cambridge University Press, 1962.

Bohannan, P., and Dalton, G., eds. *Markets in Africa.* Evanston, Ill.: Northwestern University Press, 1962.

Buchanan, K., and Pugh, J. C. *Land and People in Nigeria.* London: University of London Press, 1955.

Burns, A. C. *History of Nigeria.* London: Allen & Unwin, 1955.

Cambell, Michael J. *Law and Practice of Local Government in Northern Nigeria.* Lagos, Nigeria: African University Press, 1963.

Carter, Gwendolen M., ed. *Five African States.* Ithaca, N.Y.: Cornell University Press, 1963.

Chaffard, Georges. *Les Carnets Secrets de la Décolonisation.* 2 vols. Paris: Calmann-Levy, 1965, 1967.

Charles, Bernard. *Guinée.* Lausanne: Editions Rencontre, 1963.

Coleman, James S. *Nigeria: Background to Nationalism.* Los Angeles: University of California Press, 1958.

Coleman, James S., and Rosberg, Carl G., eds. *Political Parties and National Integration in Tropical Africa.* Berkeley: University of California Press, 1964.

Cowan, L. Gray. *Local Government in West Africa.* New York: Columbia University Press, 1958.

Crowder, Michael. *The Story of Nigeria.* London: Faber & Faber, 1962.

Crowder, Michael, and Ikime, O., eds. *West African Chiefs.* Ile-Ife, Nigeria: University of Ife Press, 1970.

Derman, W. *Serfs, Peasants and Socialists.* Berkeley: University of California Press, 1973.

Dudley, B. J. *Parties and Politics in Northern Nigeria.* London: Cass, 1968.

Dupire, Marguerite. *Organisation Sociale des Peul*. Paris: Plon, 1970.

————. *Peuls Nomades*. Paris: Institut d'Ethnologie, 1962.

Eicher, C., and Liedholm, C., eds. *Growth and Development of the Nigerian Economy*. East Lansing: Michigan State University Press, 1970.

Eisenstadt, Shmuel N. *Social Differentiation and Stratification*. Glenview, Ill.: Scott, Foresman, 1971.

Forde, Daryll C., and Scott, Richenda. *The Native Economies of Nigeria*. London: Faber & Faber, 1946.

Gardinier, D. E. *Cameroon: United Nations Challenge to French Policy*. London: Oxford University Press, 1963.

Gibbs, J. L., ed. *Peoples of Africa*. New York: Holt, Rinehart & Winston, 1960.

Guillard, J. *Golonpoui: Nord Cameroun*. Paris: Mouton, 1965.

Hailey, W. M. , Lord. *Native Administration in the British African Territories*. Vol. 3. London: His Majesty's Stationery Office, 1951.

Handbook of Commerce and Industry in Nigeria. Lagos, Nigeria: Federal Department of Commerce and Industries, 1957.

Hazelwood, A., ed. *African Integration and Disintegration*. London: Oxford University Press, 1967.

Helleiner, Gerald K. *Peasant Agriculture, Government, and Economic Growth in Nigeria*. Homewood, Ill.: Irwin, 1966.

Hill, Polly. *Rural Hausa*. Cambridge: Cambridge University Press, 1972.

Hodgkin, Thomas. *Nigerian Perspectives: An Historical Anthology*. London: Oxford University Press, 1960.

Hogben, S., and Kirk-Green, A. H. M., *The Emirates of Northern Nigeria*. London: Oxford University Press, 1966.

Hommage à Jean-Jacques Richard-Molard. Paris: Présence Africaine, 1956(?).

Johnson, W. R. *The Cameroon Federation*. Princeton, N. J.: Princeton University Press, 1970.

Kirk-Greene, A. H. M. *Adamawa, Past and Present*. London: Oxford University Press, 1958.

————, ed. *Gazetteers of the Northern Provinces of Nigeria*. 4 vols. London: Cass, 1972.

————, ed. *The Principles of Native Administration in Nigeria: Selected Documents, 1900–1947*. London: Oxford University Press, 1965.

Last, Murray. *The Sokoto Caliphate*. New York: Humanities Press, 1967.

Lembezat, Bertrand. *Les Populations Païennes du Nord-Cameroun et de l'Adamaoua*. Paris: Presses Universitaires de France, 1961.

Lenski, Gerhard E. *Power and Privilege*. New York: McGraw-Hill, 1966.

Lestrange, Monique de. *Les Coniagui et les Bassari*. Paris: Presses Universitaires de France, 1955.

Lestringeant, J. *Les Pays de Guider au Cameroun*. Versailles: n.p., 1964.

LeVine, Victor T. *The Cameroons: From Mandate to Independence.* Berkeley: University of California Press, 1964.

L'Industrie Africaine en 1969. Paris: Ediafric, 1969.

Low, V. N. *Three Nigerian Emirates.* Evanston, Ill.: Northwestern University Press, 1972.

Luckham, Alexander, R. *The Nigerian Military.* Cambridge: Cambridge University Press, 1971.

Mabogunje, A. L. *Urbanization in Africa.* London: University of London Press, 1968.

Martin, Jean-Yves. *L'Ecole et les Societés Traditionelles au Cameroun Septentrional.* Yaoundé, Cameroon: ORSTOM, 1970.

Marty, Paul. *L'Islam en Guinée-Fouta Djalon.* Paris: Leroux, 1921.

Melson, Robert, and Wolpe, Howard, eds. *Nigeria: Modernization and the Politics of Communalism.* East Lansing: Michigan State University Press, 1971.

Mémento de l'Economie Africaine. 6ᵉed. Paris: Ediafric, 1968.

Miners, N. J. *The Nigerian Army, 1956–1966.* London: Methuen, 1971.

Mohamadou, Eldridge. *Les Traditions Historiques des Peuls de l'Adamawa, Tome I: Les Férobé du Diamaré: Maroua et Petté.* Niamey: Niger: Centre Regional des Traditions Orales, 1970.

Mollien, G. *Travels in the Interior of Africa.* London: Cass, 1967.

Morgenthau, Ruth S. *Political Parties in French-Speaking West Africa.* Oxford: Clarendon, 1964.

Netting, R. M. *Hill Farmers of Nigeria: Cultural Ecology of the Kofyar of the Jos Plateau.* Seattle: University of Washington Press, 1968.

Nisbet, Robert A. *The Social Bond: An Introduction to the Study of Society.* New York: Knopf, 1970.

Oluwasanmi, H. A. *Agriculture and Nigerian Economic Development.* Ibadan, Nigeria: Oxford University Press, 1966.

Orewa, G. O. *Local Government Finance in Nigeria.* Ibadan, Nigeria: Oxford University Press, 1966.

Orr, C. W. J. *The Making of Northern Nigeria.* London: Macmillan, 1911.

Panter-Brick, S. K. , ed. *Nigerian Politics and Military Rule.* London: Athlone, 1970.

Perham, M., ed. *Mining, Commerce, and Finance in Nigeria.* London: Faber & Faber, 1947.

Rivière, Claude. *Mutations Sociales en Guinée.* Paris: Rivière, 1971.

Rudin, Harry R. *Germans in the Cameroons, 1884–1914.*New Haven, Conn.: Yale University Press, 1938.

Saint Croix, F. W. de. *The Fulani of Northern Nigeria.* Lagos, Nigeria: Government Printer, 1945.

Schwarz, Walter. *Nigeria.* London: Pall Mall, 1968.

Shils, Edward A. *Center and Periphery: Essays in Macrosociology.* Chicago: University of Chicago Press, 1970.

Skinner, N., ed. *Hausa Tales and Traditions*. London: Cass, 1969.

Sklar, Richard L. *Nigerian Political Parties*. Princeton, N.J.: Princeton University Press, 1963.

Smith, Michael G. *Government in Zazzau, 1800–1950*. London: Oxford University Press, 1960.

————. *The Economy of Hausa Communities of Zaria*. London: Colonial Office, 1955.

Sokolski, A. *The Establishment of Manufacturing in Nigeria*. New York: Praeger, 1965.

Stenning, Derrick J. *Savannah Nomads*. London: Oxford University Press, 1959.

Suret-Canale, Jean. *La République de Guinée*. Paris: Editions Sociales, 1970.

Tableau de la Population du Cameroun. Yaoundé, Cameroon: ORSTOM, 1971.

Tamuno, T. N. *The Police in Modern Nigeria, 1861–1965*. Ibadan, Nigeria: Ibadan University Press, 1970.

The Industrial Potentialities of Northern Nigeria. Kaduna, Northern Nigeria: Ministry of Trade and Industry, 1963.

Touré, Sékou. *L'Expérience Guinéenne et l'Unité Africaine*. Paris: Présence Africaine, 1959.

Trimingham, J. S. *History of Islam in West Africa*. London: Oxford University Press, 1962.

Udo, R. K. *Geographical Regions of Nigeria*. Berkeley: University of California, 1970.

Whitaker, C. S., Jr. *The Politics of Tradition: Community and Change in Northern Nigeria, 1946–1966*. Princeton, N.J.: Princeton University Press, 1970.

Williams, D. H. *A Short Survey of Education in Northern Nigeria*. Kaduna, Nigeria: Government Printer, Northern Region, 1960.

Zolberg, Aristide R. *Creating Political Order*. Chicago: Rand-McNally, 1966.

Articles

Ames, C. G. "The Highland Chieftancies (Plateau Province)" (1934). *Gazetteers of the Northern Provinces of Nigeria*. Vol. 4. Edited by A. H. M. Kirk-Greene. London: Cass, 1972.

Apter, D. E. "The Role of Traditionalism in the Political Modernization of Ghana and Uganda." *World Politics* 13 (October 1960): 45–68.

Arnett, E. Y. "Sokoto Province" (1920). *Gazetteers of the Northern Provinces of Nigeria*. Vol. 1. Edited by A. H. M. Kirk-Greene. London: Cass, 1972.

————. "Zaria Province" (1920). *Gazetteers of the Northern Provinces of Nigeria*. Vol. 1. Edited by A. H. M. Kirk-Greene. London: Cass, 1972.

Azarya, Victor. "Dominance and Change in North Cameroon: The

Fulbe Aristocracy" Sage Research Papers in Social Sciences. Studies in Comparative Modernization Series, no. 90-030 (Beverly Hills, Calif.: Sage, 1976)

Baldwin, K. D. "Land Tenure Problems in Relation to Agricultural Development in the Northern Region of Nigeria." *African Agrarian Systems*. Edited by D. Biebuyck. London: Oxford University Press, 1963.

Bayart, J. F. "L'Union Nationale Camerounaise," *Revue Française de Sciences Politiques* 20 (Août 1970): 681–718.

Beaujeu-Garnier, J. "Essai sur la Géographie Electorale Guinéenne." *Les Cahiers d'Outre Mer* 11, no. 44 (1958): 309–33.

Cole, Taylor. "Bureaucracy in Transition: Independent Nigeria." *Public Administration* 38 (1960): 321–38.

Cowan, L. Gray. "Guinea." *African One-Party States*. Edited by Gwendolen M. Carter. Ithaca, N.Y.: Cornell University Press, 1962.

Daudu, P. C. "Administrative Stocktaking: The Cases of North-Central, North-Western and Kano States." *Administration* 3 (July 1969): 301–13.

Demougeot, A. "Notes sur l'Organisation Politique et Administrative de Labé." *Memoires de l'IFAN*, no. 4 (1944), pp. 9–84.

Dent, M. J. "The Military and Politics: A Study of the Relation Between the Army and the Political Process in Nigeria." *Nigeria: Modernization and the Politics of Communalism*. Edited by Robert Melson and Howard Wolpe. East Lansing: Michigan State University Press, 1971.

Dubois, Victor. "The Rise of an Opposition to Sékou Touré." *American Universities Field Staff Reports, West Africa Series* 9, nos. 1–3 (1966).

Dudley, B. J. "Federalism and the Balance of Political Power in Nigeria." *Journal of Commonwealth Political Studies* 4 (March 1966): 16–29.

———. "The Nomination of Parliamentary Candidates in Northern Nigeria." *Journal of Commonwealth Political Studies* 2 (November 1963): 45–58.

Fréchou, H. "L'Elevage et le Commerce du Bétail dans le Nord du Cameroun." *Cahiers d'ORSTOM, Série Sciences Humaines* 3, no. 2 (1966): 7–125.

———. "Les Régimes Fonciers dans la Région du Kimbi (Fouta Djalon)." *Etudes du Droit Africain et du Droit Malgache*. Edited by Jean Poirier. Paris: Editions Cujas, 1965.

Froelich, Jean-Claude. "Le Commandement et l'Organisation Sociale Chez les Foulbé de l'Adamaoua." *Etudes Camerounaises*, nos. 45–46 (Septembre-Decembre 1954), pp. 5–91.

Hurault, Jean. "Antagonisme de l'Agriculture et de l'Elevage sur les Hauts Plateaux de l'Adamaoua." *Etudes Rurales*, no. 15 (Octobre-Décembre 1964), pp. 22–71.

Johnson, R. W. "The Parti Démocratique de Guinée and the Mamou

'Deviation.'" *African Perspectives.* Edited by C. Allen and R. W. Johnson. Cambridge: Cambridge University Press, 1970.

Kirk-Green, A. H. M. "A Redefinition of Provincial Administration, The Northern Nigerian Approach." *Journal of Local Administration Overseas* 4 (January 1965): 5–26.

Lacroix, Pierre F. "L'Islam Peul de l'Adamawa." *Islam in Tropical Africa.* Edited by I. M. Lewis. London: Oxford University Press, 1966.

————. "Matériaux pour Servir à l'Histoire des Peuls de l'Adamawa." *Etudes Camerounaises,* nos. 37–40 (Septembre-Decembre 1952; Mars-Juillet 1953).

LeVine, Victor T. "Cameroun." *Five African States.* Edited by Gwendolen M. Carter. Ithaca, N.Y.: Cornell University Press, 1963.

————. "Cameroun." *Political Parties and National Integration in Tropical Africa.* Edited by James S. Coleman and Carl G. Rosberg. Berkeley: University of California Press, 1964.

Luning, H. A. "The Impact of Socio-Economic Factors on the Land Tenure Patterns in Northern Nigeria." *Journal of Local Administration Overseas* 4 (July 1965): 173–82.

MacBride, D. F. H. "Land Survey in the Kano Emirate, Northern Provinces, Nigeria." *African Affairs* 37 (January 1938): 75–91.

Mars, J. "Extra-Territorial Enterprises," *Mining, Commerce and Finance in Nigeria.* Edited by M. Perham. London: Faber & Faber, 1947.

Murray, D. J. "Kwarra State and Its Administration," *Administration* 2 (April 1968): 130–40.

Norris, M. W. "Some Aspects of Local Government Recurrent Revenue and Their Relationship to State and Local Government Functions in the Northern States." *Administration* 3 (April 1969): 221–35.

O'Connor, M. "Guinea and the Ivory Coast—Contrasts in Economic Development." *Journal of Modern African Studies* 10 (1972): 409–26.

Onitri, H. M. A. "Nigeria's External Trade Balance of Payments and Capital Movements." *Reconstruction and Development in Nigeria.* Edited by A. A. Ayinda and H. M. A. Onitri. Ibadan, Nigeria: Oxford University Press, 1971.

Paden, John N. "Communal Competition, Conflict and Violence in Kano." *Nigeria: Modernization and the Politics of Communalism.* Edited by Robert Melson and Howard Wolpe. East Lansing: Michigan State University Press, 1971.

————. "Language Problems of National Integration in Nigeria: The Special Position of Hausa." *Language Problems of Developing Nations.* Edited by J. A. Fishman et al. New York: Wiley, 1968.

Panter-Brick, S. K., and Dawson, P. F. "The Creation of New States in the North,." *Nigerian Politics and Military Rule.* London: Athlone Press, 1970.

Platon, P. "Le Marché Camerounais, 1971." *Marchés Tropicaux et Mediterrannéens* 27 (Avril 1971): 833–960.

Podlewski, André-Marie. "La Dynamique des Principales Populations du Nord du Cameroun." *Cahiers D'ORSTOM, Série Sciences Humaines* 3, no. 4 (1966): 5–144; 4, no. special (1971): 7–190.

———. "Enquêtes sur l'Emigration des Mafa hors du Pays Matakam." *Recherches et Etudes Camerounaises*, no. 5 (1961–62), pp. 73–95.

Poréko, Osmane Diallo. "Evolution Sociale chez les Peuls du Fouta Djalon." *Recherches Africaines* 4 (Octobre-Decembre 1961), pp. 73–94.

Prothero, R. M. "Land Use, Land Holdings and Land Tenure at Soba, Zaria Province, Northern Nigeria." *Bulletin de l'IFAN* 19 (July–October 1957): 558–63.

Sklar, Richard L. "Nigerian Politics in Perspective." *Government and Opposition* 2 (July-October 1967): 524–39.

Sklar, Richard L., and Whitaker, C. S., Jr. "Nigeria." *Political Parties and National Integration in Tropical Africa.* Edited by James S. Coleman and Carl G. Rosberg. Berkeley: University of California Press, 1964.

———. "The Federal Republic of Nigeria." *National Unity and Regionalism in Eight African States.* Edited by Gwendolen M. Carter. Ithaca, N.Y.: Cornell University Press, 1966.

Smith, B. C. "The Evolution of Local Government in Northern Nigeria." *Journal of Administration Overseas* 6 (January 1967): 28–42.

Smith, H. F. C. "The Islamic Revolutions of the 19th Century." *Journal of the Historical Society of Nigeria* 9 (December 1961): 169–86.

Smith, Michael G. "Exchange and Marketing among the Hausa." *Markets in Africa.* Edited by P. Bohannan and G. Dalton. Evanston, Ill.: Northwestern University Press, 1962.

———. "Historical and Cultural Conditions of Political Corruption among the Hausa." *Comparative Studies in Society and History.* 6 (January 1964): 164–94.

———. "Slavery and Emancipation in Two Societies (Jamaica and Zaria)." *Social and Economic Studies* 3, no. 4 (1954): 239–88.

———. "The Hausa System of Social Status." *Africa* 29 (July 1959): 408–25.

Summercharges, G. V. "The Changing Relations between the Native Authorities and the New Northern States." *Administration* 3 (April 1969): 203–20.

Suret-Canale, Jean. "La Fin de la Chefferie en Guinée." *Journal of African History* 7, no. 3 (1966): 459–93.

———. "La Guinée dans le Système Colonial." *Présence Africaine*, no. 29 (1959–60), pp. 9–44.

Vieillard, Gilbert. "Notes sur les Peuls du Fouta Djallon." *Bulletin de l'IFAN* 2 (1940): 85–211.

Weber, Max. "Class, Status and Party." *Class, Status and Power.* Edited by Reinhard Bendix and Seymour M. Lipset. 2d ed. New York: Free Press, 1966.

Yeld, E. R. "Islam and Social Stratification in Northern Nigeria." *British Journal of Sociology* 11, no. 2 (1960): 112–28.

Zukerman, M. E. "Nigerian Crisis: Economic Impact on the North." *Journal of Modern African Studies* 8 (1970): 37–54.

Unpublished Papers and Reports

Boutrais, J. "Aspects Géographiques de l'Installation des Montagnards en Plaine au Nord du Cameroun." Yaoundé, Cameroon: ORSTOM, 1969.

"Cameroons under French Administration." 2 pts. Yaoundé, Cameroon, n.d.

Champaud, J. "L'Immigration Foula en Basse Guinée." Conakry, Guinea: Service Hydraulique de l'AOF, 1957.

David, Lucien. "La Formation des Cadres Administratifs en Guinée." Paris: CHEAM, 1961.

Diallo, Thierno. "Les Institutions Politiques du Fouta Djalon au 19ème Siècle." Doctoral dissertation, Université de Paris, Sorbonne, 1970 (?).

"Etude sur le Commandement Indigène de Garoua." (1934) *Documentation ORSTOM, Dossier Benoué*, no. III-979. Yaoundé, Cameroon.

Fonds Vieillard. Institut Fondamental d'Afrique Noire. Dakar, Senegal.

Fréchou, H. "L'Arrondissement de Kaélé, Etude Géographique Régionale." Yaoundé, Cameroon: ORSTOM, 1966.

Genin, M. "Etudes des Redevances Coraniques et Coutumières Perçues par les Chefs Musulmans du Nord-Cameroun." (1937) *Documentation ORSTOM, Dossier Benoué*, no. III-799. Yaoundé, Cameroon.

Hallaire, Antoinette. "Les Monts du Mandara au Nord de Mokolo et la Plaine de Mora." Yaoundé, Cameroon: ORSTOM, 1965.

Lavergne, G. "Rapport sur l'Etude du Groupement Kapsiki, Visite du Poste de Mubi." (1942) *Documentation ORSTOM, Dossier Margui-Wandala*, no. III-369. Yaoundé, Cameroon.

Lesselingue, P. "Aspects Psycho-Sociaux du Phenomène de Desserrement des Montagnards au Nord-Cameroun." Yaoundé, Cameroon: ORSTOM, 1968.

Luckham, Alexander R. "The Nigerian Military." Ph.D. dissertation, University of Chicago, 1969.

Meyer, Capitaine. "Rapport sur la Tournée dans le Boubandjida." (1918) *Documentation ORSTOM, Dossier Benoué*, no. III-242. Yaoundé, Cameroon.

N'Bady, Camara Ibrahima. "La Guinée avant l'Indépendence et l'Heritage Français." Paris: CHEAM, 1960.

"Rapport sur le Problème de la Reconnaissance des Droits Fonciers Autochtones." (1949) *Documentation ORSTOM, Dossier Adamaoua*, no. III-1209. Yaoundé, Cameroon.

Ripert, Capitaine. "Situation Politique de la Region de Ngaoundéré."

(1918) *Documentation ORSTOM, Dossier Adamaoua,* no. III-380. Yaoundé, Cameroon.

Roland, G. "Etude sur les Règles Coutumières dans la Circonscription de Ngaoundéré." (1923–33) *Documentation ORSTOM, Dossier Adamaoua,* no. I-10a. Yaoundé, Cameroon.

Santerre, Renaud. "L'Ecole Coranique de la Savane Camerounaise." Doctoral dissertation, Université de Paris, 1968.

"Situation Politique dans l'Adamaoua." (1934) *Documentation ORSTOM, Dossier Adamaoua,* no. III-385. Yaoundé, Cameroon.

Newspapers, Bulletins, Yearbooks

Africa Diary. New Delhi, 1964–1976.

Africa Report. Washington, D.C.: African-American Institution.

Africa Research Bulletin, Economic, Financial, Technical Series. Exeter, England: Africa Research, Ltd., 1964–1976.

Africa Research Bulletin, Political, Social, Cultural Series. Exeter, England: Africa Research, Ltd., 1964–1976.

Annuaire National, 1971. Yaoundé, Cameroon: République Fédérale du Cameroun, 1971.

Coup de Bambou. Conakry, Guinea. Issued irregularly in 1950.

Jeune Afrique. Tunis, Tunisia: Société Africaine de Presse.

La Guinée Nouvelle. Conakry, Guinea. Issued irregularly in 1958.

Le Populaire de Guinée. Conakry, Guinea. Issued irregularly in 1956.

Nigeria Yearbook. Daily Times Magazine Division Publication. Lagos: Time Press, Ltd., 1969–1971.

Northern States of Nigeria, Local Government Yearbook. Zaria, Nigeria: Ahmadu Bello University, Institute of Administration, 1968–1970.

Phare de Guinée. Conakry, Guinea. Issued irregularly in 1947–48.

Voix du Peuple. Conakry, Guinea. Issued irregularly in 1958.

West Africa. London.

Index

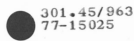